Free to be children

EDITED BY ROBYN SALISBURY

Free to be children

Preventing child sexual abuse in Aotearoa New Zealand

For the children of Aotearoa New Zealand

*For every survivor of child sexual abuse
finding their way over the hurdles*

*And for those who love them and
travel that journey with them*

Contents

Foreword 9

Preface 12

Introduction 19

1. 'Concrete baby': A survivor's story 30
   — ANONYMOUS

2. Child sexual abuse:
   A paediatrician's viewpoint 47
   — PROFESSOR DAWN ELDER,
   UNIVERSITY OF OTAGO, WELLINGTON

3. Working therapeutically with children
   who have experienced sexual abuse 64
   — SUE GLANVILLE, RETIRED CLINICAL MANAGER,
   ORANGA TAMARIKI

4. Child sexual abuse: A police viewpoint 79
   — DETECTIVE SENIOR SERGEANT NEIL HOLDEN,
   CHILD PROTECTION TEAM, NEW ZEALAND POLICE

5. Underage sex work and the
   sex-trafficking of adolescents 95
   — DR NATALIE THORBURN, UNIVERSITY OF AUCKLAND

6. Te Wairua O Tika   109
— CIARAN TORRINGTON, THERAPIST, SURVIVOR ADVOCATE

7. Sexuality education in New Zealand: What is (not) happening in schools and why you should care   122
— KATIE FITZPATRICK, ASSOCIATE PROFESSOR OF HEALTH EDUCATION AND PHYSICAL EDUCATION, UNIVERSITY OF AUCKLAND

8. Technology, new media and child sexual abuse: Time for a change   135
— DAVID SHANKS, CHIEF CENSOR, OFFICE OF FILM AND LITERATURE CLASSIFICATION

9. Living next door to a sex offender: One woman's viewpoint   150
— JUDY, MOTHER AND GRANDMOTHER

10. Kia Marama: Providing child sex offender treatment in prison   154
— ALEXANDRA GREEN, MANAGER PSYCHOLOGICAL SERVICES, KIA MARAMA

11. Singing my soul back into being   167
— HINEWIRANGI KOHU MORGAN, PSYCHOTHERAPIST, WAIKERIA PRISON

12. Hurt people hurt people   180
— DEANNA HOLLIS, MANAGER, WELLSTOP CENTRAL

13. The Good Lives Model of rehabilitation   193
— DR MAYUMI PURVIS, UNIVERSITY OF MELBOURNE
— PROFESSOR TONY WARD, VICTORIA UNIVERSITY OF WELLINGTON

14. Assessing risk and treatment change,
    and the shift towards prevention   206
    — SARAH BEGGS CHRISTOFFERSON,
      UNIVERSITY OF CANTERBURY

15. Restorative justice: Enabling a new 'normal'
    after sexual violence   217
    — DR SHIRLEY JÜLICH, JENNIFER ANNAN AND LISA MARKWICK,
      PROJECT RESTORE NZ

16. The development of constructive
    sexual behaviours   227
    — ROBYN SALISBURY, CLINICAL PSYCHOLOGIST

17. The development of destructive
    sexual behaviours   241
    — ROBYN SALISBURY

18. The pathway forward   258
    — ROBYN SALISBURY

Afterword   274
Acknowledgements   276
Appendix: Children's sexual behaviours   279
Notes   290
About the contributors   300
Index   305

Foreword

I was so brutalised inside, and then I had to live with that shame.
— Survivor of child sexual abuse[1]

WE NEW ZEALANDERS ARE A compassionate and generous people. We want nothing but the best for our young people. Our vision for childhood is one where its taonga — our children — are nourished and nurtured, and where they thrive. But child abuse, and in particular child sexual abuse, casts a sharp shadow across this vision. Increasingly we are aware of the power of this shadow and the price it demands from too many of our children. That cost is physical, emotional, psychological, indeed spiritual. It can leave children diminished and broken. The tragic fact is that New Zealand has had, and continues to have, a major problem with child sexual abuse. It is a crisis. No instance of abuse of a child is acceptable, but the rate of child sexual abuse in this country is profoundly concerning.

Participants in the Dunedin Multidisciplinary Health and Development Research Study of 1037 children were asked to report if they had experienced any kind of unwanted sexual activities that involved physical contact before the age of 16.[2] The study indicated that 30 per cent of female and 9 per cent of male participants had experienced some form of sexual abuse. That is a shocking statistic. And given the inhibitions that discourage reporting, it is likely the actual level may be higher still.

The level of concern about this issue within New Zealand has been evidenced by the insistent demand for a Royal Commission into historical abuse of children in state care, and the further call to ensure the inquiry be extended to include faith-based institutions.

The original terms of reference proposed that the Royal Commission consider complaints up until the end of 1999. This implied the naïve assumption that abuse, including sexual abuse, is somehow a thing of the past. But this is little more than a convenient myth enabling us to shelve our concern about child sexual abuse.

The Safety of Children in Care statistics,[3] released by Oranga Tamariki — Ministry for Children in March 2019, give the lie to that myth. Not only do they demonstrate that the sexual abuse of children is still happening, they also further identify that children in the care of the state are experiencing a 10 per cent rate of repeat abuse in general.

All this points to the timeliness of *Free to Be Children: Preventing child sexual abuse in Aotearoa New Zealand*. This book draws together significant contributions by writers and researchers from wide-ranging fields of expertise. Together they explore the nature of the problem and exhibit the value of a knowledgeable, informed, expert response.

Free to Be Children also draws our attention to aspects of the issue that may be new to many: the reality of child sex trafficking in Aotearoa; the challenge of keeping children safe in the digital age; restorative justice for child victims and survivors.

The Office of the Children's Commissioner is committed to prioritising the best interests of children, as this book does. We also actively commit to consulting with children, to make their views known and to give them weight. Historically, as a country, we have done that remarkably badly. Government departments, ministries, local government and community groups have too readily privileged adult voices in decision-making.

Fortunately, things are changing. Our legislation makes taking account of children's voices essential. The Children's Commissioner Act 2003 gives the commissioner a mandate to seek out children's voices, to listen to them, and to give them serious consideration (sections 13 and 14). These sections of the Act provide the basis for how we discharge our specific statutory obligations to investigate, monitor, assess and help the work of Oranga Tamariki (section 14). Our determination to prioritise the voices of children has led us to revolutionise our approach to monitoring work.

The voices of children and young people change the discussion. They rebalance emphases. They draw attention to assumptions that no longer hold. The recent student climate change strikes, demanding that attention be focused on the global climate change crisis, provide an excellent example. The distinctive value children's voices add to our kōrero is a field that would benefit from further research and exploration. This is true also in respect of children's experience of abuse.

Free to Be Children makes an excellent and contemporary contribution to the discussion of child sexual abuse. It will provoke thought on this crisis. It will broaden readers' understanding of the key issues at play. It will contribute to a better response and encourage a more professional and effective practice across all disciplines. It should be required reading for anyone working in the field, and it will richly repay careful reading.

Judge Andrew Becroft
Children's Commissioner

Preface

WHEN I HEAR PEOPLE SAY 'children are so resilient', my experiences with adult survivors of child sexual abuse always make me wonder where on earth they are coming from. Raising children is very hard work and sometimes anxiety-provoking. In talking about the sexual abuse of children the last thing I want to do is stir more anxiety. However, if a society wants to address the problem of child sexual abuse it must face the fact that children are vulnerable. Children are not sexual beings for the gratification of others, but in New Zealand too many abusers think they are. It's time for us as a country to open our eyes to the extent of this problem. We need to strengthen our resolve to address it, to get well informed and to take effective steps forward.

The unhealed psychological-trauma wounds of child sexual abuse are hugely costly: for the child, for the adult they grow up to be, for all those who love them and for our society as a whole. Emotionally or physically, survivors of abuse are called on at some point in their lifetimes to do the work of facing and working through their pain. Some do that, some do not; and while it's certainly achievable, it also takes great courage and persistence. Even when very thoroughly addressed, many survivors find that significant scars remain.

If life has brought children traumatic experiences which they haven't had good support to work their way through, some will develop overtly destructive behaviours of many kinds. Others may appear fine — they have learned to repress, deny or otherwise hide their wounds. I don't want to detract from the value of resilience; rather, I want to shine a spotlight on it. I celebrate all the coping mechanisms every sexually abused child has ever used to help themselves survive. I also know that many coping mechanisms operate at a cost, and that they have a use-by date.

Why have I edited this book? I aim, first, to bring light to this issue, then to go beneath the surface and combat taboos on talking about child sexual abuse. I want this book to be a voice for those who can't speak out or who would be at increased risk if they did. I want it to challenge the invisibility of abused children and the power of abusive adolescents and adults. That's why its authors name what happens and speak truths that some people may not want to know about.

Second, given that life is finite, it is important to me that I gather and record the wisdom of those whose many years of work in this field have resulted in great expertise. I also want to draw on the perspectives of the younger contributors, who are bringing their energy and knowledge to the field. We can't afford to lose any of this precious, hard-won learning.

Third, I want to encourage reflection, conversation and informed action. I want to support the courage of readers who are prepared to bear witness to the problem of child sexual abuse, to face the shadow. I want to inspire and empower all caring people: you can make a preventative difference and achieve social change.

THIS IS NOT A BOOK about how to heal from child sexual abuse (hereafter referred to as CSA). Much has been written about the process of recovery and all that it involves, including the neuroscientific evidence of the harm done and the effective healing processes that have been developed in more recent years. Further guidance for survivors and healers will continue to be produced as this field of expertise develops. Several of the contributors to this book have extensive experience in working with survivors. I, too, have some experience in this field, but this book focuses primarily on how to *protect* children from sexual abuse.

Following an overview of what constitutes CSA, the wide-ranging impact it can have and what we know about its prevalence, the book begins with a courageous survivor telling us something of what he has endured and about the lifelong consequences.

It then turns to the wise views of those who have devoted many years to developing great expertise in the various aspects of assessing and treating child victims, working with the whānau/family, investigating offences, prosecuting the offenders, and working to inform children and protect them.

Next is the perspective of a mother and a grandmother who found herself living next door to a child sex offender. That chapter is followed by insights into treating, researching and, where appropriate, reintegrating those who have offended or are at risk of carrying out sexually harmful behaviour. Following that, I outline my understanding of the essential developmental requirements for choosing life-enhancing sex. From this foundation I then examine what shapes destructive sexual behaviour. How do some develop a sexual interest in children?

Some of what I and these expert contributors have to say will be unpalatable. Bear in mind that the views included here are born of extensive coalface experience (sometimes personal as well as professional), deep reflection and striving to improve service delivery. I see the wisdom of each of these carefully chosen contributors as worthy of serious consideration. That said, each chapter is, of course, the perspective of its writer. I regret that I was unable to obtain a Pasifika perspective. I took too long trying to find the right person, and of course, once I did, she was very heavily committed.

HISTORY SUGGESTS THAT WHEN A significant effort is made to address the issue of sexual abuse, there is often a backlash. In the 1990s an international campaign arose to challenge, shame and undermine the credibility of both those working, speaking up and writing in the field of CSA, and the survivors themselves. The attacks were based on claims of a 'false memory syndrome', a term repeated in many media reports, before professionals were able to establish that there was no such psychological construct. So-called evidence of 'implanted memories' was found to be created by studies that in no way reflected the conditions of child trauma and were thus debunked.

More recently, we have seen the backlash when an accusation made against Supreme Court nominee Brett Kavanaugh led President Trump to tweet that 'it's a very scary time for young men in America'. Such a statement suggests that false reporting is far more of a risk than the statistics on its prevalence support. While not in this case referring to CSA, such a comment shows concern for reported perpetrators rather than for their victims, as is too often the case when CSA is disclosed. It also ignores the difficulties in establishing the existence of sexual abuse at any age, of reaching the evidential threshold and then gaining a conviction, given that offenders are often deliberate and strategic about ensuring there are no witnesses.

My understanding is that such backlashes arise for a variety of reasons. Denial can be a way of distancing oneself from unbearable sadness, fear or discomfort. Attack can be a way to defend against guilt. Unfortunately some unwell people do jump on the bandwagon, telling outrageous stories that stretch credibility too far, to the detriment of all survivors. We hear horror stories of false accusations, perhaps arising from the conflict of a messy separation or a mental illness. There is no doubt that being unjustly accused of CSA would be a nightmare. However, we cannot let such tragic occurrences deflect us from facing the significant number of genuine child sexual abuse incidents that occur every year. These, too, are outrageous horror experiences; to address them we must bear some pain.

A further caution: I want to avoid stirring hatred towards those who are maladaptively wired to desire sex with children and those who have sexually abused children. I carefully examine the evidence and understanding of what drives sexual offending against children and how we as a society can most effectively intervene to protect children. Being angry about harmful sexual behaviour is utterly appropriate, but contempt for, or the attack of, any human being is destructive. This book's task is to clarify how best we can all be constructive.

I HAVE BEEN ADVISED THAT incorporating information about children's needs, children's sexuality and the sexual abuse of children with information about those who have sexually harmful behaviours, and their needs and treatment, in one book is inappropriate for survivors. I have given this a great deal of thought. The last thing I want to do is offend any survivor of child sexual abuse. However, our reality is that we all cohabit. In order to effectively protect children, we need to consider this problem holistically. CSA is not simply a phenomenon of our current era. 'It has been a feature of every civilisation, dating back to antiquity.'[1] It is time to do something different.

Formulating a plan for reducing the prevalence of child sexual abuse requires becoming well informed. Most, if not all, of us have biases, and some will have made assumptions about what is needed. Ultimately the sole cause of child sexual abuse is that someone has chosen to use a child to gratify their own sexual, power and/or emotional needs. But that is too simplistic an understanding to be of help in stopping CSA. We have to ask: What would lead someone to make such a destructive choice?

Any major transformation is achieved first through identifying the interlinking pieces of the systems of cause and of change. *Free to Be Children* does that. Then it's over to us all to translate our grasp of the facts into effective action. This book is not a piece of wishful thinking: it's a blueprint for action. What might that action look like? The final chapter maps that out.

Working on this book has been harrowing. I thought I was well capable of bearing the pain of this topic. The dilemma, this process has reminded me, is that it *is* unbearable *and* that in order to make important progress to protect children, this pain has to be borne — by survivors of sexual abuse, by those working in the field, by me, by my contributors to this book and, to some extent, by readers. As I neared the end of this project I felt scoured out, and I was frequently and readily moved to tears. I have had times of doubt that this book will be powerful enough to generate a campaign to stop CSA in Aotearoa New Zealand and that I am strong enough to take my place in this. Please join me by doing your part to take effective, informed action in your community. Each individual reader will be able to identify from the blueprint where they have the capacity to take such action.

Prior to the genesis of this book, I had concluded that each of us is simply a little worker ant, doing what we can. I had faced my powerlessness: my concern that, despite a lifetime in the field of sex therapy, working to help people develop their sexual comfort and relationships, I could not make a significant national impact in addressing destructive sexual behaviours. Now, I have remembered that ants work in teams, have a greater intelligence collectively, and together carry far more than their own weight. And then I found myself wondering: How have we let this carry on for so long?

A NOTE TO READERS

This book may touch on tender spots or bring up painful memories in the reader. The following agencies are some of those that can provide support and professional help:

FindSupport — Here you can access a comprehensive list of the agencies and individuals in your region specialising in working with the impact of sexual abuse, whether it happened a week or many years ago. findsupport.co.nz

Safe to talk / Kōrero mai ka ora sexual harm helpline 24/7 — This is for anyone who is experiencing, or has experienced, child sexual abuse, or who is having sexual thoughts about children. 0800 044 334 / safetotalk.nz

1737 Need to talk? — A national telehealth service for anyone with mental health or addiction concerns. Free call or text 1737 any time for support from a trained counsellor.

The Harbour — Online support for those affected by sexual abuse. theharbour.org.nz

Fight Sexual Abuse NZ (FSANZ) — A support network for sexual abuse survivors of any age, gender or ethnicity. fightsexualabuse.co.nz

Male Survivors Aotearoa — Resources and support to help male survivors of child sexual abuse. malesurvivor.nz

Victim Support — 0800 842 846 (24-hour service)

Shakti Crisis Line — For migrant or refugee women living with family violence. 0800 742 584

Lifeline — 0800 543 354 (0800 LIFELINE) or free text 4357 (HELP)

Rape Crisis — For support after rape or sexual assault. 0800 883 300

Samaritans — For free confidential, non-judgemental and non-religious support. 0800 726 666

Suicide Crisis Helpline — 0508 828 865 (0508 TAUTOKO)

Youthline — 0800 376 633, free text 234, email talk@youthline.co.nz or chat online at youthline.co.nz

Women's Refuge crisis line — For women living with violence, or in fear, in their relationship or family. 0800 733 843 (0800 REFUGE)

TOAH-NNEST — Te Ohaakiia a Hine National Network Ending Sexual Violence Together. toah-nnest.org.nz

OUTLine NZ — Provides confidential telephone support and information for sexual orientation or gender identity concerns, needs and questions. 0800 688 5463 (OUTLINE)

Sex Therapy New Zealand — Specialists in working with sexual and intimacy problems. sextherapy.co.nz

New Zealand Sexual Health Society Inc. — The website of the professionals working in the field of sexual health. It will allow you to locate the sexual health clinics in your region. nzshs.org

There are three main agencies in New Zealand offering services for those with sexually harmful urges or behaviours:
Safe Network — (upper North Island) safenetwork.org.nz
WellStop — (central and lower North Island) wellstop.org.nz
STOP — (South Island) stop.org.nz

Introduction

IN ORDER TO UNDERSTAND HOW an individual can become a sexual abuser of children, and how we can stop this happening, we first need definitions of human sexuality and of what constitutes child sexual abuse. We also need data on the current prevalence of this abuse.

In any quest for clarity, I often look to literature along with psychological texts. Poets such as Anne French, David Lyndon Brown and Robin Healey remind the reader of the subjectivity and variability of the nature of sexuality.[1] Each offers their unique perspective on sexual expression, likely shaped by experience. Some are joyful and full of awe, others not so pleasant. Novelist Vincent O'Sullivan has described sex as 'the dark unfathomable current that is always there'.[2] As a sex therapist I suggest that, on reflection, we now have a good and growing understanding of the drivers of sexuality. I don't believe sex is dark unless something goes seriously wrong. In Chapter 17 I shine a torch on the sexual and psychological development of those who are sexually destructive.

The study of sexuality helps us understand the vast complexity and variety of human beings, and, conversely, knowing what drives the psyche of an individual explains much about their sexual behaviours. New Zealand-born psychoanalyst Joyce McDougall spent much of her highly regarded working life based in Britain, studying and writing in the fields of sexuality and psychosomatics (the ways in which mental and emotional states can influence the body).[3] She describes how a single erotic scenario can be used to serve multiple needs simultaneously. It can, for example, give sexual pleasure, safeguard sexual identity and be a technique of psychic survival.

American sex therapist Jack Morin adds that 'the same depth and complexity that makes eroticism so fascinating and rewarding also guarantees that a great deal can go wrong'.[4]

At the risk of oversimplifying, I consider all human sexual behaviours can be placed somewhere on a continuum that ranges from life-enhancing to destructive. This is one lens through which we can view sexuality and, from there, child sexual abuse. Some for whom sex is mundane, giving little or no pleasure, may place themselves midway on this continuum. Any sexual behaviour involving another without their informed consent is by definition destructive, as is any sexual activity causing oneself or another person distress, trauma and/or harm.

Here I use 'trauma' to mean 'coping systems overwhelmed'. Following a traumatic experience, there are inevitable after-effects, as the brain and body are swamped with an event too big to process at the time. Neurobiological studies, such as that by Anda et al. of the US Centers for Disease Control and Prevention, have now established clearly that the trauma which often occurs with child sexual abuse rewires the developing brain, leaving a lifelong impact.[5] It is only when they have safety, and sufficient support to enable healing, that the individual can do the work of processing this impact. In the absence of that, and even more so when trauma is ongoing, it is common to experience catastrophic thinking and emotional reactivity or outbursts. Hypervigilance, hyperarousal, difficulty sleeping and attempts to be in control of things and people around them are also commonly manifested as subjects try to counterbalance the sense of loss of internal control. Conversely, some people react with complete emotional detachment.

The well-known ACEs (Adverse Childhood Experiences) research has identified that childhood trauma such as sexual abuse is clearly linked to an increased risk of many serious physical and mental health problems in adulthood.[6]

What, then, is child sexual abuse? CSA is generally understood to include any sexual activity perpetrated against a minor (in this country, a child under the age of 16) by threat, force, intimidation or manipulation. Along with sexual touching and penetrative sex, this can include grooming, seduction, genital exposure and capturing images of children. Minors are deemed incapable of giving consent. While adult-to-child interactions in which the purpose is sexual gratification are clearly considered abusive, sexual behaviours between children are less clear-cut as there is no universally accepted definition of sexual abuse that differentiates it from normal sex play and exploration (as outlined in the chapter by paediatrician Dawn Elder). Although a two- to five-year age difference between children was first suggested as necessary for sexual behaviours between siblings to be regarded as incestuous abuse, this criterion is being questioned. Studies have shown this age difference to be much lower in many substantiated cases of child-to-child abuse.[7]

Far from all of those with child- and youth-focused sexually harmful urges and/or behaviours are paedophiles. This term refers to those over the age of 16 who are sexually attracted to pre-pubescent children at least five years younger than themselves, and who either act on that attraction or are significantly distressed by it. Formerly the term applied only to those for whom this age group was the exclusive sexual interest, but now it is also used in non-exclusive situations.

Some paedophiles sexually abuse children in the belief that they are expressing a deeply held love of children and that their sexual offending is not harmful to the child/children. The second part of this belief is considered by professionals to be erroneous, based on extensive anecdotal evidence. There is of course no way to safely, ethically or definitively prove or disprove this belief.

For others, paedophile and non-paedophile, the terror or powerlessness of the child or young person is part of what arouses them. For another group the harm caused to the child is simply a side effect not considered. All these people fall into the category that police detective Neil Holden describes in his chapter as preferential offenders: their sexual aims are intentional and their sexual interests primarily or exclusively focus on minors.

SOME CHILD SEX OFFENDERS HAVE a range of sexual interests in their arousal template. Some find that what is sexually arousing to them is expanded to include children by porn escalation, opportunity, or inappropriate efforts to resolve a psychological crisis. When people in this group sexually abuse minors it may be either preferential or opportunistic offending. All those who have sexual activity of any kind with minors, including capturing or distributing images of children for sexual purposes, are breaking the law and being destructive. As will be outlined in the chapter on destructive sexual behaviour, there are both predisposing and precipitating factors that lead some men and women to sexually abuse children.

Interestingly, and surprisingly for many, British sociologist Sarah Goode quotes a range of adult male-focused studies showing that between 17 and 58 per cent of men known to practise only legal sexual behaviours nevertheless show arousal to images of children under the age of 12.[8] This suggests that not all of these men will sexually offend. Some, perhaps most, put clear boundaries around their sexual practices to avoid breaching their values or breaking the law.

While it is no longer internationally accepted as a diagnostic category, the term *hebephile* is still used by some to refer to adults attracted to pubescent adolescents, and *adophile* for those whose sexual interest is in adolescents past puberty. Again, Goode cites clinical studies that found around 40 per cent of men showed arousal to adolescent images. I've been unable to find equivalent studies exploring female arousal to child and adolescent images, but it is clear that some women do sexually abuse minors.

The age at which it becomes legal to have sex differs somewhat around the world; it currently ranges from 11 (Nigeria) to 21 (Portugal and Bahrain), and in some countries sex is illegal before marriage. Such complexities of definition are just one of the factors that make it very difficult to get accurate figures of the magnitude of CSA. In New Zealand the age is 16, and I would argue this should never be lowered. Here is a summary of Sarah Goode's elegantly described reasons why:

> Child sexual abuse is harmful to children not because it is illegal but because it is inherently harmful: even in contexts where there is cultural consensus that sex with minors is ok, even without pressure, force or trickery (though these things can magnify the harm) and even when children acknowledge having given consent. It is the biology, neurology and psychology of the developing child that makes CSA harmful. Children are by definition developmentally immature; they require special protection while still developing so they can discover their own sexuality at their own pace and in their own way. Harm is 'fundamentally related to psychological intrusion and the violation of intimacy'. Child sexual abuse violates the child's autonomy and self-determination.

Adult power impacts on the child's ability to speak freely and move freely. A child doesn't want to displease and fears consequences of opposing an adult's will, is likely to be confused about what is happening and lacks the words to describe this. 'Children are prepared to sacrifice themselves for those they love.' Children may experience fear, confusion and embarrassment and have usually been socialised to not make a fuss. They often react to internal distress or overwhelm by dissociating (possum in the headlights type freeze, a trance state or a sense of being outside the body) then are further isolated because they are out of touch with themselves so can't express what they are experiencing or speak out about it. They may also fear they will not be believed.

The younger the child and the more intimate the context, the more fundamental is the distortion of the child's developmental experiences.[9]

CHILD SEXUAL ABUSE HAPPENS FAR too often in our country; of course, it ought never to happen at all. Those working in the field would agree that we don't know about all of it, and may not even identify most of it. There are many complexities involved in gathering meaningful, up-to-date data on CSA; this part of becoming well informed is difficult. There seems, however, to be more than enough evidence of a serious problem. Significant discrepancies between statistics reported from government authorities such as Oranga Tamariki and the New Zealand Police, and from self-report surveys, have led many to suggest that the majority of CSA is not reported. Even so, the Ministry of Social Development reported that during 2017 the agency was able to substantiate that 1010 children had been sexually abused.[10]

The New Zealand Family Violence Clearinghouse (NZFVC), based at the School of Population Health, University of Auckland, is a national centre for research and information on family and whānau violence in Aotearoa New Zealand. Despite our need for high-quality, research-based evidence and analysis, sadly it appears ongoing funding for this aspect of the NZFVC's work is not secure, so its 2017 Child Sexual Abuse Data Summary is the most recent available at the time of this book going to print. Interested readers can access this in full from nzfvc.org.nz; I present here just a few statistics from the summary to give a glimpse of what is known to be happening in our country.

The Ministry of Justice's sexual offences data for the year 2017/18 show that from a total of 4139 prosecutions of child sexual abuse, 2250 convictions were achieved.[11] These figures don't, of course, include the numbers of reported incidents where police were unable to obtain sufficient evidence for a prosecution. A further complexity is that changes in such agencies' reporting policies, data-capture mechanisms and prosecution guidelines result in the inability to accurately observe trends over time.

Nearly 3000 New Zealand women took part in the World Health Organization Multi-Country Study on Violence against Women. Twenty per cent reported CSA before the age of 15. Two per cent of the perpetrators were female, 71 per cent were male. For the remainder, gender was not specified. Of those perpetrators, 9 per cent were a parent, 6 per cent a step-parent, 17 per cent an aunt or uncle, 10 per cent a sibling or step-sibling, 10 per cent a cousin, and 6 per cent a grandparent. Five per cent were other family members and the remainder were non-family.

Police data summaries show that of the child sexual assaults prosecuted in 2016, roughly 40 per cent were on children under the age of 12, and 60 per cent on youths between 12 and 16 years. In the younger age group around 80 per cent of the victims were female, 20 per cent male. In the older age group the percentage of female victims had increased to around 90 per cent. Perpetrators against both boys and girls were far more likely to be male than female. From her review of the CSA research in English-speaking countries from the past 20 years, Dianna Kenny, a professor of psychology at the University of Sydney, concludes that 89–94 per cent of child sexual offences are perpetrated by males, and that 90 per cent or more of juvenile offenders against children are also male.[12] Where female perpetrators were involved, they mostly targeted boys aged 12 to 16. It is noted that most CSA research preceding the publication of this book adheres to the now outdated restrictive notion of binary choices in gender.

In 1998 the internationally respected Dunedin Multidisciplinary Health and Development Research Study asked all its participants whether they had experienced sexual abuse before the age of 16. Thirty per cent of the females and 9 per cent of the males reported a range of violations experienced, from genital touching to intercourse.

The NZFVC also reports research findings on re-victimisation, and the Ministry of Women's Affairs published a report on this topic in 2012, noting that not only are survivors of child maltreatment more vulnerable to being targeted again at later points in their development, but also that a history of child maltreatment is linked with a greater likelihood of psychological and physical health problems in adulthood.[13]

A seminal study by American sociologist David Finkelhor, who has specialised in researching CSA internationally, found that one in four girls and one in eight to ten boys report unwanted sexual touch in childhood.[14] These figures, which have often been replicated in subsequent research,[15] are generally accepted as a meaningful and accurate finding applicable to New Zealand, along with the above findings, the data reported in some contributors' chapters, and others.[16]

CHILDREN OF ANY GENDER CAN be sexually abused. Both women and men can be sexual abusers, although abuse by men is far more commonly reported. Abuse of girls is more commonly reported than of boys, for reasons that are unclear: it may be due to the fact that boys are less often sexually victimised, and/or to the silencing effect of the perceived additional shame of being a male victim in a society where men are still seen as sexual aggressors and women as victims. This effect can be heightened if the perpetrator is female, with some male survivors being laughed at or told they should be grateful when trying to report their experiences of sexual abuse by a woman. Individuals and groups who challenge the current dominant norms around gender, orientation and sexuality generally have been identified as being more at risk, not only of CSA but also of partner/other violence in adulthood.[17]

It remains unclear how much sexual abuse goes unreported. Finkelhor has suggested that it is only those men 'unlucky enough to be caught and inarticulate enough not to persuade authorities to let them off' who become known as sex offenders and on whom research on sexual offending is based.[18] If accurate, this is obviously of significant concern. Presumably this would also apply to female child sex offenders. Further, it is important to consider that in many studies the children identified are only those who were able to disclose (and who were believed, reported to and followed up by the proper authorities), and the only cases cited are those that presented enough evidence to be substantiated as child sexual abuse. There may be far more victims who fall beneath that bar.

Looking at international CSA studies, Finkelhor found in all of them that only about half of the victims had disclosed the abuse to anyone.[19] Disclosure is a delicate and sensitive process that he found to be influenced by several factors, including implicit or explicit pressure for secrecy, feelings of responsibility or blame, feelings of shame or embarrassment, or the fear of negative consequences. Ethnic and religious cultures may act as either facilitators or barriers to the telling and reporting of CSA. Ignorance of how trauma affects children, and of the metaphorical forms of expression children use in such circumstances, can undermine disclosures: when the child's testimony is deemed unreliable, or when elements of proof are unavailable or perceived as questionable, police may be forced to conclude that the evidential threshold cannot be met.

There is one final important point from American sex therapist Joe Kort that sadly requires clarification for some ill-informed individuals: child sexual offending is not determined by whether the offender is heterosexual or homosexual; it is determined by them being youth-attracted and acting on that.[20]

A GUIDE TO THIS BOOK

The first chapter provides one illustration of how bad child sexual abuse can be and the multiple ways in which it can impact. Next, following some definitions of sexuality and of CSA, this book collects the wisdom of a selection of experts in their field.

I provide a brief introduction to each contributor (my words are set in italics), followed by their chapter. Each portrays aspects of their domain of expertise. First, the focus is on children and their needs, including the work of helping children disclose and heal from CSA, the police role, community work tackling sexual abuse, children's learning needs, and our chief censor's description of the current situation and the implications of this for children. Next is the wisdom of a loving, protective mother and grandmother.

Then we read about the work undertaken with those with sexually harmful behaviours, in a range of settings. All these experts are writing in the interests of our goal of reducing child sexual abuse, so each contributor was also asked to make recommendations for the changes required to this end. This section concludes with two chapters written by me, in my role as a clinical psychologist specialising in sex therapy, to explain the development of sexuality and how this can go awry, leading to destructive sexual behaviours.

My final chapter aims to draw together important points from the foregoing chapters to provide a blueprint, a pathway, for going forward. How do we — as individuals, as communities, as a society — resolve the crisis of child sex abuse?

I thought a lot about how to choose representative examples of child sexual abuse and its impact, but I have concluded that, as no two experiences are the same, no number of stories can represent anyone or everyone else's story. I have chosen to present here a single description of severe abuse written by the insightful and honest survivor in interaction with me. This will illustrate how bad life can be for some children and how they can be affected throughout life. As it turned out, when two of the contributors to this book were invited to write about their work in addressing CSA in their communities, they chose to also tell their own experiences.

Children living in optimal circumstances can still fall prey to sexual abusers. CSA occurs across all sectors of society, and sexual abuse is not the only form of trauma to which children can be subjected. 'Concrete baby' is the story of a child abuse survivor written when he finally felt able to reflect on his life as he neared the age of 70. (Names have been withheld to ensure anonymity.) Despite enduring horrific neglect and every form of abuse possible, it was the sexual abuse that he found the hardest to reveal, for which he carried guilt and shame for the longest time, and that did the most harm. This will be painful to read, as it ought to be.

Every newborn baby arrives full of potential. The opportunity to achieve this potential is their birthright, and not only they but our society, too, thrives when they do. To realise this potential, each child must pass through essential needs and developmental stages. One model of these stages and the psychological tasks to be achieved, or not, is reproduced opposite. This man's struggles will be all the more evident in the light of this model.

Fig. 1.1: Erik Erikson's stages of psychosocial development. From www.psychologynoteshq.com/erikerikson/

Approximate age	Psychosocial crisis
Infant–18 months	Trusts vs mistrust
18 months–3 years	Autonomy vs shame and doubt
3–5 years	Initiative vs guilt
5–13 years	Industry vs inferiority
13–21 years	Identity vs role confusion
21–39 years	Intimacy vs isolation
40–65 years	Generativity vs stagnation
65 years +	Ego integrity vs despair

1. 'Concrete baby': A survivor's story

ANONYMOUS

MY HEAD GIVES MY HEART so many warnings, and many demons reside there with whom I do battle regularly. Sometimes I wonder why I exist, and other times how I exist.

When I was small and just surviving I was constantly reminded about how nothing good would ever come of me because I came from a bad family. My mother had left me and my sister at a babysitter's. She picked up my sister but never came back for me. I am unsure how I ended up where I did but I think maybe it was as a consequence of being handed around. I think it might have been common to treat children like me as a commodity simply because, where I grew up, they didn't like children; we seemed to be more of a cashflow item. I think they got paid to have us, plus they collected the family benefit.

It's no wonder I have never been on the electoral roll, filled in a census paper, served on a jury or complied with any other normal government-required action. I came across an expired passport today while cleaning things out. It reminds me of my lack of enthusiasm and trust in government agencies when I have two passports with two different birthdays; I have an old driver's licence with another date (also it's a lifetime licence, which they didn't honour, and it's expired now). They lost me when I was just a baby, and then after 53 years of paying taxes they almost refused to acknowledge I was entitled to Super.

My birthday is one of many falsehoods in my life. Although my name is made up, including the addition of my middle name (which I chose myself once I was an adult), it's always been my name as long as I can remember, so I own it. My birthday, on the other hand, is an embarrassment to me. My earliest birthday memory was never being allowed to go to other kids' birthday parties that I had been invited to, and I didn't actually understand what they were anyway.

Then one day someone said happy birthday to me (it was 27 September) and I folded it away as the day I must have been born. There were no presents or anything else, and I can't remember if I got belted that day or not. I waited a whole year for the next one to roll around and nothing happened. The following year they said happy birthday on 7 October, and it then clicked that it was just all made up.

At school my birthday was registered as 27 September (I know that because some teachers used to tell the whole class if it was someone's birthday), so it was a birthday shambles and part of my shame. When I got older and was on my own I decided I didn't need a birthday anyway, but I had to have a date to ward off questions and fill in forms, so I chose 24 September because I always thought four was a good number and I wanted a double-digit number and 2 times 2 equals 4 so it became 24. Hence my birthday is a farce to me. I could have been born in January for all I know. I should know if my real mother had actually confirmed it for me, but she was so vague that I wonder if she was my mother. Plus she would not answer even the most elementary questions.

I used to have the birth certificate for ———, which is apparently me, and that wasn't any of those dates.

The other reason I don't like birthdays is because they seemed to exist to add more pain to my life as a boy. The older girl at our place had a birthday every year and got presents (and had no shame about it, either), which just added to the mystery of why life existed for me at all. Sorry about that: once I got started I could not stop. Please know I am not sad about it.

I was told my father murdered my brother and buried him in the sandhills and that his surname was ——— and my mother's Christian name was ———. I heard it so often it was hard to forget, so when I was about 19 I wrote to everyone in the Auckland phone book with that surname (there were not very many; it was an unusual name). Some months later a person wrote back saying that his mother, who lived in Auckland, knew who I was and they all thought I was dead. He also took the time to say that if I had a good home and family I might be better leaving things at that.

I contacted his mother, who told me I had two sisters and a mother all living in Auckland. In hindsight I should have left it a few years until I was more mature and settled, but you don't know you aren't mature when you are young so I just ploughed ahead. It took time. I really didn't have any money to go to Auckland and I wasn't a great letter writer, so it took a few months to organise. I was met by a sister, and the day after that I met my mother and other sister.

It was clear my mother had no emotional feeling for me whatsoever, other than to say I looked nice (which I probably didn't) and then to just engage in very small talk about nothing in particular and more with other people than me. My sisters were only a little better. Both by then (unbeknown to me) were heavy drinkers and about to leave their respective husbands and children for younger men.

I think I was expecting too much and from people with nothing or little to offer, and I was too young to have much to offer myself. I thought I might be upset writing about this, like I usually am when I think about it, but now I understand I had my bit to play in all that as well, and I am worn out by the disappointing memories of it all. I met them all several times but with no great feeling of a sense of family, love, sadness or anything other than disappointment.

I did attempt to convince my mother that I was a good man, that I didn't need anything from her and that I never held her accountable in any way, but to no avail. After she moved to ———, I began a habit of standing outside her apartment whenever I was in that country, both when she was alive and even now if I have the chance. It's my only connection with the person who I feel could make it right. It was a fantasy that she might come out and understand my pain and make it all go away.

I never wanted her to feel in any way responsible, I just wanted her to see my soul and cleanse it. It never happened either in person or by phone, email, mail or any way. I always dressed and behaved perfectly in her presence. I wanted her to know I had not only survived, but I had also thrived (in a material way). I thought it might be the way to let her see I was a good man. The only result was that one of my sisters told me I was lucky I didn't grow up with them.

I always initiated contact, but I understand it was I who needed contact, not her. After all, I found her; she never looked for me, and in fact told everyone I was dead, including my sisters. I never really bonded with my sisters, partly because I was unsure if we had the same father and partly because I wanted/needed a mother first and family second. I gave one of my sisters money to help her out; she got angry at me for not giving her more. The other one I just gave up on. When I recently met my sister in ——— she was in the exact place I would have sat if I was looking for her. I figured that she was always headed for the caravan park where I think she lives now . . . I think anyone finding and meeting long-lost family should never have any expectations, good or bad; that was my mistake. I didn't even get to go to my mother's funeral because no one thought to let me know she had died.

I DON'T BELIEVE I AM a good person, for several reasons. I have always considered myself a fraud in that I am not what I seem to be. A bit like 'you can take a boy out of the gutter but you can't take the gutter out of him'. To survive as a child I learnt to steal, lie, fight and just not be a good person. I never lost those skills. As an adult I haven't had to use them much, but I have used all three. I am a fraud because I appear to be someone who comes from somewhere good — a person who works hard, has a brain, dresses well and has good manners — when in fact I come from nobody and nothing. I am not being hard on myself: I know I have some good things now, but I acquired them so I could appear normal.

I am a clean freak now because we were so dirty as children. I remember the dental nurse at school refusing to touch my teeth because in her opinion they had never been cleaned, and reporting that at home earned me a thrashing; some weeks later I stole a toothbrush and gave them a clean. To be honest, although I was shamed at school, I didn't know anything about hygiene and the only way I ever learnt was by experiences like that. I wasn't always able to grasp the concept either, or actually do anything about it, because until I stole one I never had a toothbrush or the other stuff you need to keep clean.

So in my adult life I dress well, and I don't let anyone wash or iron my clothes because I want to be responsible for them. I want the whitest shirts, the sharpest creases, polished shoes, and matching, colour-coordinated, age-appropriate and fashionable clothes. It's not important for me to be the best-dressed person, but to be up there or thereabouts. I am constantly experimenting with ways to iron better, get my shirts whiter or shoes shinier, or other ways to present clothes. It's actually not hard; most people just don't make the effort. It's easy to stand out. I don't want to stand out to be special; I just don't want to be ordinary. If I am going to a meeting and I am flying, I will always ask the hostess to hang my suit jacket up and I put it on when I get there. I used to do that if I visited my mother, but she never noticed.

I have been to jail (overseas, definitely not for a sexually related crime), but I don't want to talk about it. Jail is nothing to be proud of. I should have gone a few times and I am lucky I didn't. I am a tough bugger, but jail is a scary place, not for the faint-hearted, and to go twice means you are either dumb or a habitual criminal. Only the first reason is an excuse. I am not dumb.

I have always fought for the underdog. As an employer now I love when a deadbeat walks through the doors but they have something that gels with me and I give them a job, sometimes creating one that didn't exist. I am not good at it — they hardly ever work out — but I think maybe one day something I did will help them survive, if not thrive.

I am a white boy when it suits me, which is most of the time; but I think my inner self connects with being someone darker, although I don't openly admit to feeling that way. Māori are very iwi-orientated and if you don't know your history it's difficult to connect. Hence my aversion to openly belonging.

I get much pleasure from being told to do things instead of being asked. I am unsure what that's about; I suspect it means that I don't have to think, I just do it. When I was little, Mrs X (a foster mother whose surname changed regularly depending on whom she was dealing with) never asked me to do anything; she told me. I learnt that staying out of trouble even for a few minutes meant do it now, do it fast (not too fast, make it last) and do it well, and then wait for the next instruction. When there was nothing to do, violence or sex became options, so it was better to be working under instruction. Actually, though, since I left home 99 per cent of the time I operate being in control and alert for dangers and opportunities. That sounds a bit contradictory, but both are true.

MY ENDURING MEMORY OF MY childhood is of being hungry every single day. There was always plenty of food in the house: it just wasn't for some of us. I even went to the grocer's and picked up the food and to the butcher's to watch him cut up the weekly order, but I never considered it my food or our food: it was their food. The chosen ones would eat a full meal while some of us had a potato and maybe a bit of cabbage. Lunch was a stale sandwich and breakfast was what anyone left on a plate. To this day I still eat cold food as easily as hot because I grew up eating cold bits of leftovers and drinking cold tea.

We had a feast of luncheon sausage once when a foster sister stole three slices and hid them in the dirty dishwater and I made her give me half. I stole a mouthful of cold sago once that was in a big pie dish and swallowed it without tasting it. I got caught and it turned out it was two-day-old porridge that was going to the chooks. I was sat down, given a spoon and made to eat the whole bowl. Another time I had to eat a whole bowl of green apples for a similar offence.

When I was about five I used to go to the local grocer's on my trike to collect the groceries. All my childhood I got the groceries, I am not sure why; I was given a list and money and away I went. On one particular visit the two ladies who ran the shop asked if I would like to bag apricots for them. They took me to a separate building behind the shop which was full of stuff and there was a big wooden box full of dried apricots. My job was to fill paper bags with apricots. Needless to say, left alone I gorged myself on them while filling the bags. I was so fixated on eating that I never noticed the time; they forgot I was there and I got locked in when the shop closed. Not for long — but I would have happily stayed there all night eating my way through the box. What a great day in my life, second only to the luncheon sausage day.

I stole sandwiches from other kids at school or sometimes they just gave them to me. If I got caught, the school would ring home and I would get a belting when I got home. Food was always a constant search for me; everything else took second place because the hunger never ever went away. I hated school holidays; there were fewer chances to eat and more likelihood of getting beaten.

I could relay numerous stories of not eating, being forced to eat as punishment, watching other people eat and spending almost my entire childhood being hungry, but they are all similar so I have touched on only a few. Eating food was my prime objective as a child and I can't explain how very important it was . . . I don't have a sweet tooth and count the number of fizzy drinks I have ever had probably on both hands. But even now I have bad eating habits. I forget to have breakfast, mostly. I can easily do without lunch. My excuse is that it's too close to dinnertime. I feel like I don't want to get complacent in case it all happens again. I prefer eating on my own or in public facing away from other people.

I have inherited some negatives from my everyday childhood eating experiences, including not being willing until recently to share food off my plate. Most of my adult life I have insisted on my own packet of fish and chips, which I could not bear another person taking even one chip from. I lost all my teeth at a young age due apparently to lack of bone growth in my jaw. For a long time I used to poke teeth that fell out back into their holes, but eventually I could afford to go to a dentist. He indicated my problem was unusual and that it's usually attributed to malnutrition. I never consider a use-by date on food. That's for fools: food is food.

I HAVE DISCOVERED THE BEST way for me to write calmly is to make bullet points, which is something that I have used regularly in my business life. I want to be clear that I don't think I am unique. I think lots of little New Zealanders live my story every day. I am just writing about some of my experiences and even then I am only scratching the surface.

Beatings

- I am sure there must have been some but I can't remember a single day in my childhood when I wasn't verbally abused or slapped or punched or kicked or beaten with an object; one or more of those things happened every day.
- I was beaten with fists, sticks, boots, household utensils, a whip, belts, had my hands put on the oven and probably some things I don't recall.
- I have been hung in a sugar sack under the shower, which was turned on with cold water, and then taken down and put — still in the sack — into a cold bath full of water. The whole time they were telling me I was in the clutches of the devil. I was thinking I just needed to make sure I didn't drown; I didn't believe the devil stuff.
- Once I was trapped in a galley kitchen with no escape and was punched and then kicked in the face when I fell over; I lost my front teeth and both my eyes closed over for a day or two with swelling.

- Slapping was a minor inconvenience. You got a whack around the face just for breathing.
- Hidings with a stick were common. You had to go find your own stick and hand it over and then stand there and get belted. The trick was to get one that would last just long enough to satisfy them. If it broke too soon I had to go and get another one.
- Punching, kicking and other hidings were only when they got out of control with either alcohol or just plain rage.
- Only one other child consistently got beaten and starved. There were only four of us in total that were there all the time; a big Islander boy got given food and the foster parent's daughter got food, too. Neither of them ever offered any to the other girl or me. The others were transient, mostly in between welfare homes or borstal. They were there for months, not years, and got food and little or no beatings because they were not staying and were often checked on.
- I frequently wonder why someone didn't rescue us. The neighbours must have heard, seen and known, schoolteachers must have known something was amiss. Too late now.
- There was a probation officer who brought young men to stay a few times. He can't ever have looked inside our house or he would have known things were wrong. The young men he brought there must have told him about it, though. I don't know why no one ever talked about what they saw. They must have just thought it was normal.
- My biggest problem was that after about age six or seven I would not be humbled, I refused to cry, I refused to bow my head and I learned to suck up the pain like it wasn't there. It *was* there; I just would not acknowledge it. Not my smartest move ever — it just made things worse for me — but I could not give in to them. I didn't do it to aggravate them: I did it because it was all I had left of me.

Sexual abuse

- This is the most difficult thing I have ever written about. I have never talked about this in depth before in my entire life.

- I experienced sexual abuse since my earliest memories.
- At first it was by seeing other people having some form of sex (my foster 'father' with young girls). I didn't realise what it was, but because it allowed me to fly under the radar, even if only for a few minutes, it didn't really concern me.
- I don't know how old I was when I was first visited in my bed by my foster father and he felt my privates and made me feel his. This happened at least once a week, and not long after I was forced to suck him as well.
- The whole process was silent. He usually held me by the hair and just pushed me down and stuck it in my mouth.
- At first it was brief, but later he started coming in my mouth and would hold me there, making me swallow.
- He was also doing at least one girl at the same time. Not us both together. If he wasn't at me he was at them.
- I think eventually they (the girls) must have liked it because they started coming in my bed and playing with my penis and asking me to lie on top of them. I would only do that if they left their clothes on. I didn't like it, but they wouldn't let me sleep otherwise.
- Some of the older boys at the house would do them properly.
- We had a series of young men live with us from time to time who I now understand were homosexuals or transsexuals and they would on occasion just throw themselves on top of me and dry-hump me until they came and then they would let me go. That could happen any time; they seemed a bit out of control to me. They were too heavy and I couldn't get them off, so I used to be wary of them all the time.
- The father of the house penetrated me when I was about eight and he got caught by his wife, but she just told him to fucking wash himself before he came to bed. I got thrashings from both of them the next day.
- He preferred me sucking him and coming in my mouth, but when he was drunk he would hold me down and penetrate me and started having orgasms in me.
- Then she (the foster mother) started saying it was time I was

'educated', as she called it, and made me do all kinds of sexual acts on her, including penetrating her. I wasn't old enough to have an orgasm so she said she liked it because I would just stay hard. She smelt bad, she wasn't a clean person; and he smelt as well.
- It wasn't a daily event; it might not happen more than once a fortnight or, if I was unlucky, him and her in the one week. Not together, always on their own.
- I think she knew about him because sometimes with the girls he would actually do them in her bed while she was asleep, which I don't think you could sleep through.
- It didn't stop until I was about 12, and by then I was an angry ant and, although small, I was over people touching me and bashing me. I am not sure how they knew; it just happened. He was going to bash me one day in front of her and I remember thinking I am going to bash him back. He stopped and said something like 'oh you think you are big enough, do you?' I have never been big — even now I am a small man — but he backed off and I never got bashed or molested again.
- I can't describe how bad it was. I actually thought in some way it was my fault, but it was also just another event to add to the daily grind of trying to find food, getting another hiding and just for good measure being used as a sex toy. It was just another thing to learn to turn off from, to be detached from and not let it weigh me down.
- In my adult life I have struggled with human touch and I have struggled with emotion. I strive to remove myself as far as possible from that life. I am always looking out for danger.
- These events when I read them don't look like much, but it went on for years. I once worked out I must have been raped at least 1000 times.

I USED TO RIDE TO school with a boy. One morning when he came to meet me he told me his granddad had died and then he started crying. I pushed him off his bike and rode to school without him. He was upset and crying and all I could think of was at least you had a granddad. I thought he was like me, a hard man, a survivor, but I guess in hindsight he was being human.

I have rarely been deliberately unkind in my life, but I was then and wish I hadn't done that, but I had no skills to show empathy.

I have some enduring friends from early adulthood through sport. I was a ferocious if only average rugby player, so I was always a good bloke to have on your team because I didn't mind a bit of biff and could sort things out (it was tolerated then). I think every rugby team has 20 players, five of whom have no courage and are tolerated, 10 are good players and good blokes to know, and that leaves five who fit me like a glove. They are brave, funny, bloody good players and they are always going to be your mates forever even if you don't see them very often. I have a few of those in my life.

I liked school and I liked learning, but to be frank it's hard to concentrate when you are planning on how to feed yourself mostly out of the school bins (some very good lunches go in there) and how to steal a uniform or parts of one because it's the only way you can blend in and not stand out. I always had a ragtag uniform; either it wasn't the right colour or it was very badly mended. Once I had grey pants with a black patch the size of a dinner plate on the bum. I was ashamed every day. I think when I concentrated I was a good student, but with so many things going on at home I didn't manage school well. One of the saddest days of my life was when I decided to run away and that meant leaving school. I remember sitting in the locker room thinking this is my last day of school, no one knows, no one cares. Now I don't write that well but I can read well. I am OK without it, but I wonder what I might have been with an education. In other ways running away was a red-letter day. I left when I was either 13 or 14: I stole a pound note, walked to the railway station with my little brown suitcase (God knows what was in there), got on the train and went off into the sunset. I only had a few pennies left after the ticket but I survived, and survived well, almost from day one.

THE EVENTS THAT LED ME to surviving well after I first boarded that train as a young boy were simplistic and typical of early 1960s New Zealand. Kind, unquestioning (they wouldn't have got answers anyway) ordinary adults gave me accommodation opportunities, work opportunities, and taught me a few basic skills like saving money for a rainy day, personal hygiene and good manners.

By the time I was 15 and a bit I found out that I had a work ethic that matched any adult's. I was desperate to fly under the radar and not be discovered. I pretty much kept to myself apart from working and playing rugby. I became immersed in the good and bad side of rural Māori life. I had one good friend whom I worked with, played football with and hung out with. After work on a Friday we bought a huge packet of fish and chips, went back to his place and shared them with his younger siblings. I had my own packet. His mum and dad had gone to the pub and would be home again late Sunday afternoon. If there was no football we would go to the dump on a Saturday and throw stones at the rats, and on Saturday night we would go eeling in the creek with all the little kids in tow. My friend knew how to prepare and cook them like little steaks with an onion ring on top with bread and butter as a side.

Pretty much that's how I lived for the first year: boarding, work, football, rats and eels. We did go to the pictures a couple of times. The best part of all was that I felt safely hidden away. No one came looking and after a while I realised they probably never had. I found out that it's normal to eat three times a day (not a lesson I really picked up on), that hard work brings rewards, that life isn't all bad when you are in charge of yourself. My runaway years were a very special time in my life, although some of it was sad as well. I remember spending a whole Christmas Day alone once, I think because people assume everyone has either someone or somewhere to go. Man, it was a very long day and brought home to me that I really was alone in the world. I didn't see it as survival then because I had already survived, but I was confused. The first time I held a girl's hand her palm was sweaty, but on reflection it was probably mine. The first time I kissed a girl I missed and kissed her forehead because I had never had or given a kiss before. It was a major disappointment. Her forehead just about knocked my tooth out.

NOW THAT I AM AN adult I can see that there are some things that would have made a difference:
- If I had a real name.
- If I had a birthday.
- If I ever got a present.
- A hug.
- A cuddle.
- A kind word.
- A lolly.

- A fizzy drink.
- A mother and a father.
- Food that I didn't steal.
- A safe bed with a lock on the door.
- Peace instead of 24-hour high alert trying to stay out of harm's way.

What I would change about me now if I could:
- Not worrying that people might find out that I come from a bad place.
- Not looking over my shoulder and assuming everything is a threat.
- Learning how to cry.
- Being more kind to myself and not working so hard.

I struggle with relationships and friendships because they come with expectations. In a relationship it's not enough to be a good provider (which I am), you also need to be a lover, romantic, caring, have empathy and lots more, and I only have some of those things in very small quantities. Friendships are the same: they come with expectations that you will remember their birthday, that you have a birthday and that you listen with empathy to their woes and not just offer solutions. In short it's easier to avoid friends than have them, mostly. I am learning to value friends now; but how long has that taken?

Writing this story about my life has also triggered a father-figure interest for me. I have spent my whole life looking for a mother; how come I have had no interest in a father figure? I have three thoughts about the parents I never had.

- They together combined to give me the right mix of genes that allowed me to fight my way through life with some success. Thank you.
- I miss not having a sense of history about where I come from and whom I am related to. I miss not having a family (I think), I miss not having happy memories of a childhood. I miss not knowing what I might have been or could have achieved with nurturing parents. No thanks for that one.
- I miss not being able to show you that I am a good man, a hard-

working man, a successful man, a man that I think most parents would be proud of. Your bad luck.

I never consider myself a victim. I have endured some harrowing early experiences and, without my being aware, some of those have impacted on my adult life; however, they also gave me unique skills that I use to this day. I can endure a lot of pain that might otherwise stop most people. I have drive and a relentless attitude that I can achieve anything. Sometimes I can't, but I give most things a better than average nudge. I can see trouble before it arrives and usually take appropriate action. In a business sense I have boxed well above my weight. I can't believe someone with little schooling can still have success in business. Being a successful business person gives me pleasure now, as does providing opportunities to ordinary people who have potential. I care about the vulnerable and I'm glad there's more help for people now, but in my business I see so many people abuse the system and that makes me feel less charitable.

IN MY ADULTHOOD I HAVE discovered I have an aversion to touch and sex. It's not that I don't think about sex. In fact, the more I think about it the harder it gets. I think I put too much pressure on myself to be normal, or at least what I thought normal was, and although I had a willing and lovely partner I just could not get over my mental barriers.

I was always interested in older women, but I didn't do much about that — or at least, not that I want to write about. I don't want my story to be about sex, even though in one way or another it has had a huge detrimental impact on my whole life. I never found or looked at women for beauty. I always looked for a mothering look, but I learned it's not normal so I suppressed those thoughts. I could never understand what men saw in younger women. To me they are to be looked after because they don't understand the consequences of lust. I could only appreciate their youthful beauty as I imagine a good father might. I don't want to talk about my adult sexuality other than to say it was a disaster and a constant embarrassment to me and almost as painful as my childhood. Why? It shows me what a terrible effect my early years had on me.

I sought professional help in my adult life to try to deal with my difficulties with touch and personal relationships. I think for it to be successful you have to make yourself vulnerable and be willing to change. I wasn't ready for either of those things. The only person I really trusted was myself. I remember when the counsellor tried to talk to me about my needs as a child, I told her I was a concrete baby: I didn't have needs.

I carried other people's guilt with me; the things they did to me I thought were my guilt and shame. I didn't want people to know what happened to me in detail because those things still haunt me even today. Some of the people who did those things to me were still alive and I didn't want to light my revenge fire and end up in prison or worse. I don't think I am anything special, but I might have been. I regret my life and the wasted potential. I don't think I have achieved as much as I could.

I'M PLEASED THAT I HAVE written this with you. I'm enjoying feeling better about myself. I never want my mood to go down again. To be raped is one thing. But to have a man (if you are a young, unwilling boy) stick his cock in your mouth and fuck it until he comes and then make you swallow him? Then after a while you do it because you just want it over with and he thinks you love it. A couple of hundred of those and you start to climb into a very, very deep cave. I want to be out of there and never go back. I am almost 70 now, I am professionally successful, but the events of my childhood have tainted my entire life. I still yearn for a cuddle from my mum and a manly conversation with my dad. I don't have any children and I am grateful for that because I would have no idea how to be a father.

When I met this man he was immaculately dressed, and clearly a successful businessman. He stressed that he had 'never looked for a handout'; he paid for the treatment he received and did not think of himself as a victim. Nor did he want me or the readers of this book to think of him in this way. When he left, he kept close to the wall as he made for the door, keeping maximum distance between us, avoiding turning his back to me.

We met again six months after he wrote his story. He reported being pleased he had done this, that his nightmares had reduced by 80 per cent, and that the remaining nightmares were different than before. He told me his hope for having contributed his story was that one more little person could go to sleep each night feeling safe.

When I asked for his recommendations for protecting children from sexual abuse he answered that he thinks every child should at the very least be accounted for, from birth, on a regular basis. 'I don't understand even now how I could have got so lost in a system with no name, no history and no one checking up on me. How can that happen?'

The next day he added, 'As a child, I was quite withdrawn with adults. I think I would have shown visible signs of neglect and abuse, but no one spoke out or investigated. I think teachers, in particular, should, without becoming involved, be able to raise red flags for more qualified and trained personnel to investigate. I don't think children will speak up because of the consequences and their own personal shame.'

The presence of loving adults is crucial for child well-being. Professor Dawn Elder recognises child sexual abuse in New Zealand as one of the most important health problems affecting children currently. She sees being well informed about the development of child sexuality in particular, and child development generally, as essential steps in reducing the prevalence of child sexual abuse and achieving convictions when crimes have been committed. Using her decades of experience as a paediatrician, Dawn clearly describes myths that can interfere with the accurate identification of child sexual abuse, and she provides crucial information to help us clear away these misunderstandings.

Dawn is head of the Department of Paediatrics and Child Health at the University of Otago, Wellington, and a consultant paediatrician at Wellington Hospital. Since 1991 she has been examining children and adolescents for the medical assessment of alleged sexual abuse. Having carried out nearly a thousand new patient assessments in this context, Dawn brings huge expertise to this book, as she does to her teaching role in New Zealand and the state of Victoria, Australia, which benefits medical students, doctors, nurses, allied health professionals, and child protection detectives in the New Zealand Police. Professor Elder was a member of the Family Violence Death Review Committee, a national committee of the Health Quality and Safety Commission from 2011 to 2016. She is currently chair of the New Zealand Paediatric Society Child Protection Clinical Network.

2. Child sexual abuse: A paediatrician's viewpoint

PROFESSOR DAWN ELDER
UNIVERSITY OF OTAGO, WELLINGTON

I HAVE BEEN WORKING IN the area of child sexual abuse since 1991 and have seen and assessed literally hundreds of children. My role is to undertake a medical assessment, mostly in a non-acute paediatric clinic setting, but sometimes as an after-hours acute referral and very occasionally in the mortuary. Although the primary intention of the referral is to consider whether sexual abuse has occurred, it also provides an opportunity for a general medical and health assessment. Most of these children have experienced sexual abuse, but sometimes the medical assessment is able to determine that the symptoms the child has presented with relate to another diagnosis. In some cases we are just not clear whether or not anything inappropriate or criminal has happened.

There is today increased awareness of the prevalence of child abuse in our communities, and while this may have resulted in earlier disclosure and therefore recognition of sexual abuse, there are no current data enabling us to confirm that.

Increased public awareness can also have a negative side. Parents may start to find the following questions disturbing their peace of mind: If child sexual abuse is so common, when is it going to happen to my children? Has it happened already? Will they be safe if I let them walk to school? Is my child's sore bottom an indication she has been sexually abused? As a father can I still hug my daughter?

In this chapter I share with you my experience of the problem of child and adolescent sexual abuse by addressing some myths that have caused confusion over the years, while also explaining the role of the medical assessment in this context. I also share my thoughts on how we might move forward to better address child sexual abuse in New Zealand.

COMMON MYTHS AND MISUNDERSTANDINGS

1. Young children are not sexual

Infants are born with sexual organs — these don't just arrive with puberty. Infants and toddlers may exhibit genital interest, but it is usually self-directed. By age three, children when asked are able to report whether they are a boy or a girl. Girls may be quite fascinated by their father's or their brother's penis since this is a recognisable body part they do not have. They also may wonder why males urinate standing but girls sit.

Both boys and girls may try to touch their mother's breasts. Younger pre-school children may imitate breastfeeding with a doll if a younger sibling in the house is being fed this way. Interest may also be expressed in the breasts of other women. From around age three or four children can be voyeurs: they poke their nose around the door when adults are dressing and exclaim gleefully 'I can see your boobies' or 'I can see your bottom'. Despite this rather impertinent interest in the bodies of adults around them, children become more aware of keeping their own bodies private as they approach school age. The actual age at which this happens is variable and will depend on the way the adults around them react to both adults and children being naked around the house.

Some parents have a very low tolerance of nudity in the home, while others are more relaxed and may leave the bathroom door open and walk freely from bedroom to bathroom without clothes on. The key issue here is intent. If a parent finds pleasure in being naked in front of their child or finds it sexually arousing to see their child naked, then that is a type of sexual abuse. For example, men reporting sexual abuse by their mothers in childhood describe being invited into the bathroom when their mother was in the bath to have a conversation with her and feeling very uncomfortable about it, but not being able to say 'no'.

As adults we can at times be pretty naïve about how young children learn and develop. It is endearing when a young child imitates a parent doing a housework task, but the same child is likely to be reprimanded minutes later for using a swear word they heard their parent say the day before. Children are sponges and absorb both positive and negative experiences. Sometimes they just copy what adults do without fully understanding what it means. When children exhibit sexualised play it is always important to remember that they may have learnt about sexual matters from accidental observation rather than because of direct involvement.

2. Young children view sexual differences and sexual matters the way adults do

We often interpret child behaviour through an adult lens. We have decided that we need to keep genitalia covered, or that checking out a little brother's penis is wrong, and so we evaluate this as a sexual matter, when in fact the child is just trying to learn about the world around him or her and the physical differences between the sexes. Context, however, can be everything.

Imagine the scenario of a three-year-old girl coming into the kitchen when her mother is cooking dinner. She has just been in to see her father, whom she hasn't seen all day, and found him in the shower. She is very interested in what she has seen and so tells her mother that she saw Daddy's penis. An appropriate response from her mother might be something like this: 'That's exciting — now go and wash your hands because we are having dinner when Daddy is ready.' Now imagine if a three-year-old girl comes back from a weekend access visit with her father and the relationship between the parents is strained. What effect will the statement 'I saw Daddy's penis' have then? The circumstances may be exactly the same for the child, but the adult may interpret it quite differently. For the child this event is still just part of the voyage of discovery about the differences between the sexes, but for her mother it may become a reason to believe her child has been sexually abused by her father.

For children who live in small families where the children are of a single sex and there is no parent of the opposite sex around, there may not be opportunities to see what the genitalia of the other sex look like. For these children a natural way to work this out is by playing games with peers. These games may involve undressing and exploring each other's bodies. This is usually at the level of 'I'll show you what I look like if you show me what you look like'. The games are usually played with non-sibling peers. When parents become aware of these games they may be concerned that this play is inappropriate and seek advice, or even report the incident to child protection services for investigation. If the children are the same age, there should be no need for concern as long as children are not being coerced into the games; this play is about curiosity rather than sexuality, although it involves a degree of developing sexual awareness. If there is a child who is significantly older, then the reasons for that older child being involved need to be explored.

Some children will go through a phase of displaying their bottom provocatively towards adults and finding the whole thing quite hilarious. It is the comments of caregivers that can label this as a sexualised behaviour by saying to the child, 'Don't do that, it's rude!' This will probably have the opposite outcome to that intended, as the knowledge that what he or she is doing is 'rude' is likely to encourage the child to repeat the behaviour to get the same reaction. Ignoring the behaviour or saying 'Don't do that, please' in a calm, disinterested manner is more likely to extinguish the behaviour, as the child soon realises there is little point repeating a behaviour that is not attracting attention.

3. Fathers should be careful how they respond affectionately to their daughters in case their daughters accuse them of sexual abuse from a recovered memory later in life

One particular aspect of the media debate on child sexual abuse has been the issue of recovered memories. Specifically, this relates to the psychological phenomenon whereby adults recover a memory from their childhood that has been repressed so that it has not been readily recalled up until it is remembered, usually, but not always, in the process of therapeutic intervention. Some adults, usually women, have reported recovered memories about a sexual contact instigated by their father or a male acting as a father figure. Publicity around this phenomenon has caused some fathers to be cautious about how they interact with their daughters. This is because of an erroneous belief that normal father–daughter interactions, which may involve physical expressions of affection through non-sexual touching, could in later life be interpreted by the adult child as having been sexually inappropriate.

If your four-year-old child has expressed great delight in seeing her father's penis for the first time and was able to work out why he 'pees' standing up, will that come back as a traumatic recovered memory about seeing her father's penis later on? I would say no: not if that first experience was treated by the child's parents as the normal childhood developmental experience that it is. If a four-year-old female child is scared in the night and her mother is out of town, is it appropriate for her to snuggle up in her father's bed for reassurance when she is having trouble sleeping? Yes.

Why do we not always accept this as a society but we accept a four-year-old boy snuggling up with his mother? In real life both fathers and mothers need to help infants and young children with daily intimate activities, such as toileting or taking a bath. Parents need to understand when their children need support and reassurance, and perhaps help and supervision, and when they need privacy. (Children will make their own decisions about when they want or need these things, anyway.) Most parents get this balance absolutely right, but some don't. That is when a line can be crossed and the act may become more about the adult's sexual gratification than the child's safety. An example would be insisting on watching your child — male or female — in the bath beyond the age when that is necessary to ensure their safety.

4. Masturbation is a sign of possible sexual abuse

Hopefully we all now accept that masturbation does not lead to blindness, but parents and caregivers can still be concerned if they observe younger children masturbating overtly. Children below the age of five years are not modest about their body, and if they find that touching the genital area is pleasurable, in much the same way that eating an ice cream is pleasurable, they may 'eat their ice cream' in public. Children are not going to view this activity through a lens that says it is a sexual activity. Put simply, like eating ice cream, they find the experience enjoyable, so they are not going to understand why an adult thinks they should stop.

Masturbation is a self-soothing behaviour, and most young children living in happy home environments will be easily redirected from overt masturbation; they can be told that if they want to do that they can do it in their own room in private. If children are masturbating frequently, the question that needs to be considered is: Why is this child needing to self-soothe so often? This behaviour is not unusual in cases of parental separation where there is acrimonious disputed custody. In this context it may be interpreted by one parent as being an indication of exposure to sexual abuse, whereas it is more likely to be a mechanism by which the child finds comfort while the adults around them argue.

Excessive and developmentally inappropriate masturbation, though not specific to sexual abuse, can be associated with exposure to sexual abuse. An example would be an older child (of an age when they would usually be very private about their genitalia) overtly masturbating in a public family area in the home where they are living.

5. If a child has been sexually abused they will surely tell somebody that they trust about it

This may seem to be a reasonable assumption. A number of mothers of the children seen in our clinic have told me during the consultation that they, too, were sexually abused as a child. Accordingly, they have sought to ensure their child knows that if anything were to happen to them they could tell their mother and she would help. Yet despite this there has often been quite a delay in the mother being aware about what has happened, and sometimes the circuitous way in which she has found out is distressing. For example, her daughter might tell their friend at school, the friend tells her mother, the friend's mother tells the school, the school makes a report to the statutory authorities, and then a social worker makes contact with the mother and she hears the news for the first time.

There are a number of reasons why this is so. Child sexual abuse is a secret activity. Many perpetrators will want continued access to the child, so they may bribe them with gifts. The child might not like what happens but likes the gifts. The perpetrator will tell the child that this is their secret. Some children receive very serious threats about what will happen if they tell. Young children are concrete thinkers. If somebody tells them they could be chopped up and buried in the garden, they are likely to take that threat at face value.

Some older girls in a family may allow abuse to continue because they want to protect younger sisters now approaching the age they themselves were when their father started abusing them. Some children, sadly, may not realise it is not the norm to have these things happen within a family. If you are meant to keep it a secret, how will you know that this doesn't happen in your school friends' families?

When children do keep a secret for a long time, what do adults do? They say 'Why did you not tell me?', often with a real sense of betrayal and anguish in their voice. It is very hard not to say this if you are a distraught parent. It is easy to blame the child for keeping the secret, but the real culprit is the adult who perpetrated the abuse and swore the child to secrecy.

6. Perpetrators of child sexual abuse are always male

It is true that those who sexually abuse children are usually male, but it has become increasingly clear that women, including mothers, can be perpetrators, too. Both male and female children can be targeted. For many years this has been a problem for the victims of abuse by female perpetrators: they have summoned the courage to disclose, only to be greeted with disbelief. Also, as a society we can give conflicting messages: a male school teacher having sex with a young female adolescent is bad, but when an adolescent boy is approached sexually by a female teacher it may be viewed almost as an opportunity for the boy. In fact, in both scenarios there is a clear power differential and potential for significant psychological harm.

7. Sexual abuse of boys is rare

While it is reported that sexual abuse is less common in boys than girls, it is also thought that there has been considerable under-reporting of sexual abuse for male children, such that the true prevalence is not clear. Young males in the past may have been less likely to be believed. Also, as they are more likely to have been abused by an adult of the same sex this can add to the confusion that they feel. Today, fortunately, there is increasing recognition of male child sexual abuse. Non-incest paedophiles may put themselves in a position where they have ready access to children (for example, priests, coaches and group leaders). Many of these children will be male.

8. Child sexual abuse offenders are usually strangers to the child

The news about young children being approached by strangers in the community may become big stories in the media, but children are far more likely to be approached sexually by somebody they already know. Often this is a family member, but it may also be a friend of the family or a person they have met through community activities, such as in church groups, or sport and other organisations that provide structured activities for children. This also explains why many children do not report sexual abuse. Society is more prepared now to accept that some religious leaders and sports coaches sexually abuse children, but in the past many children either kept silent or were ignored when they did speak up because what they were disclosing was just unimaginable to the recipient of the disclosure.

9. Children lie about sexual abuse

This can be true, but children are far more likely to lie to cover up a genuine case of abuse than make a false allegation. Imagine you are an eight-year-old girl who loves her dad most of the time but doesn't like it that he sometimes comes to her bed at night and does weird things with her. She finally tells her friend at school. A social worker comes and talks to her also at school. The next day she is taken away from home to stay with her grandmother. Her mother has told her she has lied. She is taken for an evidential interview where she has to again tell strangers what she told her friend and the social worker.

Her grandmother tells her she doesn't have to worry any more because the police have taken her dad away. Her father is gone and her mother is distraught. She feels that she has caused all this to happen. Perhaps what happened with Dad wasn't that bad after all? The child will blame herself — wrongly, of course — for all the trouble she has caused. Why would she not decide to change her mind about what she has disclosed? How can she, at her age, ever envision life returning to normal? If a young child makes a clear disclosure about sexual abuse it is likely to be true, whether or not that disclosure is later retracted.

A related issue, touched on earlier in this chapter, is when very young children make incomplete statements that adults misinterpret. If a three-year-old comes back from a weekend with Dad saying 'Daddy hurt my bottom', what does this mean? For some there will be a leap to 'I think my child has been sexually abused'. What are the other explanations? Well, maybe the child needed their bottom wiped after toileting and Dad rubbed a bit harder than Mum usually does. Or maybe he gave the child a little smack on the bottom for a minor misdemeanour. Maybe he was playing 'horse rides' with his daughter over his ankle — she was only in her undies and already had a slightly sore red bottom because of her bedwetting, and so this innocent game left her in discomfort. In such cases, nobody has lied, but some might leap to wrong conclusions.

I have seen a very small number of young adolescent girls who have presented after making false allegations of sexual assault. They were all troubled young women with histories of abuse and neglect and most of them had had previous involvement with child protection services. One appeared to have significant mental health issues, and the others appeared to have made the allegations as a way of seeking help for other trouble they were in. The statutory agencies were able to clearly identify these allegations as false before any charges were laid.

10. When a young girl says she has a sore bottom we should think about sexual abuse

While young children who have been sexually abused can complain of genital and anal pain, there are many more who have purely medical reasons for such complaints, and yet the site of the pain causes parents to suspect sexual abuse. An important mantra in paediatric medicine is that common things occur commonly. Constipation is common in children and sometimes this can lead to an anal fissure occurring.

Wetting and toilet accidents are common in young girls, and this can result in irritation to the genital area from sitting in wet or damp underwear, as mentioned above. I have seen little girls who wet themselves at school because if they went to the toilet at playtime the other girls might go away and play without waiting for them. So when a little girl or a little boy presents with a sore bottom a careful medical history and careful examination should be undertaken. If the child has not made any clear disclosures about sexual abuse, then that diagnosis will be way down my differential diagnosis list.

11. Young girls now use the correct names for their genital area

Unfortunately this is not true. There is a prevailing attitude that it is very good that young girls talk about their vagina rather than using euphemisms like 'down there'. In a feminist context this is seen as part of taking control of your body and knowing its functions. The problem is that the term is not being used in an anatomically correct way. This doesn't really matter most of the time, but it does matter when little girls make disclosures about sexual abuse that include anatomical descriptions.

So, let's describe a pre-pubertal child's genital anatomy. If you are starting from the outside you come first to the external genitalia. These are the labia majora and the labia minora — sometimes referred to as the outer lips of the genital area. If you gently part the labia there is a small space called the vestibule. Both the vagina and urethra open into this space and the clitoris sits at the top, above the urethra. This whole area, which is the external genitalia, may be called the vulva. At the base of this space is the hymen, and, more internal than that, usually not readily visible on routine examination, is the vagina. Beyond the hymen, the vagina represents the beginning of the internal genital organs. The introitus is the opening that leads into the vagina. The hymen sits at the entrance to the vagina and is like a margin around the entrance of the vagina, rather than a complete covering. The surface skin area that includes the external genitalia, the anus and the area between the two is referred to as the perineum.

In pre-pubertal girls the hymen is usually tender to touch and there is none of the lubrication of the tissues that occurs after puberty. Parents of course need to understand the anatomy themselves in order to explain it to children. Personally I find it useful to talk about the front bottom and the back bottom with children when asking them to describe symptoms, but it doesn't work very well with the children who already think of the anterior area as being their vagina and so think I am a bit weird.

12. The physical examination will prove that sexual abuse happened

This is why we need to know that young girls do not understand their own genital anatomy. Let's say a seven-year-old girl has said that her Uncle Bill put his penis in her vagina. What could that mean? Well, if she thinks her labia is her vagina it might just mean that the penis went through the labia and not into the vagina at all. Does this matter? Surely if Uncle Bill's penis is anywhere near this young child's genital area that is wrong and he should be charged with the crime of sexual assault. Yes, but what crime and what penalty?

The penalties, if he is convicted, will be different depending on how far 'in' it can be proved the penis went. On further questioning we might find that it hurt a bit, but not much. He tried to do it a few times and told her not to tell anyone. She hasn't had any other genital symptoms. A genital examination will be described as normal. The case is put to trial and the evidence is presented to a jury. What are they going to think? They are going to see a little girl having an evidential interview on the screen and a large adult male in the defendant's chair. They are going to assume he has a normal adult-sized penis and she has a small vagina. They are also likely to assume that child sexual abuse is like adult rape where a penis goes right into a vagina. They are going to think that if Uncle Bill really put his penis in this little girl's vagina it would have hurt and it would have caused a lot of damage. There is no reported damage: therefore this little girl must be lying. This is where the medical expert who has examined the child has a role to explain why a normal genital examination does not indicate that nothing happened.

There are many inappropriate things that can happen to a child that are of a sexual nature and relate to the child's sexual organs but which do not result in physical injury. These can include touching with a finger, genital-to-genital connection without penetration, and having the child sit on your knee while the male perpetrator has an erection. Some acts, such as attempted digital or penile penetration, could cause superficial injury that will have healed without a trace by the time the child makes a disclosure and is referred for examination.

Back, too, to the question of what the little girl means by 'in' in this context. An adult, especially a non-expert sitting on a jury, may assume she means 'in' to describe adult penile–vaginal sexual intercourse. But to a seven-year-old child 'in' could mean between the legs, through the labia or around the labia. It is not that this makes the act non-abusive; it is still clearly a crime against the child. However, it is not a physical event that will result in an injury that a doctor will be able to see on examination some months later and cite as evidence of sexual abuse.

13. Young girls who have been sexually abused have lost their virginity

I have been asked this question a few times by mothers of the young girls I have seen. 'Is she still a virgin?' I have also been asked this question in court. 'Was she a virgin, doctor?' For court my definition of a virgin is a young person who has never had consensual sexual intercourse. We still live in a world where there is an expectation that there are definitive anatomical differences to be visualised in a young woman examined before and after her first sexual encounter. We read phrases like 'the hymen was broken' and stories about marital beds being checked for blood on the morning after the wedding night. The pathologists in detective novels are always confident to state whether the deceased was a virgin.

Here are a few facts. The hymen never completely covers the entrance to the vagina. The only exception to this is when there is an imperforate hymen, a very, very rare congenital anomaly. There are some types of hymen that are more substantive, with smaller openings, but they are also fairly rare. So there is usually no 'breaking through' the hymen the first time you have sexual intercourse. Part of the design of puberty is to prepare the body for sexual connection and procreation. This involves changes in the hymen, which becomes more elastic and capable of stretching, and also an increase in the lubrication of the entrance to the vagina. Lubrication also further increases when there is sexual arousal.

These changes enable sexual intercourse to occur without damage occurring and often without discomfort. When on rare occasions I do see some evidence of injury to the genital area, it often heals well, and I may say to an older girl, 'I can see where you were hurt but I only saw this because I used my special light. Nobody else will be able to see it unless you tell them what happened.'

14. The forensic tests will prove that the sexual abuse happened

One of the most important differences between child and adult sexual assault is that, in by far the majority of cases for pre-pubertal children, disclosure is delayed and forensic material is no longer available. Also, there are differences in the sexual acts that occur with children, as described already. Because of this, if there is ejaculation of semen it is much more likely to occur on the external part of the child's body than deep into the vagina, as may occur with adult or adolescent sexual assault. Forensic evidence is much more likely to be found at the scene where the assault took place than on the child's body at the time of examination. Even when the child has presented relatively early after the assault, they have often already had a bath or a shower and their clothes may have already been put in the wash.

15. A positive forensic or sexually transmitted infection test will prove the identity of the perpetrator

In the age of DNA this definitely can be the case. However, we all leave quite a bit of our DNA around wherever we go, and there have been some cases where stray DNA pick-ups have led to wrongful convictions. This is theoretically likely to be more problematic for children, when we are relying on DNA from a scene rather than from semen found high in the vagina of the victim.

This can also be an issue when a very young child presents with gonorrhoea. Since this is a sexually transmitted disease, there is an extremely high suspicion that the child has been sexually abused. This does not, however, mean that we will automatically find an adult with gonorrhoea who abused the child. Firstly, they are not going to put their hand up and say, 'Oops, I think that might have been me.' Secondly, even if a suspect does agree to testing, he might test negative because he has already been treated. So forensic evidence is great when it all fits, but its reliability always needs to be tested and sometimes it is just not available.

CHILD SEXUAL ABUSE IS NOT A MYTH

So far I have described some situations where sexual abuse has happened and some where we might determine that it has not occurred. So, while this distinction is important, it is also important to be very clear that currently sexual abuse is one of the most important health problems affecting children in New Zealand. The true incidence is difficult to determine: partly because of variations in definition in epidemiological studies, but also because many children still do not tell, and some may have been so young when the abuse happened that they have no retained memory of the event. Also, the available local population studies provide information about childhood experiences that are now some years ago.

So what New Zealand data do we have? An Otago women's study reported that 32 per cent of women had had unwanted sexual experiences before the age of 16.[1] A Christchurch health and development study reported in 1996 that in their cohort of just over 1000 18-year-olds, 10.4 per cent reported sexual abuse before the age of 16 years (17.3 per cent of females and 3.4 per cent of males). Family dysfunction was associated with an increased risk of CSA.² A Dunedin multidisciplinary health and development study asked about a history of child sexual abuse at 26 years of age. As Robyn has reported in her introduction, in this cohort 20 per cent of the group — 30.3 per cent of women and 9.1 per cent of men — reported some form of sexual abuse before the age of 16.³

In comparison, less than 1 per cent of New Zealand children have current diabetes or a new cancer diagnosis each year, and yet our health and support services for children with diabetes and cancer are much better organised than services for children who have been sexually abused. Why is this so? It does seem quite extraordinary when one considers the possible long-term adverse effects of exposure to sexual abuse, which are discussed in some detail in other chapters in this book.

It is not that we have no services. We have the New Zealand Police, who investigate referred cases and determine whether a crime has been committed. We have Oranga Tamariki, who investigate referred cases and address child safety and care and protection needs. But what about the physical and mental health needs of these children? How do we assemble all these components of the assessment of child sexual abuse in childhood? Currently there is only one place in New Zealand where this is happening routinely to some degree, and that is Puawaitahi, the multi-agency child protection unit at Starship Hospital. There are services around the country, but they are not as well organised and connected.

The big four areas of abuse in childhood are physical abuse, sexual abuse, emotional abuse and neglect. (Emotional abuse includes exposure to family violence and the adverse effects of living with caregivers who are driven by substance abuse or are experiencing untreated mental illness.) Emotional abuse can be a component of all forms of abuse. Paediatricians and general practitioners have always found assessment after physical abuse to be more straightforward than assessing for sexual abuse, neglect or emotional abuse. However, the reality is that it is not unusual for all of these forms of abuse to coexist.

There are many things that we need to do better to improve our track record with the assessment and management of child sexual abuse in this country. In health I would consider two things to be particularly important:

1. We need to make the right diagnosis. This includes being more confident in defining what is *not* sexual abuse as well as being clear about what *is* abuse. This means ensuring that clinicians working in health can recognise what does and does not suggest child abuse, as well as ensuring that this understanding is shared by those at Oranga Tamariki and the police investigating referred cases, and also those involved in the courts in the cases that go to trial.
2. We need to have better services in health, both within hospital-based systems and in the community, for children who have been sexually abused. These services, especially follow-up services, need to be free to families, appropriate to the needs of the child, and offered in a cohesive manner so that support, investigation and treatment services all run smoothly together.

All forms of abuse can have significant effects on mortality and morbidity in childhood. The now famous Adverse Childhood Experiences Study (ACEs) in the United States has been very clear that adverse childhood experiences affect physical as well as mental health. We need to view child abuse like childhood cancer, with a high risk of very serious short-term and long-term effects on those affected. If we were to provide services for children affected by abuse in New Zealand in the way that we provide services for children affected by cancer, then I think we would begin to see better outcomes for those affected by sexual abuse in childhood.

I opened the preface of this book with a statement about resilience, often misunderstood to encompass no more than the ability to maintain control in the eye of observers. Sue Glanville understands in great depth and breadth how child sexual abuse affects children of all ages and what is required to address that traumatic impact. Given her awareness of how fundamentally essential to well-being it is to be effectively seen and heard, she has spent a lifetime refining how to professionally delve beneath presenting behaviours to provide gentle, skilful responses. This allows a child's brain to integrate the aftermath of the trauma and re-establish, or achieve for the first time, the sense of self-mastery and belonging that is essential to healthy functioning.

I met Sue when we were both studying as mature students in Massey University's clinical psychology programme. She reports feeling privileged to have worked with many children and young people for over 36 years, initially as a social worker and since 1992 as a clinical psychologist.

In 2002, through a collaboration of the community with those who had developed great expertise in the field of child abuse, a multi-agency child protection centre was developed in central Auckland. Designed to be as easily accessible as possible for whānau/family, Puawaitahi brings together investigation, assessment and treatment services from New Zealand Police, Oranga Tamariki, Starship National Children's Hospital and Auckland District Health Board to provide coordinated, efficient and effective services for children thought to have experienced abuse or neglect. Sue became manager of the then CYF Specialist Services Team in 2006, and therefore a member of the Puawaitahi management team.

Now retired from her role as clinical manager for Oranga Tamariki at Puawaitahi, Sue has extensive experience in identifying and assessing child abuse and neglect, helping children to safely and appropriately disclose the painful secrets they are holding, and ensuring they get the professional help necessary to become safe and to heal from their experiences.

Sue shares with us here some of her precious psychological expertise and experiences in the domain of child sexual abuse. I learned years ago whenever discussing work with her that I need to brace myself to hear some of the horror stories. It takes great courage and strength to sustain such work, along with much compassion; fortunately this daughter of a West Coast fishing family has all of those characteristics in abundance.

3. Working therapeutically with children who have experienced sexual abuse

SUE GLANVILLE, RETIRED CLINICAL MANAGER ORANGA TAMARIKI

NGĀ MIHI NUI. I INTRODUCE this chapter by acknowledging the children and young people from whom I have learned so much over many years working in the area of child abuse, and my colleagues in a range of professions who undertake the difficult but important work of helping tamariki and mokopuna to find their voices to talk about and heal from their trauma.

I first encountered the far-reaching impacts of child sexual abuse four decades ago, when I worked briefly as a prison officer in a women's prison, then later in a residential setting with female adolescents. The long-term emotional and psychological effects of trauma related to sexual victimisation in childhood were common, although largely unidentified in both populations. The majority of adolescents in the residences I worked in were there for delinquency and other antisocial behaviour, and were absconding from often neglectful and abusive homes. Intervention was largely custodial to prevent reoffending, rather than to identify and address the cause of offending.

I was reminded as a prison officer that my role was custodial. The severity and impact of the emotional pain of some of those women and girls, and my own feelings of powerlessness to help, led me to seek knowledge and skills beyond my tertiary social work qualification via training in clinical psychology.

My intention in writing this chapter is not to attempt to provide an exhaustive list of specific treatment strategies for child sexual abuse, but rather to share some of my experiences of working therapeutically with children.

EVIDENCE-BASED PRACTICE AND PRACTICE-BASED EVIDENCE

Therapeutic work with sexually abused children carries a great responsibility for therapists and clinicians to ensure that interventions are informed by assessment and supported by research and evidence of efficacy. My own research (1992) for a master's thesis explored factors that influence therapists' understanding of the impacts of sexual abuse and the treatment strategies they used. Some reported their understandings derived primarily from their personal experience of sexual abuse, while others relied on formal training and evidence-based research to inform their practice.

At that time, clinical research in the area of sexual abuse was in its developmental stages when compared to the significant body of knowledge of both the impact and effective treatment that has developed since. Many therapists relied on therapeutic methods that appeared to ameliorate emotional and behavioural symptoms of psychological trauma. Just as the prevalence of child sexual abuse may never be known because of the conditions of secrecy in which it occurs and other difficulties involved in identifying victims, in 1992 the processes involved in healing from sexual abuse trauma proved to be just as elusive. Back in 1992 I wrote: 'While awaiting expansion of the professional literature and the development of more effective means of making use of information from survivors (of sexual abuse) themselves, practitioners must continue to identify for themselves the variables involved in effective clinical intervention.'[1]

Before undertaking formal training in psychology, in my role as a residential social worker I attended an intensive four-week therapy training course facilitated by a therapist who was to have a profound influence on my subsequent work. This influence lay primarily in combining the evidence-based/empirically supported theories and practice of psychology and other therapeutic modalities with varying degrees of research-based evidence. Many of the strategies I utilised prior to my formal clinical training nonetheless continued to prove to be effective vehicles for vulnerable children and young people to be able to talk about traumatic experiences, and to gain some mastery of emotional and behavioural expressions of trauma.

UNDERSTANDING THE IMPACT OF ABUSE

The impacts of childhood sexual abuse are now well documented in the clinical literature. They are diverse and include short-term and long-term effects, which are mitigated or exacerbated by a range of individual, family, cultural and socio-political factors. A young person with no major adverse childhood experiences, a history of family support and adequate emotional resources experiencing a first trauma at age 17 will likely emerge from that experience with fewer enduring problems than a child who has been sexually, physically and emotionally abused over a period of time, with a history of resulting disrupted attachment relationships, and who has poor family and social support.

Children's short-term, emotional responses to trauma commonly include fear and anxiety, and these need to be managed during the initial crisis of disclosure. A familiar and trusted adult is the best therapist for the child at this stage, and psycho-education about trauma — including reframing the child's reactions as normal reactions to traumatic events — is essential, as is support for the child's family and/or caregiver. Sadness and depression may develop after the initial crisis, along with feelings of guilt and self-blame. The violation of trust that results from dependent children being abused by an adult they have looked to for nurturance and protection may impair attachment relationships with parents and siblings. Interpersonal and social relationship difficulties may continue into adulthood and result in: unstable intimate relationships; mental health issues such as anxiety and depressive disorders, disorders of personality and social functioning; substance abuse issues; and antisocial behaviour and difficulties with authority.

Children's behavioural responses to trauma frequently include regression to an earlier stage of development when the child may have felt physically safe and protected. I have observed this in children with younger siblings and have helped parents understand that a child's aggressive behaviour toward the younger sibling represents a yearning for safety. Young children may fear — and commonly express in therapy — that the resources of their parent or caregiver are not enough to be shared.

Regressive behaviour may involve speech ('baby talk'), loss of bladder and bowel control, and a need for constant close proximity to a primary attachment figure, including sleeping with the parent. The needs of traumatised children may be perceived by parents or caregivers to be excessive or overwhelming, and caregiver support and reassurance is important to protect against further harm to the child arising from unintended rejection. Usual behaviour management strategies such as 'time out', or otherwise removing the child from the proximity of their attachment figure, may need to be moderated until the child is more secure.

Behavioural responses to psychological trauma may be described as either over- or under-responding. Over-responding may be likened to 'feeling too much', with under-responding 'feeling too little'. Over-responding involves activation of the innate fight–flight response in situations where there is no actual danger present, but something in the environment has triggered memories of the traumatic event, causing the child to 'overreact' in ways that may involve angry and aggressive behaviour. Under-responding is also referred to as 'numbing' or 'denial', whereby the child copes with overwhelming emotions or perceived threat by withdrawing and appearing to caregivers to be unfeeling.

Humans — adults and children — respond to events in the best way they can with the resources they have available to them at any given time. Trauma responses represent the child's available coping resources and it is by exploring these responses *as* coping resources, and helping the child to develop insight into how helpful these resources are, that we begin the therapeutic process of identifying maladaptive coping responses and exploring and practising new, adaptive ones.

Asking people to give up a maladaptive coping response — for example, cutting — in the absence of a more functional response has been described by American psychologist and child trauma expert John Briere as 'asking the person to hurt without a solution'.[2] Therefore unlearning patterns of emotional and behaviour expression learned as survival mechanisms is central to effective therapy with traumatised children, regardless of whether the trauma is related to emotional, physical or sexual abuse or neglect. Sadly, many children experience multiple sources of trauma.

THERAPEUTIC INTERVENTION: WHAT INFORMS THE CHOICE OF INTERVENTION?

Assessment

Effective therapeutic work is informed by comprehensive assessment of the child's emotional and behavioural functioning; comparison of current and pre-trauma development; the nature and severity of trauma responses and the impact of these responses on the child's daily functioning; and resilience — individual protective and buffering factors that include perceptions of mastery and self-efficacy, sense of relatedness to others, and emotional responsiveness.

I have found that a child-focused assessment requires both standardised and non-standardised use of assessment tools to obtain valid information. This is particularly so for children who are unable to complete psychometric testing because of acute presentations of trauma, including anxiety and mistrust, and disrupted development. Assessment of parental and family support is essential to identify the level of support available to the child, the parent/caregiver's commitment to therapy, their own needs for information and additional support, and the family and cultural contexts.

Interpretation of assessment data carries with it considerable responsibility, particularly with regard to diagnosis. Because childhood is a time of rapid development, including brain development, the risks of labelling and misdiagnosis are important considerations, particularly with regard to accessing the right intervention. For example, abuse-related trauma mirrors and includes a number of presentations such as attention deficit issues, mood and conduct disorders, anxiety/depression, and disorders of attachment.

I have seen many children and young people who have been prescribed medication for attention deficit hyperactivity disorder (ADHD) but who have not been assessed for abuse-related trauma, and whose over-responsive (hyperactive) behaviour is actually associated with trauma-related brain and autonomic nervous system dysfunction. Similarly, children diagnosed with externalising behaviour disorders such as conduct disorder and oppositional defiance disorder (ODD) also often have underlying and undisclosed abuse-related trauma.

Accurate diagnosis is essential for ensuring access to appropriate mental health services for children with abuse-related trauma and appropriate medication where necessary. However, it is important to maintain an open and inquisitive mind and, as far as possible, to continue to test hypotheses regarding diagnosis while joining with children in a search for the meaning and function of trauma symptoms.

Knowledge of child development

Knowledge of child development, and particularly the critical development periods for exacerbation of harmful effects of abuse and for opportunities for healing, informs effective intervention. Erik Erikson's psychosocial developmental tasks have been integral to my clinical practice with children.[3] Erikson proposed that the completion of certain developmental tasks in the direction of mastery at critical developmental stages paves the way for the successful completion of subsequent tasks. He proposed that the primary developmental task of infancy is the acquisition of basic trust versus mistrust, and that an infant's ability to trust that the environment is safe and will meet his/her needs is the foundation stone for attachment and the successful completion of all later tasks.

These include: achieving a sense of autonomy versus shame and doubt in early childhood (the 'terrible twos', when children become aware that they have agency in the world and can influence their environment); industry versus inferiority in middle childhood (young children's interest in positive reinforcement for effort and achievement); and the important adolescent task of developing a sense of identity versus role confusion as they begin to transition from reliance on parents toward increased identification with peers in readiness for the next stage of individuation as young adults. Erikson saw these tasks not as an either/or dichotomy, but as a continuum along which psychosocial development proceeds in the direction of the task. This model has informed my focus for therapeutic intervention because it 'fits' with the concept of 'making good' deficits arising from disrupted development and identifies critical periods for reparation to occur.

Knowledge of trauma and trauma-informed interventions

In Aotearoa New Zealand it is estimated (various sources) that between 60 and 90 per cent of children referred for outpatient mental health services have been exposed to psychological trauma related to neglect; physical, emotional and sexual abuse; family violence; and natural disasters, such as the Christchurch earthquakes.

A number of studies have demonstrated the effectiveness of trauma-informed and trauma-focused therapeutic interventions for assisting children who have been sexually abused. The purpose of an extensive project by Benjamin Saunders, an American expert on childhood victimisation and trauma, was to encourage the use of mental health treatment protocols and procedures that have a sound theoretical basis, a good clinical–anecdotal literature, high acceptance among practitioners in the child abuse field, a low chance for causing harm, and empirical support for their utility with victims of abuse.[4]

Trauma-focused cognitive behaviour therapy (TF-CBT)

The Saunders study found that trauma-focused cognitive behaviour therapy (TF-CBT) met the highest standards of empirical support for effective treatment of children presenting with child-abuse trauma. A practice-based study conducted at Puawaitahi,[5] the multi-agency co-location of Auckland District Health Board, New Zealand Police and Oranga Tamariki Clinical Services child abuse specialists in Auckland, resulted in a manualised treatment programme which is used internationally. Recently, in order to directly target traumatised children's need to better regulate emotional reactivity, a sensory modulation component was added as a result of a follow-up study.[6]

Briefly, TF-CBT supports children through a series of stages. These include: psychosocial strengthening; teaching coping skills; trauma processing (exposure to frightening memories in the safety of the therapeutic relationship); and targeted interventions for specific issues — for example, grief and loss, anger, guilt and shame.

Children, and especially very young children abused before gaining language, may store trauma memories somatically — as bodily sensations rather than as accessible cognitive memories. Young children often need physical soothing when distressed, and can be helped to learn to moderate their responses to trauma-evoking stimuli through the use of sensory methods, both for self-soothing and to teach them to self-regulate their emotional responses. For example, children are able to select from a 'sensory diet' in a specially equipped room that includes objects of different shapes and textures, weighted toys (which support some children to feel secure and 'grounded' when distressed), coloured fairy lights, bubbles and musical instruments.

As well as TF-CBT, therapeutic interventions available to children at Puawaitahi include play-based therapy, animal-assisted therapy, art and drumming therapy, and parent–child interaction therapy (PCIT). PCIT is an intervention that supports positive parent–child attachment; it also teaches parents and caregivers positive behaviour management techniques which may interrupt the negative cycle of interactions that can increase the risk of further abuse. In cases where children have been sexually abused, PCIT may be undertaken with a non-offending caregiver after the child has completed the TF-CBT intervention.

WORKING THERAPEUTICALLY WITH CHILDREN

I want to share some of the insights I have gained from working with children and young people regardless of the model of therapeutic intervention.

Importance of informed consent

Children do not usually self-refer. Informed consent can be obtained as an initial engagement task, and agreement to work together may be verbal — for example, 'to get to be the boss of troubles and worries' — or written, depending on the child's presentation and developmental stage, and reason for coming to therapy. I might say, 'My name is Sue. It is my job to talk to children who have been hurt by someone [if the child has made a clear disclosure of abuse] or who have troubles or worries because of something that happened to them.' Then pause. 'I talk to lots of children.' Pause. 'We talk about happy things, sad things, funny things, and sometimes yukky things.' Pause. 'Some children find it hard to talk about some things at first and that's OK. You don't have to talk about anything you don't want to talk about, but I can listen to anything you have to say.'

I am careful about the language I use with children and the potential for unintended messages. For example, 'I can listen to anything you have to say' is different to 'anything you *want* to say'. Many children don't want to talk about frightening experiences, but can be supported to do so with explicit permission.

When children know the therapist is used to talking to other children about abuse, they become aware that they are not alone or different. I have become aware of intense scrutiny by some abused children who have developed heightened empathy, to assess if I can in fact hear what they have to say. Early in my work with children, a little girl who had been sexually abused by her mother's partner and emotionally abused by her mother told me, 'I don't want to make you cry. Mummy cried when I told her.' This child's estranged mother told her at the conclusion of a later supervised contact visit, 'Look after yourself [name]'. The little girl looked at me and said, 'But I can't look after myself, can I, Sue?'

Conveying your caring purpose

A respected colleague conveyed this concept during a professional development session at Puawaitahi. He quoted an anaesthetist describing his caring purpose to his patient. 'I am the doctor in charge of the sleeping medicine. My only job is to keep you safe and make sure you stay asleep.'[7]

I always tell children at the start of every session that my job is to listen to children with troubles and worries and to help keep them safe. I end every session by asking them if there is anything we need to do together, or that I need to do, to keep them safe until next time. This expression of concern has on occasions supported further disclosures of abuse, and expressions of feeling unsafe.

Developing and modelling expectations for sessions/working together

It is also important to convey to children the purpose of meeting together and to practise doing this. I have heard therapists from differing professional backgrounds struggle to explain their role to children, who need to understand the therapist's caring purpose more than their professional title. Children need to know how many times they will come to see the therapist and how long each session will last. I use a sand-timer with coloured sand to show children how long we will spend together, and have had a hard-to-engage and oppositional child turn the timer upside down to start again when the sand ran out!

I tell children I sometimes get things wrong, and I teach them how to correct misunderstandings or misinterpretations, and praise them for doing so. Then we create a picture or map of why we are meeting and what we will do together — to learn to be the boss or in charge of unwanted or frightening thoughts and feelings, for example. At the start of every subsequent session I remind the child of our agreement, explore what has happened since last time, and check if our agreement is still relevant for them or whether we need to change it in line with progress or setbacks. The TF-CBT programme outlines the model's sequential steps for trauma processing and coping skills development.

Entering the child's frame of reference and creating a safe environment

The importance of understanding the child's world and working within their frame of reference and at their pace cannot be overstated. I adopt a curious approach — 'I am wondering', 'I am thinking' — and invite the child to 'tell me if I get things wrong'. I mirror the child's language to enhance engagement, taking care with older children not to appear to be patronising or mocking them.

An important first thing to do with children at the start of therapy is to help them to identify a trusted adult: someone they can get help from if/when they don't feel safe. In the child protection space this may be difficult for some children. Time needs to be taken to explore their perceptions of, and trust in, familiar adults and authority figures. Young children can be helped to identify supportive adults by tracing an outline of their hands and writing the names of trusted adults on the fingers — for example, a family member, a family friend, or a teacher — to create their special 'helping hand'.

I also help children with self-harming thoughts and/or behaviour to name a specific adult who can keep them safe, and then ensure that caregivers know who that person is. It may be someone other than the person caring for the child. It is important to include child mental health crisis services for actively suicidal children and young people.

WHAT ENHANCES COPING IN CHILDREN WITH ABUSE-RELATED TRAUMA?

Learning or relearning emotional regulation

Young children's emotional coping is significantly affected by their capacity for emotional regulation — the ability to 'down-regulate' emotional states and to self-soothe in response to emotional distress. Emotional coping abilities develop in the first three years of life during the critical period for attachment, when rocking, stroking and physical proximity to an attachment figure helps the child develop internal emotional regulation and self-soothing abilities. Children who have never had a secure attachment to an adult may not have developed the ability to down-regulate strong emotions (such as fear and anger) and the heightened arousal to stimuli such as noises or smells that trigger memories of abuse.

Teaching and practising coping skills

Explaining the 'fight or flight' response using stories and pictures can help children understand and develop mastery over frightening feelings and behaviours. Reframing these feelings and behaviours as strengths, rather than deficits or problems to be fixed, can empower children to explore and practise new ways of coping, and to unlearn patterns of emotional and behavioural expression developed as self-preservation.

Supporting indirect expression of self and feelings

Abused and traumatised children do not respond well to direct questioning because questions further tax already depleted emotional resources. Instead, I consider 'What can I give this child?' to support their self-expression.

Young children are more likely to project frightening emotions onto non-human figures, such as toys or pictures of small animals, assisted by sand-tray, art, drumming and animal-directed therapy. For example, a young child who had been exposed to severe emotional trauma developed externalising behaviours — aggression and defiance — in response to overwhelming feelings of vulnerability. He was diagnosed with conduct disorder and ODD. Recognising he was unable to acknowledge these feelings directly, I showed him a picture of an angry tiger chasing a frightened-looking monkey and wondered aloud what the monkey might be feeling. The child said angrily,

'Stupid!' Avoiding questions, I 'wondered' if and when the child might have felt 'stupid'. He told me, 'When my teacher asks me a question and I don't know the answer.' I invited him to name this feeling and he said, 'Oh Oh!' I wrote 'Oh Oh' on a small glass jar and invited the child to choose, from an assortment of coloured sand, the colour that could be 'Oh Oh' and to put the sand into the jar to show how much 'Oh Oh' he felt when his teacher asked him a question and he didn't know the answer. This led to exploration of other feelings and, eventually, to situations in which the child had felt frightened and abandoned, with congruent emotional and verbal expression of those feelings. For one particularly traumatic experience, he said, 'There isn't enough sand.'

I have found the use of toys — holding a tiny doll or toy to my ear, and showing caring purpose and modelling empathy — supports children to talk about traumatic experiences. 'Dolly wants to say something to me about [a feeling the child has identified] but she says it's hard to tell me.' Feelings may be named or represented, for example by using coloured sand, or painting colours after the child has chosen colours 'that look like' their feelings.

I have given very young children the doll to take home with the invitation to 'listen carefully to what dolly has to say'. A very young child who had been treated for a sexually transmitted disease climbed on my knee when she arrived for the following session and told me someone had hurt dolly's private parts. With empathic listening and responding, the child disclosed sexual abuse. It is important for forensic purposes to note that the doll is not intended to represent the child, but is a receptacle for the child's emotional expression and feelings they may project and then be able to own within the context of a safe and caring therapeutic relationship.

I have used therapeutic stories extensively in my work with children. American clinical psychologist, therapist and author Nancy Davis describes brain images obtained during traumatic recall (flashbacks), showing that the right side of the brain — where images, vision and emotions are located — was extremely active. 'By contrast the left side of the brain, where speech and logic reside, was completely shut down.'[8]

In stories such as 'The Bunny with a Sore Heart' and 'The Princess and the Boxes', Davis uses metaphors and symbols — 'the language of the right brain' — to support abused children to express trauma-related feelings and help them heal. Davis has recently updated her stories to include multi-sensory trauma processing for older children and adults (as yet unpublished).

Finally, I believe that maintaining a curious and playful stance is necessary to guard against the therapist and child becoming overwhelmed with the painful processes of trauma expression and healing. Small steps toward self-efficacy are celebrated with bubbles and balloons, and the conclusion of therapy with a treat of the child's choice — often party food.

I want to finish with an example of the effective use of metaphor and playfulness given at a training workshop.[9] 'Remind me to tell you about snakes and marbles,' the presenter told his fascinated audience just before a break. Later, he recounted working with a traumatised child whose obsessive-compulsive behaviour was severely impairing her ability to function in the world. To illustrate the power of symbolic representation of symptoms — in this case, anxiety — and ineffective coping as attempts at mastery, the therapist described randomly rolling marbles across the floor during sessions.

> Child: 'Why are you doing that?'
> Paul: 'To keep the snakes away.'
> Child: 'But there aren't any snakes!'
> Paul: 'See — it works!'
> Child: 'That's silly — doing that doesn't keep them away. There aren't any snakes.'

AFTER THERAPY

At the conclusion of therapy it is important that children continue to develop self-confidence and coping skills. Self-empowerment courses facilitated in Auckland by therapist Morgan Libeau aim to 'reduce anxiety, fear and misinformation' and support children and young people to develop and practise new skills: for example, saying aloud how they feel about unwanted behaviour, or telling someone when they feel unsafe.[10] The following are written statements children (whose names have been changed) have made about the course:

> I loved the feeling that I used to be someone small and shy, but now I feel clever and strong and brave! It was fun and I won't forget it! That's a promise. (Dana, 12)

> I feel stronger, more capable, more aware, more informed, more confident [about] how to help myself, [how to feel] less vulnerable and how to stay calm. (Rebecca, 13)

And this from Georgia, 12:

> Sexual abuse is not okay,
> kids just want to run and play!
> We don't want to worry about things
> get into fights run and scream!
> That is why we took this cource [sic].
> Now I feel I can knock down doors!

FUTURE DIRECTIONS

I have worked in the area of child abuse for more than 30 years. For the past 16 of these I have worked collaboratively with child protection specialists at Puawaitahi — the 'one-stop shop' or multi-agency centre model — to identify, investigate and provide effective interventions for children and young people who have been sexually abused. An inclusive, collaborative response in the form of a multi-agency investigation and multi-sensory interventions is the most effective way of ensuring all children and young people who have suffered sexual abuse have access to the same resources to help them heal.

The multi-agency model, with its emphasis on collaborative best practice, and multi-agencies such as Puawaitahi as centres of excellence in the identification, investigation and treatment of child abuse, should be accessible to all abused children and young people in Aotearoa New Zealand. That will require the statutory agencies currently responsible for the investigation and treatment of child abuse to cooperate with a genuine commitment to co-locating in multi-agency, purpose-built and child-focused centres throughout the country.

It was suggested to me by a detective senior sergeant of my local police force that Neil Holden would be a very good person to talk to for this book. We agreed to meet at a café halfway between our two cities — and Neil biked there. I had anticipated our meeting would take about an hour. Five hours later I stumbled back to my car and carefully drove home, recording device long since full and switched off, head buzzing.

Drawing on his long history with the police, which dates back to before the introduction of specialist child protection teams, Neil provides a well-honed view of the police role in responding to child sexual abuse. He describes the expertise required to investigate this crime in its many manifestations, and why all the work that has gone, and continues to go, into developing the skills required is so crucially important to the goal of this book.

Neil has astutely recognised that child protection is not much protection if it's only after the fact. Fortunately, he also has the tenacity to persist in this field. While he and I both see the huge value in the police continuing to carry out their investigative role effectively, he also identifies changes that will need to occur in order to reduce the prevalence of child sexual abuse in this country.

4. Child sexual abuse: A police viewpoint

DETECTIVE SENIOR SERGEANT NEIL HOLDEN
CHILD PROTECTION TEAM
NEW ZEALAND POLICE

Portions of this chapter involve my personal views, which are not necessarily those of the New Zealand Police. When case studies are used to address a point, these are from real cases but have been altered to remove any identifying features.

FROM THE EARLY TO MID-1980s a number of police investigators across New Zealand (and internationally) saw the need for the response to child abuse to be handled by specialist investigators and officers. These fine men and women sought to change the random assignment of enquiry cases across the then generalist detective. This endeavour coincided with increasing research into the maltreatment of children, and — probably more importantly — with an awareness of the need to reassess the way information was gathered and to create a specialist child interview. At the time, I was a trainee investigator and detective constable in a satellite Criminal Investigation Branch office of around 16 staff, and my detective sergeant and I were the only local volunteers.

Thirty-odd years on, I have no idea why I put my hand up. There was no shortage of other work (the child abuse portfolio was an extra duty, not an alternative option), plus I was busy with 'normal' life stuff, such as building a house, starting a family and playing sport. I had no history or compelling drive to right particular wrongs; my wife and I had grown up in safe, loving families within a central North Island town.

Within two months, I dealt with a 12-year-old girl who was raped by a relative. We muddled through, doing our best to treat her right and gather evidence. On a warm Sunday morning, while his family was at church, I approached the accused man at his home. We spoke in his sun-porch as I tried to display calmness and sincerity and invited him to tell the truth. He did, even providing unknown graphic detail through his tears. We had taken action and had a positive outcome (for us anyway: he went to jail), but we stepped from that case into the next with no wraparound support for the victim.

Fourteen years later, as a detective sergeant, I dealt with the same girl again, now a woman of 26, when I arrested her grandfather for sexually abusing her daughter, an infant of 18 months. The cyclic nature of badness can haunt the vulnerable like an hereditary disease. I have no explanation for why I am still involved in the work — but I am. It can follow people like me in the same fashion.

Today I am an investigative manager still working in the field, and the following is my view of the police child protection response and the tools developed to assist our fact-finding endeavours. As a working group plus our multi-agency collective we have come a long way, and we have learnt many lessons — a lot of them painful, a good number born of our errors. It is good to report that currently there is far less reluctance for police staff to get involved in the work. My view is crystal clear: the police response to child abuse, more especially sexual abuse, is the most important business we undertake. Child abuse and family harm are a blight on future prospects — we owe it to do our best, and to always improve.

THREE PREREQUISITES FOR TRAINING AND WORKING IN THIS FIELD

When speaking to investigators and other groups, I often begin with these three fundamentals:

1. Police recognise the high number of victims of sexual abuse across our community in a range of scenarios, including reported, unreported (the majority), historic, recent or still occurring. Given that police recruit from our communities, there will be staff who fit these criteria. It is important we acknowledge and respect all people so affected.

2. The topic of abuse requires sensitivity and confidentiality. When we discuss investigations and incidents it is only for the purposes of learning, and we strive to respect personal information and details.
3. Outside of professional wellness checks, there are valid natural coping mechanisms for police and other personnel working in this field. Keeping a distance, not getting emotionally involved, and even on occasions 'dark humour' are all tools that can be used to retain a sensible balance in a testing workplace. Inappropriate language and humour needs prompt addressing, with an emphasis on altering behaviour or redeploying staff to other duties.

THE CHILD PROTECTION PROTOCOL AND BEST-PRACTICE APPROACH

Since those early days of seeking a specialisation, a multi-agency approach to child sexual reports (along with reports of physical and serious neglect) has been developed. The current commitment by the New Zealand Police and Oranga Tamariki is the Child Protection Protocol (CPP), a nationally consistent approach to reports of serious child abuse that was established in 2010.

The CPP outlines the police role in investigating crimes, holding offenders to account and preventing future offending. Oranga Tamariki addresses care and protection concerns and takes action to keep children safe. The protocol exists to ensure timely, coordinated and effective action by the two agencies where the victim is under 18 years at the time of referral.

This best-practice approach for all forms of abuse will often include a medical component, in which expert practitioners address medical, forensic and wellness requirements. A summary of the currently 23-page CPP protocol is:

- Joint referral across the principle agencies — initial information sharing.
- Consultation — local-level information sharing and detail discussion.
- Agreement on an initial plan — creation of an initial joint

investigation plan (IJIP) to establish and record what needs to happen, when and by whom. This will address initial and formal interview requirements, plus medical and support aspects.
- Details to be recorded in respective databases (police and Oranga Tamariki).
- Each organisation to follow its own objectives while adhering to the CPP. For police this will predominately be to stop the abuse and to provide support as soon as possible. Police also consider the potential for a mass allegation investigation (MAI), where other victims may have been created. This is important for instances of child sexual abuse; while not necessarily common, it requires willingness to think the unthinkable.
- CPP monthly meetings — case data is recorded and updated across the agencies once a month.
- CPP closure — each agency will advise the other when matters are resolved and closed.

WHO ARE THE VICTIMS AND OFFENDERS?

All corners of our community are affected. I have dealt with families across the privilege spectrum; no social group is immune to child sexual abuse. Some locations generate more calls, which could be due to a willingness to report within a particular community and/or to accept that child abuse may be happening. Our busy Wellington Child Protection Team occasionally finds it easier to work cases in the lower socio-economic parts of town than in the more affluent. Families in the not so well-to-do areas can be less overawed by the presence of police in their neighbourhoods and homes. In contrast, when we visit more affluent parts of town we can encounter disbelief and resistance; sometimes people are more concerned about neighbours and friends finding out than about addressing the abuse in their midst. (I will return later to this stigma.)

Strictly speaking, child protection teams respond to sexual matters that affect children aged under 18 years at the time of reporting. Adults reporting CSA are referred to the adult sexual assault (ASA) squad; however, we may also lead or oversee cases where the reporting victim is now older but the case warrants our expertise: for example, where a suspect appears to be a preferential child sex offender, as will be explained below. Our files range from the most serious — sexual violation by rape or unlawful sexual connection[1] — through to a range of indecent touching and acts, as well as actions where online contact is linked to arranging for a sex act to take place.[2] Online offending has become widespread, and many countries have enforcement in this area. The New Zealand Police OCEANZ unit based at police national headquarters is world-class and constantly delivering results that reinforce the growing need to be active in the world's largest public place: the internet.[3]

THE CHILD PROTECTION DETECTIVE

The modern detective is a multi-skilled practitioner; far more of a super-sleuth than in my early days in the role. They understand the abuse environment; they're good at investigative interviewing, and they know a lot more about human behavioural science. They have a wider comprehension of the impact and demands of their role. I admire them greatly.

Specialisation is now the status quo, with all main centres across New Zealand having child protection teams that can interview, investigate and process. The equipment, approaches and training are always improving, which is appropriate given the growing number of reports coming forward. I don't believe this increase is necessarily because more abuse is occurring, but rather that awareness and disclosure have improved. This high workload now means constant monitoring of our staff's case-load allocation, with a focus on children's (and others') safety, risk, priority and timeliness.

In each case our investigators are encouraged to ask: What does good look like? What would be a good outcome? Once focused on that, we extend the perspective to ask: Whose good? Their good or our good? A victim's or a family's good? Or even an offender's good? What lens, or lenses, are we best to look through?

From there, basics must be followed, such as policy and process compliance (adherence to CPP protocols, for example) and rules for admissibility of evidence in court. Fairness is a vital component and is generally an uncomplicated test that detectives follow well. Sure, there can be breaches and mistakes can be made, but they are less common now there is a robust quality-assurance process. Our information and data collection process should be diligent and sensible. Technology is helping as new systems and approaches roll out regularly. Recorded information has to clearly capture our logic, actions and professional views so that anyone in the present and future can understand what occurred and why.

Alongside police upskilling is an enhanced understanding of child abuse by the public and in the courts. For example, we no longer need to explain 'grooming' or DNA; these are concepts and advances that jury members now (mostly) grasp. The public also has a better awareness of child exploitation material — sometimes wrongly named child pornography[4] — and of child sex offenders. This growing understanding has enabled an increase in reporting, which is a move in the right direction. However, my impression is that juries can also expect more from the investigation, and on occasion feedback to the police has been that a lack of explicit evidence (for example, video of the sexual abuse occurring or forensic evidence) can mean no positive court outcome. This is regrettable, not least because court cases predominately rely on a child's testimony against that of a lawyer-equipped adult. Discussion and action begun in recent years, aimed to improve sexual abuse victims' encounters with the court system, is in my view long overdue and certainly needs to continue.

THE DETECTIVE'S FIELD CRAFT

The science of reporting

There is no science behind this — perhaps there should be; rather, the 'science of reporting' is a phrase I have coined to discuss and promote a concept. Police react to reports or indicators of abuse. Reporting rates have risen as the public better understands the reality of such abuse, and stigma is replaced by a need to address issues. For police the information coming forward has been likened to a flood, a stream or a trickle, depending on the volume. If we don't respond in an appropriate and timely manner we can hinder this information input. We need to manage the delicate early stages as best we can — hence my phrase.

Questions we ask ourselves: What can we do better? Who speaks to whom, when and in what environment? Critically, where and when is the vital child forensic interview; what is the setting; how do the professionals portray themselves; are we turning our minds to deliver the best approach for known circumstances? If a supporting parent is uncomfortable with a police response, more often the child will be influenced and we receive reduced buy-in. Our Wellington team and others around the country operate from a stand-alone, purpose-designed building, often alongside Oranga Tamariki staff. We strive to address reporting concerns and improve in this vital area.

Pillars of support

It has long been accepted that police alone cannot address sexual violence. The support and expertise within partner agencies, governmental and otherwise,[5] are critical in addressing offending and victimisation. Fortunately this collaboration is now standard practice as we seek input in policy creation, training, research, field work and mutual encouragement.

Another aspect investigators must consider is a case's pillars of support. Supporting the child is a given, but that may not be enough if their mother, who is perhaps the person who brought the offender into the family unit, isn't also supported. On many occasions a child will love the abuser, who may be a close family member. Therefore we ask, where do pillars need to be placed and what support will be most effective? This continues through an investigation and after it, and as we approach any court case. It is a hard thing to get right, but awareness is a critical starting point.

> When 15 years old, she started believing her mother's boyfriend, her step-dad, was also doing sexual things with her sister, younger by four years. She too had been about that age when he started abusing her, touching and rubbing that slowly progressed to full violation and sexual acts. She had thought it was only her. A number of times she told him she wanted it to stop, she would tell somebody, but he said if she spoke up he would have to leave and her mother loved him.
> She knew her mother did. Family and friends knew he went out of his way to make her happy, happier than she'd ever been before. Finally, she plucked up the courage and told her mother. At first, the mother didn't believe her, didn't wish to consider anything was going on. The love of her life had said the girls might say something; that they didn't like him and would make him go away. The mother stumbled over what to do.

Finally the mother confided in a trusted friend, who, without hesitation, told the police. This offender was clever. Getting wind that a disclosure was probable, he disappeared. Child protection investigators tracked him down. He denied everything, calmly speaking about the girls' inappropriate behaviour and of their being jealous of his love for their mother.

He faced 13 sexual charges and the matter went forward for trial. Investigators had quickly realised that several pillars of support needed placement around the mother, and that if they were not in place then the girls would suffer. The offender had fully manipulated her as he patiently went about securing his preferential sexual conquests. For him the grooming process was all about controlling the family unit's dominant adult, and it worked — for a while.

He finally pleaded guilty before trial, although the sentencing process was equally harrowing for the girls and their mother. The police process was successful; however, nobody won, given that the case deeply affected all concerned.

Victim awareness

Detectives look to understand the drivers of demand. This involves an awareness of clients, be they victim, witness or suspect. A non-judgemental understanding of victims comes with the knowledge that any person can be affected, but it is also important for investigators to know that, with the right input, most will move on to lead lives that are not fully ruined by the abuse. They have been affected and influenced, without question, but they have not been destroyed. With appropriate action, support and/or care plans, which are enabled to work well, prospects exist for favourable outcomes. I balance this with the observation that some victims are seriously affected — sometimes permanently — and can have terrible, shortened lives.

Many decades ago, a nine-year-old girl was molested by a known sex offender behind some trees in a public place. Her friends were playing in the park nearby but she was too scared to yell out. It was over in minutes and he let her go after ejaculating onto her body. His forceful grip had hurt her arm and shoulders, and she ran away from the park to sit alone for about an hour, not knowing what to do. Slowly she wandered home. That evening she told her older sister, who, after hesitating, told their mother. The woman sent the nine-year-old to bed without dinner, and took all her clothes and hid them. When her husband got home from the pub, he was told and became angry. As he swore and cursed across the house, the little girl pulled her sheets over her head and cried, not understanding her father's fury. The next morning her parents acted normal, as if nothing had happened. At the breakfast table, her father said, 'What happened yesterday, we will never speak of again.' His wife smiled meekly and they never did. Sometime over the next week the mother burnt the clothes in an outside fire.

The abuse was the injury. A horrid thing for such a young child. But the avoidance and incorrect attribution of wrongdoing was the wound. A rankling, seeping wound that remained open until her suicide nearly 40 years later.

There is shame in sexual abuse, but far worse is the hurt, self-destruction and underachievement that occurs when victims are ignored or unheeded. Society, not the child, is to take the shame.

Suspects

Suspects emerge from the same broad spread of community members as their victims. From educated and working to dysfunctional and/or unemployed, I have dealt with a huge cross-section. Alongside considering these factors, detectives need to know who and what the suspects are sexually. That doesn't mean their gender or sexual orientation, which is nearly always irrelevant, or their marital status, which is completely irrelevant; rather, where is their sexual motivation? We screen all the available information — statements, case detail and previously captured data — to see if elements of preference are revealed.

Indications of preference help investigators formulate an offender approach. A simplistic way to put this is to say that there are two types of child sexual offender: the preferential and the opportunistic offender. Both can be sinister, destructive and abusive, and both can have a serious impact on their victims, but I believe that the preferential offender is the more dangerous of the two. They are motivated to have sex with the victims of their desire, which can be determined by age, gender, race or vulnerability.

Preferential offenders can also be excited by certain positions or actions, and sometimes by violence and/or domination. Since sex with children is illegal, these individuals need to plot and manipulate. It's important to avoid detection, as they need to escape so they can reoffend. There will be planning before, during and after the offending. The grooming will be calculated and often done to appear normal so as not to raise suspicion. Grooming after the abuse is also very common and is done to reaffirm suppression and silence. We therefore look for patterns around non-disclosure: how it was achieved and manipulated.

Preferential child sexual abusers are paedophiles and adophiles. Pre-pubescent sexual offending is less commonly reported to police, but this may not reflect true prevalence, as it is accepted there are difficulties and dynamics that hinder younger children's abuse being brought forward. Preferential offenders present a danger similar to adult serial rapists because of the massive damage they do before they are captured. In my experience, a preferential offender is fortunately not as common, but is harder to capture and convict than the opportunistic sexual offender.

Opportunistic sexual offenders do not cause less harm or merit less police attention. The preferential versus opportunistic assessment police use is aimed at assisting the investigator, and is never the basis for minimising an abuser's actions.

A lesson I learned many years ago is that, sadly, normal people, sometimes with otherwise apparently blameless lives, can do terrible things, including sexually abusing children. These can be opportunistic offenders who abuse an adolescent child. Sometimes supposedly good people do foolish and truly dreadful things, driven by alcohol, drugs, escapism or rampant sexual desire, or fuelled by pornography, with often a ridiculously misguided sense of entitlement. Offenders take advantage of immaturity and innocence, and of a child's own risk-taking, experimentation or natural curiosity.

> The mother's new boyfriend finally moved in after 14 months of a committed relationship. Her two children, the 11-year-old girl and nine-year-old boy, liked him, and as a unit they settled down. The man did not have children and life quickly moved into a routine.
>
> Two years later the girl was generating issues for her mother,

who had little tolerance. These were normal teenage problems, which the mother either ignored or heavily penalised. There was little consistency. The mother and daughter hardly engaged, so the man became their communicator and person of reason. The girl would wear inappropriate clothing in the home, but never when her mother was around; just him. She flirted with him, showing off her latest dance moves. He had no idea this was a young woman practising her femininity in what should be a safe environment. Nobody ever told him this was what young people did, to not read anything into it and to remain the adult in the situation.

In a moment of utter stupidity, he touched her on the leg. It wasn't just a touch, but something done sexually. The girl froze; she didn't know how to respond and did not make any comment. She also didn't tell her mother. How could she? She was the one being provocative. Plus her mother would explode, as always.

Everything changed for the girl. Because she hadn't said anything, he took this as further encouragement — it was their special relationship, he thought. He spoilt her, was always on her side and made her life easier. She saw things as tolerable, so stayed friendly with him. Then he touched her again, this time on her buttocks, holding his hand there. She didn't move, he sensed her discomfort and didn't do anything more. In terror, she later told her best friend, who told other girls. Finally a teacher was told and a report came forward.

Effective child protection investigators have the ability to not be swayed by dreadful acts and to adopt a manner and approach appropriate for each suspect. Treating people with respect is a start, as investigators look to obtain truthful accounts. It doesn't always work. One reason is the subject matter itself. The stigma associated with being a victim of child or any sexual abuse is less of a problem today, although it is still a notable factor. Fortunately, more people are coming forward for assistance, and not necessarily to police. However, there is even more stigma attached to being a child sex offender — and many say rightly so. I don't necessarily disagree; but I often see this stigma as an obstacle to an offender telling the truth and thereby taking ownership of their wrongdoing and enabling a victim to move forward, as well as creating an opportunity to address their own flaw or flaws.

Owning up to having sex with a child currently only provides jeopardy, and the only likely reward for confession is a lighter sentence. I have dealt with men who have been terrified by the situation and mortified by their behaviour, which they greatly regret. They then engage legal counsel, who nearly always advise them to say nothing. The consequences of admitting all and revealing this utmost failing are so high. Over the years, investigators have argued, 'So what? They should have thought of that before they did the crime.' True enough; however, most offenders don't think.

The better question is: How can we move forward in the best interests of a victim? The noblest answer is the appropriate ownership of wrongdoing. For police, encouraging offenders to take ownership is a key investigator goal. The approach I promote is one of respect for the offender with a focus on their actions and not their personality; fairly collating the best evidence; and respectfully maximising the benefits and minimising the jeopardies of telling the truth. I understand that an offender's plight may not evoke sympathy, and certainly that isn't the angle being promoted here; rather, being aware of it is part of pursuing the best approach and outcome for the investigation.

Most lawyers do their job well: they work for the best interests of their client with a holistic understanding of the crime; but in my experience some will not, instead supporting their clients with a possible escape route via acquittal at court.

> The octogenarian man sexually assaulted his partner's granddaughter, touching her genitals under her clothing a number of times. Finally, he was caught in the act and made partial admissions at the home. Police were called and he was arrested by uniform branch.
>
> I saw him at the police station and noted his lack of police history, good upbringing, a wide law-abiding family, plus healthy work and community involvement. It wasn't hard to uncover signs of dementia along with other ageing attributes.
>
> Before speaking to this man I approached his lawyer and said what I thought. Police hadn't yet spoken to the little girl, but here was an opportunity to have the grandfather's open account and the taking of ownership, which he indicated he wished for. I felt both

the child and the family would have been better served if he spoke openly and before her.

The experienced lawyer did not disagree, but would not allow a statement. That was always his advice to police detainees and he would not deviate. Then, after the child's statement, the man would still not be interviewed, again on the advice of his lawyer. The matter dragged through the courts, family members turned on each other and the child went through the full process. Finally, months later, it was resolved when he pleaded guilty just before trial and used his medical condition and age to avoid jail. To me, that was a dreadful process for all concerned — except the lawyer.

PREVENTION

The mission of the New Zealand Police is to make this the safest country in the world. Along with striving to deliver a more responsive police service which targets and catches offenders, prevention first is a key strategy. I have pondered for years on how to achieve prevention first in child protection. How do we provide more than our present response model? Child protection isn't much protection when it's only after the fact.

We cannot patrol all homes and other locations to watch over every vulnerable child, or evil and/or stupid adults. But there are societal principles that forever need promoting, such as protective rights around children and an absolute intolerance of abuse.

We can send a message by promoting our enforcement success: If you abuse a child, you will get caught, so don't do it. But this has an impact on only one sector of the population. While I have long ceased to be surprised when historic complaints are made, I have often wondered, what was this person thinking when they did this years ago? Did they not think that the child would one day speak up? I now understand that imagining the future is impossible for some: the here and now is their priority or limit. The risk of being caught is more often than not a preventative only for the principled: for those who understand right and wrong and that actions have consequences.

Our present court approach is penalty-based, and while punishment can incentivise behavioural change, I believe it has its limitations, even given the stigma and shame associated with sexual offending. We need more thinking and discussion in this area to identify how best to protect children in the present and enhance their futures.

Across the globe, child sex offender registers operate in a practical, secondary prevention fashion; although given resources are finite, the challenge is to find an assessment tool that best identifies those more likely to reoffend. All countries with registers face the same challenge: in order to identify and focus on the high-risk, we need to determine who they are.

Societal issues such as child poverty do not cause child sexual abuse, but they can create the opportunity for abuse to occur, so we need to work to address them across our communities.

Society's ambivalence about rampant sexualisation is also of concern. Shifts in entertainment, social media, music, advertising and attitudes have resulted in a desensitisation of standards around pornography and a drop in behavioural standards. A better understanding of sex and the body is a good thing, but society needs to catch up with recent developments and what I regard as an overload, and to work on achieving a balance around respect and appropriateness. A large part of our workload is children committing sexual abuse on other children, which can no longer be considered learnt behaviour from an adult. Now it is likely absorption or collection from any number of modern-day forums.

Parental awareness is crucial to child safety. Parenting has always been hard, but it has also changed. Social media, the distractions of other devices and the need for both parents to return to work are some of the major changes from the child-rearing models of the past. As a result parents can be unaware of what their children are doing and with whom — including online. Children who are disconnected from the adults in their lives are vulnerable. We see this often.

Overcrowded homes with multiple and changing sleeping arrangements, such as frequent guests, sometimes hardly known, feature commonly in our cases. Children must have an absolutely safe sleeping arrangement, everywhere and every time.

Alcohol and drug abuse are long established as risk factors for child abuse, and this is exacerbated now by the scourge of methamphetamine. Enhancing services to help people address such addictions is important.

Family violence and harm can be heavily intertwined with child sexual abuse, although most children are sexually abused without any physical force or violence; intimidation and/or coercion are more likely. All the ongoing developments in addressing family violence will have a beneficial impact on reducing child sexual abuse.

NOW IN THE TWILIGHT OF my policing career, having specialised in sexual and child abuse for the larger part of it, I'm proud of how we have handled most of the thousands of cases that have come to us. Sadly a number have not gone well, for a multitude of reasons, some mine, and for that I carry regret. However, right from those first quasi-specialist endeavours we have never stopped learning. We continue to evolve and improve, to chase what good looks like. So many times I have thought, *This is the most courageous young person I've ever met* — and then I meet another.

The authors of the previous three chapters work, or have worked, within key stakeholder organisations, responding to and working to reduce child sexual abuse. The next two chapters come from individuals who strive to make a difference in their community.

I consider myself to be well informed about child sexual abuse, and aware of the production and online trading of child sexual abuse images. And yet, until it came to writing this book, I managed to largely close my mind to the horrifying fact that there are also people who directly exploit children — even their own child or grandchild — for monetary gain. I had dismissed it as 'something that happens overseas', after shaking my head about those (men, to my understanding) who travel overseas to pay to have sex with children. Until encountering Natalie's work I had not opened myself to think about the children in this country put in this position, the factors that make them vulnerable to this occurring, and the people (sellers and buyers) who abuse children as a sexual commodity.

Natalie Thorburn is a social worker and researcher. For the past two years she has worked as a policy advisor for Women's Refuge while completing her PhD. Her research covers two related topics: underage sex work, and the sex-trafficking of adolescents. The latter involves force or coercion by another person. She has been able to identify some of the factors that lead girls as young as 11 to be prostituted. Natalie has described how the experiences they then encounter exacerbate the harm already done, and why it is difficult for these young people to engage with social services for support and safety. This is qualitative research, essential to build sufficient trust with those who took part; therefore it does not allow comment on prevalence or trends.

Natalie's enormously credible work has opened my eyes to this phenomenon occurring in our own country, and it is part of what we must consider in addressing child sexual abuse in Aotearoa New Zealand.

5. Underage sex work and the sex-trafficking of adolescents

DR NATALIE THORBURN
UNIVERSITY OF AUCKLAND

SEX WORK WAS DECRIMINALISED IN New Zealand in 2003 for those 18 and over. Despite it being illegal to purchase the sexual services of those younger, the research shows this activity is definitely taking place, albeit to an extent that is difficult to measure accurately. It's important to distinguish between adult sex work as a legal industry, and prostituted young people who become involved as a result of constrained choices or — in the case of trafficking — no choice. Applying the word 'prostitution' to young people is intrinsically harmful and inappropriate, as it assumes legitimacy, likening it to adult involvement in the sex industry. The term 'survival sex' is often used to reflect young people's use of transactional sex to meet their basic needs well before they could be seen as legally, developmentally or socially capable of giving informed consent. Others have suggested that this should be described as child sexual abuse. However, my research shows the value in understanding the specific phenomenon of transactional child sex.

THE CHALLENGES OF RESEARCHING VULNERABLE ADOLESCENTS

This research and its findings are far from disconnected academic theory.

There are many ethical challenges for researchers dealing with competent adults who are physically safe and who have a sense of agency in negotiating their social environments. The challenge of navigating ethical issues with young people, whose cognitive–emotional processes are potentially impacted by previous trauma, and who in many instances lack autonomy, freedom or basic safety, makes the research much more difficult and requires a lot of thinking through.

Many of my participants had complex histories of abuse, and many had not had the chance to work through this abuse or even name it as such. It was often difficult to ascertain how safe — both physically and emotionally — they were when they made contact, and there was a risk of retraumatisation through participation. These risks required careful safety planning. I used many of the same strategies with participants as I did with social work clients who had experienced trauma, and aimed to explore their lived experiences as deeply as they felt comfortable with.

What follows is information drawn from the stories of underage sex workers and young adolescents who have been sex-trafficked in New Zealand.

UNDERAGE SEX WORK (USW)

Circumstances known to precede USW

Childhood trauma, the involvement of child protection services, being in foster care, experiencing poverty and the normalisation of male violence towards women are all recognised as antecedents to underage sex work. So, too, are home environments featuring a lack of consistency or a lack of emotional responsiveness and reliability from parents or caregivers.

Trauma plays an integral role in creating vulnerability to exploitation. Childhood trauma — including sexual abuse and physical violence, homelessness, and separation from family of origin — has been shown to negatively impact on the developing brain. Trauma influences the brain chemistry, the development of normal thinking processes, beliefs and emotional and social skills. Such experiences also distort the normal analysis of risk and safety, and severely impair the development of distress tolerance. Variables such as the age and stage of development at the time of the trauma, its severity and duration, the child's supportive networks and individual temperament, and the nature of the relationship between victim and perpetrator all mediate the effects of childhood trauma.

It is worth looking a little more closely at the role of trauma in the lives of underage sex workers, given that this can both contribute to young people becoming sex workers and be exacerbated by aspects of the underage sex work itself.

Child sexual abuse often precipitates early involvement in sex work. Previous studies have shown that the prevalence of child sexual abuse among adolescent sex workers ranges from 40 to 60 per cent, and this is likely to be a conservative estimate, given the inherent barriers to disclosure. There is also some evidence that sexual abuse may condition young people for sex work. Through the abuse and reward patterns played out between the perpetrator and victim, children can begin to form associations between sex and the subsequent gaining of tangible rewards. It can also normalise abuse, especially abuse from men, leading victims to consider abusive relationships with older men who exploit them as normal.

Changes to cognitive processes, psychological well-being, self-worth, relationships and perceptions of what is normal sexual behaviour result from abuse. Traumatic responses can then be reactivated by sex without free consent, replicating the dynamics of the initial sexual abuse. Feelings of stigmatisation, shame and disgust about sex beginning at the initial victimisation may also be reinforced by the act of being prostituted.

Girls who have been sexually abused may not always be able to name the abuse as such. For example, one participant spoke about a sexual relationship that began when she was 11 with an adult male who was a friend of her father, and referred to this as a 'love' relationship. Another referred to the adult man who had been exploiting her at age 11 as her 'partner', as though it was an adult romantic relationship.

My participants made connections between the defence mechanisms they employed to deal with sexual abuse, and the methods that enabled them to distance themselves from the sexual act while working, such as dissociation and mental distraction. One said: 'It wasn't like having sex for cash was any different than being raped by my cousin. It felt exactly the same as it did when my cousin had sex with me. Or when my boyfriend did, or the business suit guys, or the cops. It was all the same. I didn't feel any of it.' Another said that childhood sexual abuse 'prepares you for sex work; it makes it not such a big impact as if it was someone who hadn't been abused going into that environment, you know'.

A lack of parental responsiveness affects adolescents' ability to effectively integrate experiences and leaves significant scope for peer influence. Under 'good enough' home conditions, adolescents learn how to take part in adaptive and meaningful activities even when distressed, through observing their primary caregivers model this and being taught emotional coping skills by parents and the family's collective emotional climate. Participants showed poor distress tolerance skills, a result of not having had anyone providing or modelling effective strategies to deal with distress as they grew up. As adolescents, participants linked this lack of capacity to tolerate distress (and their corresponding self-harm and suicide attempts) to their unmet need to find a secure home base that would protect them as they began to explore their own identities.

They also outlined numerous coping strategies designed to avoid facing distress. Several made connections between what they considered 'extreme' behaviour and the drive to avoid feeling overwhelming emotion. Survivors of abuse are more likely to have high levels of trauma-related avoidance and intrusive symptoms such as flashbacks in adolescence than at any other time. Coping strategies included such escape behaviours as drug and alcohol use, suicidal and self-harming behaviour, continual involvement in party environments, physical transience and casual sexual encounters. Participants all used illegal drugs, and spoke about the value of substances in blocking out their distaste for the sexual interactions and the shame they later felt about them. Although participating in street work often made them feel tough or was exciting, they were aware of constant risks of violence and sexually transmitted diseases.

All the physical and cognitive changes associated with adolescence as a developmental period are compounded by the absence of good enough parental responsiveness. This concept is defined in detail in the development of sexuality chapters in this book; fundamentally, it involves the willingness and ability to recognise what an infant or child is feeling and needing, then to empathise, comfort and guide according to age. Adolescence is a major identity-forming period: interactions with primary caregivers begin shaping the identity, then young people shape it further as they seek to gain self-esteem and self-knowledge through interactions with peers. These peer interactions have a notable influence in the shaping of both individual identity and behavioural decision-making. This is exaggeratedly so for adolescents who have been made vulnerable by inadequate parental input.

This often interacts with other factors — including broader social norms. The ways that we teach children to play and interact effectively condition their later behaviour. Boys are taught from a young age that being powerful, dominant and aggressive are positive traits, and girls are taught to be submissive, caring and sexually desirable, and these behaviours lend themselves well to the dynamics involved in sexual exploitation and other types of violence. This becomes particularly obvious in adolescence, when teenaged girls are expected to show the 'right' level of sexuality — neither too chaste nor too sexually active — positioning them as moral gatekeepers of sexuality.

All these factors lead to a culture that both silences and takes no action about exploitative sexual situations. (While the recent #MeToo phenomenon is challenging this, it remains to be seen how deeply and thoroughly change can be achieved.) Gendered beliefs, such as the assumption that men have sole decision-making power regarding the initiation of sex, and that women's needs are secondary to men's, seemed to act as one of the foundations of sexual violence, and of the acceptance of sexual violence, for the girls in both studies.

Each of these dynamics contributes to the development of rigid internal working models about gender and ideals about male and female behaviour that create vulnerability at the individual level. The saturation of gender-based beliefs and violence within participants' environments reinforces this at the relational level. Witnessing intimate partner violence between parents, and subjection to sexual abuse from male family members, further fortifies these gender-based sets of beliefs, which then shape future expectations about male–female relationships. The physical and sexual violence witnessed and experienced in childhood by those who are involved with sex work while underage or who are trafficked for sex is therefore likely to have independently contributed to them accepting as normal being victimised by intimate partners, strangers and clients in adolescence.

Destructive power structures in some of the research participants' lives meant that sexual decision-making rights lay with others, rather than themselves. Known men were viewed as 'nice' despite coercing participants into sex, and sexual relationships between adults and minors were not typically viewed as abnormal or indicative of harmful behaviours. 'When I met Max, he was, like, real nice . . . he was the first guy I fucked. Uh, he told me I was pretty and stuff and made me feel good about my body, even though he was, like, twenty and I was, like, eleven.' Similarly, violence was only regarded as 'bad' if it was extreme — otherwise, it was normalised as an expected part of a woman's life. Clients' preferences for strangling and choking workers were tolerated without complaint, despite physical injuries and safety fears. Both male and female participants disclosed this type of violence, often from repeat clients who paid extra after causing pain or injury.

Physical violence within intimate relationships was rarely questioned or seen as unacceptable. A lack of caring others and the consequent emotional vulnerability of participants appeared to contribute to their tolerating mistreatment; violence seemed to be the preferred option over being alone or in state care. Three had regular partners who were physically violent, and the reasons given for the violence were jealousy, the participants' involvement in sex work, and control. Two blamed themselves for the violence, believing that it was unintentional and that if they had been better partners there would have been no cause for violence.

Participants also had varied understandings of consent. Unwanted sexual acts were deemed to be abusive only if they involved penetration. The one incident that featured both violence and penetration was the only sexual incident that was clearly defined as rape, and the participant then rescinded this label as she spoke about her inaction at the time. Sexual encounters between girls selling sex and people in positions of power were also normalised and not framed as abusive.

A desperate need for income and a need for housing also make young people extremely vulnerable to being inducted into underage sex work. US studies show that between 20 and 50 per cent of young people who become homeless will engage in underage sex work. Studies into economic deprivation and early entry into sex work have found that between 18 and 61.4 per cent of participants identified their status of financial deprivation as being the chief motivator to entering sex work.

CONSEQUENCES OF USW

We've seen in detail how attachment disruption, child sexual abuse and a lack of parental responsiveness combine to create a common pathway into USW. Peer relationships have an increased role in shaping identity, and a gender-based power differential then further restricts autonomy and agency in sexual decision-making. Desensitisation to violence is common. This is often accompanied by a sense of powerlessness to escape, difficulty building trusting or meaningful relationships, low mood, poor concentration, self-harming behaviours including drug and alcohol use, eating disorders, dissociative disorders, and possible poor sexual health outcomes such as diseases and pregnancy. Emotionally, victims are likely to feel invisible and worthless, and these feelings may persist throughout their lifetimes. Victims are also at risk of significantly poorer mental health outcomes.

The results are young people who both create and encounter barriers to seeking help. The extent of an individual young person's traumatic response to abuse is dependent on a number of variables, including: the frequency with which the abuse occurred; its severity, degree of violence, and whether there was physical pathology; the number of abusers; whether the abuse occurred concurrently or in discrete instances; and the relational proximity of the abuser to the victim. Cumulative exposure and intra-familial abuse contexts have both been shown to result in significantly worse mental health outcomes.

Notably high levels of avoidant, intrusive and arousal symptoms in young people engaging in underage sex work have been linked both with their prior histories of penetrative sexual abuse and with the legal restrictions and cognitive immaturity that place them in higher-risk situations than adult sex workers. In addition, it is likely that psychosocial stressors such as homelessness or involuntary transience, addiction and tenuous socially supportive relationships interfere with the opportunity to heal from adverse experiences. As young people using sex for survival are more likely to demonstrate these clusters of risk factors and fewer protective factors, magnified mental health implications following traumatic events are anticipated.

Difficulties engaging with helping services

Typically, adolescents engaging in underage sex work view social service practitioners and figures of authority with distrust; they anticipate punitive or stigmatising responses. Seeking help to leave underage sex work behind may also be hindered by the circumstances that prompted their initial involvement; fear of shame or stigma may also be a barrier. These sex workers (generally working on the street or in people's homes) are also likely to internalise society's differentiation between moral and immoral victims, leading to fixed negative expectations about helping providers' responses. In addition, addiction to drugs and/or alcohol may add to adolescents' reluctance to engage with formal systems. Moreover, social services practitioners' awareness of adolescent involvement in underage sex work is uneven, which is conceivably a factor in the professional perception of adolescents involved in this work as being 'hard to reach'.

When offering support to girls who have been selling sex, professionals at mental health and social service agencies need to be able to work around lives that are chaotic and engage with young people whose thinking and emotional processes are also likely to be chaotic. Interventions need to be trauma-informed, and staff need to be able to offer empathic engagement without judgement in the process of trauma resolution work. If participants feel ashamed after seeking support, they are unlikely to try to do so again.

Participants had grown up with drug use, unpredictable responses and violence or abuse as the family norm. Adolescents who had then formed links with drug subcultures sought out peer relationships based on mutual involvement in substance use, and these peers then further normalised their use and related activities. Family disorganisation compounds these chaotic experiences in the lives of individuals.

In order to retain existing support systems such as peer groups, these services may be delivered using a group-work or peer-support model. This should be accompanied by strategies aimed at improving emotional regulation: teaching the skills of recognising and naming the feelings being experienced, and communicating or otherwise processing and releasing those feelings to avoid using destructive coping strategies such as substance abuse or self-injury.

These individual-level interventions are only one part of a need for change, however. More broadly, greater attention to consent and relationship education should be given, and in particular should be targeted at high-risk groups. The prevalence and normalisation of intimate partner violence should be actively combatted at individual, community and societal levels, and helping professionals need to be educated about the implicit messages that are transmitted to children by child sexual abuse and witnessing intimate partner violence. Further, the pervasive presence of gender-based inequality needs to be addressed through universal public policy and health promotion awareness-raising approaches.

'WE DON'T HAVE SEX-TRAFFICKING IN NEW ZEALAND'

Victims of sex-trafficking are globally known to be at risk for a wide range of adverse outcomes, but sex-trafficking is commonly believed not to happen in Aotearoa. New Zealand has a robust legislative framework to safeguard adults doing sex work; the work itself is decriminalised, and trafficking legislation disallows exploitative behaviour. However, this trafficking legislation is underutilised, and domestic sex-trafficking has attracted no prevention efforts from the government. While initiatives to assist identification and intervention are common practice internationally, they do not exist here. Rather, there was significant misunderstanding of the concept, with social service staff putting experiences of exploitation into the categories of sexual violence, family violence or sex work, rather than trafficking.

The international literature suggests that most victims of trafficking and/or forced prostitution have backgrounds of economic marginality, trauma and abuse, and that traffickers often exploit these vulnerabilities. Most trafficking victims were sexually and/or physically abused prior to being trafficked, indicating that pathways from initial victimisation to secondary abuse by intimate partners must be understood in order to understand young people's vulnerability to sexual exploitation, including trafficking. Currently, no other research exists regarding the methods used by abusers to recruit, entrap and exploit victims through sex-trafficking or forced prostitution in New Zealand.

Internationally, victims of sex-trafficking are generally picked up by screening from medical professionals and social service practitioners, but in New Zealand there are no screening initiatives or pathways for accessing helping services for domestic victims if practitioners become aware of them. Generally, frontline medical and social service practitioners buy into myths about what trafficking is — for example, that it only affects foreign victims and involves the crossing of an international border, or that all sex work is trafficking. Both create problems for understanding what trafficking really is. In addition, with few exceptions, moral judgements appeared to colour practitioners' perceptions of women who had been involved in commercial sexual transactions, which prevented them from asking enough questions to ascertain whether the sex work was by choice.

Signs of trafficking include the following:

1. Social factors: isolation and the presence of a controlling other.
2. Medical factors: untreated or repetitive gynaecological issues and/or the presence of marks of ownership, for example a tattoo.
3. Psychological/emotional factors, for example anxiety, depression.
4. Delay between injury and presentation for help, fearfulness.

As well as demonstrating a lack of active screening, the research into trafficking found that many New Zealand health and helping practitioners were unable to identify the dynamics of sex-trafficking that differentiate these situations from sexual violence, family violence, or sex work. The findings also showed that practitioners are largely unaware of the distinguishing features of victimisation, and that there are substantive barriers to safe practice.

HOW RECRUITMENT AND ENTRAPMENT OCCUR

Young people's vulnerability to recruitment into trafficking or forced prostitution is shaped by a number of interrelated factors. Research from the United States indicates that the majority of victims are intentionally recruited from locations frequented by vulnerable young people, such as those who are homeless, in poor socio-economic areas, in state care, or addicted to substances. Histories of abandonment, abuse and disruption to primary relationships create intense vulnerability ('push' factors), and these young people are then sought out and exploited by abusers who can offer necessities like love, affection, alternative homes and safety ('pull' factors).

Methods used by traffickers to groom and ensnare young girls included flattering, giving affection and acting as a 'boyfriend' for girls whose sources of affection were scarce. This initial period of love, generosity and protection creates the positive emotional connection victims feel for their abusers. While this was true of some victims in New Zealand, others did not 'love' the abuser; their compliant behaviour was motivated almost exclusively by fear, rather than the desire to maintain the abusers' positive perception of them and resulting positive treatment.

Both love and fear have been shown to be instrumental in preventing victims from objectively considering their relationships with their abusers, typically in conjunction with subcultural standards of behaviour that normalise violence or coercion. Young people are acutely vulnerable during the transitory period immediately after leaving families of origin or state placements; they need money, food, shelter and protective, affectionate attachment relationships. Most of the young people who took part in this New Zealand research were outside the school system.

Both pregnancy/child-rearing and surveillance were used as a means of control over victims — despite this being rarely acknowledged in international studies. Managing care of children while in situations of forced trafficking or prostitution was reportedly very difficult for participants. The threat of bringing the care of children to the attention of authorities was used to ensure compliance; correspondingly, participants in relationships with their children's fathers often perceived the situation as too difficult to exit from.

A lack of options for childcare and the absence of social support meant that desperate measures were often resorted to in order to ensure the safety of children during working times, such as convincing an acquaintance to hide the child in the car until they had earned sufficient money for the day.

Victims also reported being watched, and living in fear of being caught doing something they were not meant to do (for example, staying home from work for a day) and receiving a beating.

Physical and sexual violence were used both as methods of punishment and as assertions of dominance, control and the abusers' apparent superiority within the 'relationship'. Being subjected to beatings, being raped (particularly as a punishment) and being threatened were all experiences commonly reported by victims. The most common precipitant to such punishment was refusing to continue to earn money through sex. All victims reported lack of a secure attachment relationship in childhood and all but one had been subjected to violence, thus developing an internal working model in which violence was accepted as normal. Violence was generally blamed on them. These young women had trouble reconciling the abuse that was occurring with their original experiences and expectations of their boyfriend.

Given that abusers who recruit and entrap adolescent girls into forced prostitution and sex-trafficking use a range of tactics to foster control and dominance over victims, it's important to consider the dynamic and complex nature of victim–abuser relationships when identifying such situations and when working with victims. As with other studies, this research revealed highly variable tactics — with the exception of the 'love-illusion'. The compelling vision of 'love' as a deterrent to escape and disclosure appeared to be equalled by overwhelming fear for both self and others, illustrating the need for tailored intervention strategies to elicit, validate and productively work with victims' disclosures.

Further, the design of interventions oriented toward safety-seeking must extend beyond the victim–abuser dyad to account for potentially multiple abusers with significant collective power, and also for potentially multiple or secondary victims (including victims' children) who may have extra constraints to autonomy. The power of this love-illusion cannot be overstated, and must be the primary object of attention in any design of support services.

CONCLUSION

Young people in these situations are being exploited in a way that invariably leads to later struggles. They are routinely subjected to abuse and violence, and rarely find avenues for support that they find helpful. There are a number of things that need to be in place to address this. The first is a raising of awareness of the unacceptability of the use of young people in prostitution, and this must start with the updating of a national plan of action on youth exploitation. The next is to introduce and embed consent and respect education at all schooling levels, as this type of exploitation is always accompanied by gender inequality and the sanctioning of abusive relationships more generally. This needs commitment from all sectors — police, justice, social services, health and education — to identify and support young people who are being exploited, instead of maintaining our current response, which is typically interpreted as punitive, shaming or stigmatising. Finally, we need to begin targeting the buyers of underage sexual services.

REFERENCES

Thorburn, Natalie, 'Consent, Coercion, and Autonomy: Underage sex work in Aotearoa New Zealand', *Aotearoa New Zealand Social Work* 28, no. 1 (2016): 34–42.

———, 'Surviving Shame: Adolescent sex workers' experiences of accessing and avoiding helping services', *New Zealand Journal of Counselling* 35, no. 2 (2016): 14–26.

———, 'Sexual Trauma, Memory, and Implications for Police: Lessons from the literature', *Australian Policing Journal*, 2017, retrieved from https://apjl.com.au/

———, 'Practitioner Knowledge and Responsiveness to Victims of Sex Trafficking in Aotearoa/New Zealand', *Women's Studies Journal* 31, no. 2 (2017): 77–96.

———, 'Sexual Exploitation in Adolescent Dating Relationships: Recruitment and entrapment of victims', *Sexual Abuse in Australia and New Zealand* (SAANZ journal), 2018, retrieved from https://www.anzatsa.org/saanz-journal/browse-saanz-articles/

———, 'Researching Underage Sex Work: Dynamic risk, responding sensitively, and protecting participants and researchers', in *Handbook of Research Methods in Health and Social Sciences*, ed. P. Liamputtong (Singapore: Springer-Verlag, 2019).

——— & I. de Haan, 'Connecting Through Chaos: Escape behaviour among sex-working adolescents in Aotearoa New Zealand', *Kōtuitui: New Zealand Journal of Social Sciences Online* 12, no. 1 (2016): 32–40.

I first heard of Ciaran Torrington as she was being interviewed on the radio about receiving the latest in her ever-growing list of honours, which includes her invitation to speak to the United Nations Commission on the Status of Women in New York in 2018. Ciaran expressed strongly held views on what needs to happen for a community to tackle child (and adult) sexual abuse. I realised she would be a valuable contributor to this book.

Ciaran's powerful drive to change attitudes and help abuse survivors is born of personal experience. At the age of 16 she dropped out of school, left home and was on a benefit. Nine years later, she began what she called her 'fight back against the impact sexual violence had on my life' and embarked upon a lengthy period of study that led to a master's degree in psychology. Now an ACC-registered sexual abuse therapist and assessor, she lives in the Far North, where she has worked in the healthcare sector of the Kaitāia community for over 19 years.

Ciaran has campaigned for more support for survivors in Kaitāia since 2014. She developed the concept Te Wairua O Tika ('the spirit of belonging to right'), which aims in part to establish a connection between sexual abuse therapists and police that increases disclosure, strengthens clients' resilience through the justice system, improves outcomes and promotes healing for the victims.

In 2018, along with other survivors, Ciaran founded HEALnz, a trauma charity. She has received Best Contribution to Social Good by an Individual — Social Innovation Awards and a Local Hero Medal for her work.

6. Te Wairua O Tika

CIARAN TORRINGTON
THERAPIST, SURVIVOR ADVOCATE

TO TELL YOU WHERE MY work in the world of child sexual abuse began I have to step deep into the early origins of my childhood. All my life my mother said that I changed when my sister was born, suggesting I was jealous. I remembered how each time I heard it I would cringe as if I had done something wrong. One of the last times I spoke to my mother, I challenged her that she said this because I had regressed back and had become incontinent again and she agreed. Today this is a recognised sign of sexual abuse or other trauma in children. I was two years and two months old when my sister was born.

For those of us who are sexually abused before the age of five the trauma becomes locked into us and woven into our identity. Our memory is fragmented, disconnected; we have behaviours we don't understand and memories that don't make sense or that we don't want to, or can't, fully remember. Even with the later external validation of confessions or convictions, memories will often remain fragmented; that is the nature of trauma's impact on developing brains.

My own most painful memory of sexual abuse is trapped in my body. If someone close to me hooks their leg over mine or even just around my right ankle I am instantly overcome with an incredible sense of heat and nausea. I try to fight this feeling, but the longer their leg holds me down the hotter and sicker I feel. The sense of suffocation and being trapped is overwhelming. It takes everything not to panic, struggle and scream even now, some four decades later. I believe that people shy away from even trying to comprehend what the experience of sexual assault is for a young child: what it's like to be held under the weight of a person who is harming you. I thought I was going to die, and to this day that's what my body believes, no matter how much I tell myself that I'm safe now.

ESSENTIAL STEPS TOWARDS CHANGE

Understand the impact of child sexual abuse

When we look to the future and ask how we are going to stop child sexual abuse, then the first step is to start accepting the reality of how harmful sexual abuse is. Hurtful comments that minimise our pain, such as 'get over it', 'stop being a victim' and 'you've just got to forgive', suggest the trauma from sexual abuse is some kind of choice. Being sexually offended on by so many different people in the earliest years of life has rewired my brain. There are parts of me that will always be trapped there. I have lived with the impact of dissociative post-traumatic stress disorder (PTSD) all my life. I have struggled with major depressive disorder and dysthymia, a chronic low mood that can last decades. I have had to learn how to be happy, to feel joy. I've had to fight to be here, to not want to die, to find meaning to my life, and yet people continually minimise the suffering I and others have experienced. A key problem this country is facing is insufficient understanding of the impact of sexual abuse on the victims. If we don't understand them, how can we help them?

You will notice that I am happy to call myself a victim. I'm also happy to use the word 'survivor' because they both represent who I am. I do, however, resent being told that I *have* to call myself a survivor, and that 'victim' is in some way a dirty word. Surely I should be allowed to define myself as I see fit? As a therapist I know that accepting your victimisation is a key part of healing from PTSD, so please allow me to reclaim in this chapter the word 'victim' for myself and the people I care for. I am a victim, a survivor and now a warrior as I speak out against sexual violence.

Acknowledge all victims and offenders, regardless of gender

The second step towards change is to start acknowledging all victims and offenders. The concept that rape is a war of men against women has gained significant momentum in our society, but it excludes male victims, female offenders and all good men out there, and it has become a barrier to changing sexual violence in society. In 2008 I was at a Stop Sexual Violence conference in Taranaki. The event was gender-focused: men barely got a look-in as victims, and the idea that women were all victims was also very dominant. I remember I had popped out from the main conference room, only to find a woman crying in the hall. I asked her what was wrong and she said to me, 'No one cares.' I asked her what she meant by this. She said, 'No one cares about me in there. They act as if women don't harm, and yet the person who sexually abused me was a woman.'

The denial that women are offenders goes back to the earliest days in the feminist movement. In one of the first books of sexual harm, *The Courage to Heal*, there is a story of how a woman came out to a group of women that her mother had sexually abused her, and how the group attacked her for her disclosure and denied her claims.[1] You can see this prejudice clearly within the media today in their reporting of child sexual offending. Whenever a male is convicted the word 'paedophile' is used routinely, but this is rarely — if ever — applied to the same situation with female offenders. Even worse, the media often describes female offenders as 'loving' their victims, which in some way legitimises their sexual abuse.

On my first day of school at five years old, two girls took me into the bathroom and sexually abused me. The sick feeling of terror in my stomach and the sense of violation was exactly the same as when males offended on me, but society continues to rate my suffering as somehow different; and when I disclosed to a feminist about the abuse, she said to me, 'Oh, those poor girls, it must have happened to them, too.' This belief that females don't offend or, if they do, that it's not as harmful as when males do it, has to change if we want to stop harming the victims and start catching the offenders amongst us.

Acknowledge all offenders, regardless of age
We tend as a society to minimise the harm done by youth offenders who sexually assault children. When these girls took me into the toilets to harm me, and later when I was taken into the forest to be assaulted by a group of boys, I thought the world terrifying. I had willingly followed these children and was so shocked when they turned on me. From a victim's perspective,

being sexually abused by peers seems over time to become normalised and accepted, and then nowhere feels safe. The advocates for young offenders and the sex offenders programme will repeat the line that these children who harmed me are 'victims too'.

All I can say is: no, they are not. Once you cross over to the dark side you don't get to sit beside me and tell me you are the same. These children who assaulted me knew that they were hurting me and they liked it, and that makes them responsible for their actions no matter what their age. I never liked hurting anyone, and that's a key difference. The most common feeling that youth offenders show towards their victims seems to be anger: 'You made me do it, it's not my fault.'

When the youth sex offender is given more support than the victim, this represents a travesty of justice. I have seen a young rape victim harm herself after a poorly managed restorative justice process forced her to be in the room with the person who raped her and pressured her to forgive. On another occasion, when a child sexually abused two other children at a local primary school, the school not only failed to report it to police or Oranga Tamariki, but also pressured the parent of the abused child to just accept the school's handling of the situation because it 'wasn't the offender's fault: he had problems'.

Women, too, need to take some responsibility

The concept of rape being a war against women also puts women into a passive role, as if they play no part in the perpetuation of sexual violence in our society. This creates the misconception that all women are on the side of rape victims. I was part of a women's group that passed a resolution at their conference petitioning government to run workshops to build empathy toward sexual abuse survivors. It was the first time I spoke publicly of my own sexual abuse and I was shaking, but the resolution was passed unanimously. It hurts some four years later that this women's group never actually petitioned government for the survivors in their club (the resolution was not passed through at executive level because it was deemed 'not relevant'), and when I suggested to an executive member that we needed to push for a commission of enquiry into sexual abuse I was told flat out 'No'. If we are to change sexual violence, then women's beliefs need to be challenged, too. They sit on the same juries that are not convicting offenders; they protect the sex offenders amongst us and prevent victims from coming forward.

Mothers, and indeed parents, play a key role in victims coming forward. Sexual abuse survivors frequently tell me it is fear of the impact on their mother that stopped them from coming forward as a child and, years later, as an adult. If every parent in Aotearoa sat their children down, no matter what age, and said, 'If anyone hurts you, no matter who, I promise I will always love you, believe you and protect you, no matter what', and really meant it, then how many disclosures of sexual abuse would we hear and how much healing would be possible in this country?

Be seen to be fighting for the victims of child sexual abuse
Without that overt parental support, most victims of sexual abuse are oppressed by a crippling sense of loneliness. When no one helps you, when no one fights for you, you carry this burden all your life: a sense that you weren't worth fighting for. And if no one else fights for you, why would you even bother to care for yourself; why would you value your life? On a world ranking, New Zealand has a relatively high suicide rate, and here in the Far North we have the highest in the country. Research shows a clear link between suicidality and trauma, and my own personal and professional experience backs this up. If we are going to confront sexual abuse in this country we need to begin fighting for the victims amongst us.

I think of all the times as a child when I hoped for help and it didn't come. After one assault at four years old I was admitted to hospital. I kept waiting for someone to come and ask me what happened, but no one did. A year later, I was in hospital for 10 days, and each day a team of doctors would come in and peer at me and wonder what could explain my erratic heartbeat, headaches, malaise and white pallor — but again, no one asked if I was OK.

I clearly remember the day the police officer came into the primary school where I had been sexually abused on the first day at school. It wasn't long after the abuse, and I remember looking at him, thinking, 'Don't you know? Shouldn't you know?' I later learned it was even reported in the local newspaper — a rare thing for 1977 — that children were being sexually assaulted in the area I lived in, but no police officer ever came to my school to talk about sexual abuse.

I was sexually abused again at 11 years old, and this time when I reported in my evidential interview being shown videos of a woman being gang-raped and murdered and then waking up with a naked man slobbering all over me, I was told by a police officer, 'Sounds like you liked it.' No, I did not like it! It took another two years to tell myself that, after working my way through all the guilt and humiliation and deciding he was wrong.

Later I found out there was no point in reporting because, at the time, the word of a child against an adult was insufficient in the eyes of the law without any other evidence. Nowadays, with a maximum possible sentence of 20 years, I saw someone get four years when convicted for a similar crime, but back then another police officer rated me as a 2/10 for severity. Boy, did it hurt reading that years later in my retrieved police file; the pain caused had been way higher than that, and it took me into my twenties to get past what that officer said and then to face the sexual abuse that occurred before this.

I spent my whole childhood waiting for someone to turn up to save me, but no one did. *Where are all the heroes?* my young mind asked. *Why does no one care?* I was defiant, suicidal and self-destructive, and now people started paying attention, but it was too late for me to care. When I was 14 years old I was at school reading a book that turned out to be about sexual abuse; the words of the girl in the story hit me, and there in the middle of class I began crying. It was the first time I could acknowledge I was hurt. A teacher noticed and we had a talk and she suggested counselling. On my own I reached out for help and was one of the first to receive ACC counselling and an accepted sensitive claim for sexual abuse. This validation from the government was huge for me: someone acknowledged I was hurt, that this wasn't OK. I hadn't received that before and it meant a lot.

The counselling helped me acknowledge I was hurting, but it couldn't change my dysfunctional environment. I left home and school at 16 years old. I found out many years later from an IQ test that I had a processing speed that was in the top 2 per cent in the world, but there I was on a benefit, with no hope and no future. My story was typical. Too many young victims drop out of school and withdraw from society. We know now, too, that if you are a victim of sexual abuse you earn less money across your lifespan.

Use models of healing appropriate to the individual's needs

It was after 18 months of counselling in my twenties that I finally started to understand myself, but it wasn't enough; our knowledge of trauma was still so limited at that time. My studies into psychology were a way to dig deeper.

It was during this I first came across Te Whare Tapa Whā ('the four-sided house') as a holistic concept of healing for Māori. Conceptually Te Whare Tapa Whā works well for trauma victims because intrinsically it represents being whole again and where to start. Trauma impacted on my connection to my body (tinana); my thoughts, feelings and how I communicate (hinengaro); my attachment to significant others (whānau); and the identity I had constructed from the trauma (wairua). To heal I needed to address all these areas of my life.

At the time I was coping with a chronic illness as well as PTSD from childhood. The concept resonated with me and my path of healing; it gave me hope and direction, and an understanding of what I needed to change. Later a Māori therapist was the first to encourage me to become a trauma therapist, and she encouraged a holistic approach for wellness based on Te Whare Tapa Whā. Over my years working as a therapist in Kaitāia I evolved a Trauma Informed Te Whare Tapa Whā (TITWTW) approach for sexual abuse that was effective for both Māori and Pākehā with complex trauma. It was based on my own personal knowledge, professional supervision and training, and experience as to what does really bring change.

Agencies and communities need to collaborate and communicate

What led to my first attempts at social activism on sexual violence was a day in my clinic when client after client came in with a story of how, after becoming a victim of sexual abuse, the people in their community had hurt them through failing to support and understand the impact of trauma. These people were their whānau, health professionals, government agencies and social services: people who could have — and from my perspective should have — known better. I realised then that nothing was going to change unless I tried to do something to support these people I cared for.

When I stepped out of my counselling room in 2014 and started speaking out for victims it was based on the assumption that society had changed: that it now cared about sexual abuse victims and was ready to address it. Boy, was I wrong! I certainly wasn't prepared for the challenges and the risks I faced in speaking out, nor for the apathy and lack of support for victims I found in my community.

Moments that stand out include a meeting where people from the sex offenders' programme mainly showed up and I was told that we couldn't implement any change in town for victims that would 'upset the offenders'. I think my mouth dropped open! When I approached police to build more support for victims to come forward, one police officer suggested to me that I get a man to speak for me because police 'won't listen to a woman'. It would have been funny if it wasn't preventing progress; I faced brick wall after brick wall when I started asking for change.

At another meeting, where I pushed for Medical Sexual Assault Clinicians Aotearoa (MEDSAC, the acknowledged expert body in New Zealand on sexual assault and abuse medicine) facilities in Kaitāia, I was told that 'no one actually wants to go to police', even though the lack of MEDSAC services was identified as a real gap for Kaitāia. A year later, when I approached the district health board and ACC about increasing services, they had no idea that our community even considered it a problem. It feels so hopeless when everyone around you seems to have given up. There are too many offenders, they say, so we just have to accept it here in Kaitāia.

I've faced aggression and intimidation from speaking out in forums about sexual abuse run by the government and TOAH-NNEST (Te Ohaakii a Hine — National Network Ending Sexual Violence Together). It's been 40 years since I was sexually assaulted, but I still can't speak out. How disempowering is that for me and the victims I represent? When all those working towards addressing child sexual abuse can be trauma-informed and respectful of individuals' voices, then not only will they reduce the prevalence of more CSA, but victims and survivors will also step forward in their healing process.

Communities need to build relationships with police

The progress I made with the Criminal Investigation Branch is perhaps thus far what I am most proud of in making a pathway for victims who are too harmed and too scared to come forward of their own accord. This has been a real challenge for me because I had to change beliefs about the police that I had held since my evidential interview at 11 years old — that going to the police was harmful and a waste of time. What pushed me to change was the arrest of James Parker, and then of the other sex offenders that followed. (Parker was arrested in 2012 for committing multiple sexual abuses against pupils during his tenure as deputy principal of Pamapuria School.) This had an incredible effect locally. It triggered a town full of trauma survivors — including people in their seventies — to come forward about their abuse.

It restored faith in the police and encouraged people to report offenders.

I, however, faced a personal dilemma. Was I obstructing victims, by not recommending that they approach the police? Many of the victims I have worked with have gone on to study and have a career because I suggest to them they can if they want to, but I realised I also needed to have the same meaningful conversation about reporting to the police. When I did that, I was amazed at how many felt they wanted to come forward. Clearly I was standing in the way. Clearing a path to help so many people come forward has been a huge challenge for me, given my own history with the police. (At 13 years old I used to fantasise about killing myself in front of them to show them how much they had hurt me.) But I'm so glad I did, and it has been very healing watching highly skilled police officers respond to victims in a way that makes the victims feel so validated and supported.

My role now is to build that connection with the police because it is the sense of working as a team — therapist and police — that really anchors victims. I build the police up so much that victims almost expect the officer to fly in like Superman.

One day I will never forget: I had told a victim that the local detective sergeant was like a father to the victims in the community, knowing that she connected her sexual abuse to the loss of her father. When the officer arrived she threw herself at him, hugging him tight. She was a little woman and he was a tall man and she made it just to his waist. He looked surprised but, full credit to him, he hugged her back, and in that moment he became the anchor she had been missing all her life. I have learnt that police play a powerful role in helping victims heal and in protecting the community, and I believe there is untapped potential in how police and therapists can work together to convict offenders. The more I was aware of the massive pressure within the community to not report offending, the more determined I became to overcome it. Over the past few years I have helped many victims come forward, and for each it has brought a sense of peace and closure, regardless of outcome.

One thing I've learnt is that the evidential interview is critical to deciding whether to arrest and then convict offenders, because of the need to reach an evidential threshold in order to prosecute. As a therapist it can take years to gently draw a trauma story from a victim. The police get just one shot, and often the anxiety of being with police overwhelms victims, making it difficult for them to tell in detail exactly how they were harmed. Most who think of reporting have one sentence to say: 'I was raped.' This is their adult perspective; as children they wouldn't even have had that much language to describe what was done to them, but in a court they need to be able to slow it down and give every possible detail, including body memory and how they felt; that's an incredibly hard thing to do for deeply traumatised people.

Juries need to be educated about child sexual abuse

An added problem is that juries expect a victim to show emotion, but PTSD typically causes a person to dissociate from their traumatic memories and shut down. To win a trial you have to work against the survival mechanisms of PTSD; this is hard for anyone to do, even with good support.

Adopt a community-wide trauma-informed approach

A trauma-informed approach has worked successfully in communities overseas. It takes the perspective that the social problems of self-harming, suicide, bullying, substance abuse, gangs, violence (including child sexual abuse), poverty and crime within a community stem from the traumatic histories of the residents. To alleviate these social problems we need to acknowledge and treat the trauma at a community level. We need to provide physical and psychological healing, as well as social support and a strong sense of identity. There is currently little or no identity for trauma survivors among a public that is largely poorly informed, unsupportive and often hostile towards their sexual abuse story.

Acupuncturist Teri Stout and I work out of a house of healing in Kaitāia to create a TITWTW approach to support victims of sexual abuse. I access healing through the mind as an ACC sexual abuse therapist, while Teri accesses healing through the body as an acupuncturist and energy healer. Together we create a team and a home that provides social support, and we present a strong sense of identity in that we are both CSA survivors.

We also take this TITWTW approach into our community. We have conducted sexual abuse educational workshops, and in 2018 went together to the Commission on the Status of Women at the United Nations in New York to speak out about the challenges faced by rural women. I formed the charity HEALnz with Teri and other survivors to promote, encourage and support the human rights of all people impacted by trauma within the community through membership, mentorship, advocacy and education programmes. We launched our website healnz.org to mark 125 years of female suffrage, and made our commitment to Te Wairua O Tika.

Since I began standing up and telling my story I have wanted to change how we address sexual violence in this country, but I have struggled to define my purpose — what my message is, and what role I am meant to play in this fight for change. This really hit me after Humans of Kaitāia, the local branch of Humans of Aotearoa (a group committed to bringing forth stories from people who are making a positive contribution to their community), published my confronting story in the local newspaper.

I was really surprised by the support that I felt online. I was 'real', people said. People acknowledge me on the street in a way I had never experienced before, in part because I had stood up and said things that needed to be said. But it was the real sense of change I felt in people that touched me deeply. I know now I am here to help other victims to feel stronger, to show that there is a path, that they are not alone. I'm in a town that sometimes feels like overwhelming darkness, but I am determined to be a light that encourages victims to come forward, to convict the offenders, to save our town.

Observing the ways children in my family have made use of the sexuality education they were privileged to receive has moved and delighted me. I recall a niece, now in her thirties, rolling out from under her dad's tickles at about the age of four, leaping up, putting her hands on her hips and stating assertively, 'I'm the boss of my body and I want you to stop.' How many other New Zealand children, past, present and future, would have benefited or could benefit from learning that principle?

This little girl was privileged to have a father sensible and respectful enough to respond appropriately; but even without that, children need to be armed with this knowledge. At a similar age, my eldest grandson announced to me that bottoms were private. I asked if he wanted me to let him wipe his own bottom now, but he didn't: he just wanted me to know what he'd been learning at daycare and, clearly, thinking about. It didn't stop him a year or so later asking me if he could see my vagina, but it did provide a good comeback line.

As Dawn Elder has established, children are sexual beings from birth. Their sexuality is theirs to develop in their own individual way and in their own time. To do this there is so much they need to learn. Sexuality is complex — for all of us. Some have family/whānau who can help them learn; some do not.

As will be seen in the chief censor's chapter following this one, children from a young age now potentially have access to legal and illegal sexual material, and thus it is surely essential that they develop the language, the life skills and an understanding of their own values to allow them to process what they are exposed to, voluntarily or otherwise. If our children and rangatahi are not familiar with models of healthy sexuality, how are they to evaluate what they see on their friend's device or what is being done to them by someone they know?

In this chapter, Katie Fitzpatrick, associate professor of health education and physical education at the University of Auckland, now answers questions about what is happening in our pre-schools and schools to address the ever more complex needs of children *today. In 2015, at the request of the Ministry of Education, Katie wrote the curriculum guidelines document to help schools teach sexuality education in developmentally, socially and culturally appropriate ways. She explains why it is so crucially important that this should happen, and if indeed it does.*

7. Sexuality education in New Zealand: What is (not) happening in schools and why you should care

KATIE FITZPATRICK, ASSOCIATE PROFESSOR OF HEALTH EDUCATION AND PHYSICAL EDUCATION, UNIVERSITY OF AUCKLAND

MOST NEW ZEALANDERS WOULD AGREE that young people should be informed, have access to information and learning, and be able to ask questions about the things that matter to them. Many would also admit, however, that we are not as open as we could be when it comes to talking about sensitive issues such as sex and sexuality. At the same time, the internet, popular culture and social media are flooded with a wide range of messages about sex, sexuality, gender and bodies. Not all of these are positive or helpful, yet teenagers and children are increasingly looking online for answers to questions they are curious about.

In some ways, we are experiencing a new kind of generation gap between parents and young people. While online games, social media and streaming are absolutely the norm for contemporary children and young people, this is not necessarily the case for many parents and caregivers, who lament 'losing' their teenagers to screens for large portions of the day. But while parents may feel at a loss, young people have many positive experiences online, and the internet is a powerful source of information, engagement and entertainment for young people (just as it is for adults).

In the area of sexuality, young people frequently search for answers to questions of health, biology and relationships, and pornography is very accessible. A recent survey of New Zealand youth showed that one in four had viewed pornography by the age of 12, as had two-thirds of teens aged 17 and under.[1] The same study also showed, however, that New Zealand youth are aware of problems with the open availability of online pornography and would like to see changes. Other studies show that young people are looking for opportunities to discuss, question and debate issues of sex and sexuality in spaces that are open, safe and non-judgemental.[2]

While media headlines are dominated by alarming stories about young people and pornography, abuse and risk, human sexuality is much broader and more complex. It is worth taking a step back from the fear and panic and considering what we as a society want our young people to know, care about and be able to do. As an educator who has spent my career thus far teaching, thinking and writing about issues of health in education, I want today's young people to be well informed, to have a social conscience, to know about their own bodies, and to be able to engage in respectful relationships with others. I want them to feel confident, to be able to critique the images and values they are fed by the media and internet sites, and to be able to reflect on and act on their own values.

Now, this is quite an ask in a society where we don't talk about or study human health and sexuality. It is also quite an ask for young people to develop these skills when families are short on time, and when many people are simply too embarrassed or worried to know how to open up conversations with children and teenagers. No adults I know would suggest that relationships — particularly intimate relationships — are easy. And yet we don't give young people the chance to learn about the complexity, the messiness and the challenges of human relationships, as well as their joys and their risks.

The final point I want to make in the introduction to this chapter is that talking about this stuff is actually not enough. Talking about sexuality and *learning about sexuality* are different things.[3] You would not expect your child to gain adequate knowledge of maths or history or science simply by talking about it at home. Rather, you expect them to study these subjects at school, in order to read, debate, learn, discuss, construct and gain knowledge. So in order to understand and practise human health, young people need to study it at school. While studying health is of value in its own right, it may also help protect young people as they become adults. Having knowledge about a subject is a form of empowerment because we can't help but feel more confident in our decisions if we are better informed.

Health education is a formal part of the school curriculum in New Zealand, and so is mandated in all state schools from years 1 to 10. Sexuality education is part of health education and so should be studied (alongside food and nutrition, drug and alcohol education, and mental health). But while health education 'should' be a usual part of the school timetable, many schools do not offer it, and so sexuality education does not get the time needed in most schools. This means that opportunities to learn about sexuality — including consent, relationships, the role of various media, and interpersonal skills and friendships, for example — are absent in some (many) schools. A further problem arises because of perceptions about sexuality education.

Here's where things get mixed up: some parents assume that when young people learn about sexuality at school, there is a greater risk of them becoming sexually active. Many people feel fearful about this, and so prevent young people from learning about their own bodies, their feelings and their relationships with others, as well as issues in society, laws, how to communicate well and how to begin to understand themselves. This fear goes away when we see learning about sexuality as just another area of study. And, as mentioned above, knowledge tends to be empowering, while ignorance is always disempowering.

So what is (or should be) happening in schools? The law requires young people to attend school up until the age of 16. While we know that the schooling system is not perfect, the time they have at school allows young people to engage in a wide range of experiences and to learn a diversity of knowledge and skills. School is the ideal place for the formal study of health and well-being.

In 2015 the Ministry of Education released a new curriculum document to help schools teach sexuality education. I led the writing of that document — *Sexuality Education: A guide for principals, boards of trustees and teachers*

— and I will return to a discussion of it shortly, but first let's understand how the school curriculum is structured and where learning about health and sexuality fits.

Schools base their overall programmes on a document called *The New Zealand Curriculum* (Ministry of Education, 2007). That document covers learning aims across seven curriculum areas, most of which will be pretty familiar: mathematics, English, science, technology, languages, social studies, and health and physical education. The final area — health and PE — is divided into seven key areas of learning, or topics: sport studies, physical activity, food and nutrition, sexuality education, mental health, outdoor education, and body care and physical safety. So, sexuality education is one area of focus in the wider curriculum. This means that schools are required to teach it, just as they are required to teach, say, history (as part of social studies) or algebra (as part of mathematics).

The new sexuality education guide mentioned above recommends that 12 to 15 hours per year of learning time be dedicated solely to sexuality education. The rest of health education of course requires more time. The recommendation of 12 to 15 hours is based on the Education Review Office's (ERO) evaluation of programmes in 2007.[4] ERO's most recent review, however, shows that most schools fall short of this, and some schools don't offer sexuality education at all.[5] This is a serious problem.

If schools do not offer health education, then young people miss out on the opportunity to learn about a diversity of health issues that affect them every day. *The New Zealand Curriculum* states that health education enables students to 'develop their understanding of the factors that influence the health of individuals, groups, and society: lifestyle, economic, social, cultural, political, and environmental factors'.[6]

Health education helps students to 'develop competencies for mental wellness, reproductive health and positive sexuality, and safety management, and they develop understandings of nutritional needs'. It enables them to 'build resilience through strengthening their personal identity and sense of self-worth, through managing change and loss, and through engaging in processes for responsible decision making'. These are all skills and knowledge that would be ideal for everyone to learn. Furthermore, the curriculum notes that health education helps students to 'demonstrate empathy . . . [and] develop skills that enhance relationships'. They then (ideally) 'use these skills and understandings to take critical action to promote personal, interpersonal, and societal well-being'.

While these are somewhat lofty goals, don't we want a society where our young people are engaged in such learning? The problem is that schools have many competing pressures, and only a few schools give adequate timetable space to health education. Ideally, health education should have at least two lessons per week in every year level. Moreover, New Zealand law currently allows parents and families to withdraw their students from sexuality education classes. While this is something of an anomaly and is problematic, it does mean that schools can (and should) offer programmes that meet that curriculum and students' needs, with families making the choice to withdraw their children if they choose. There is, however, emerging evidence that engaging in sexuality education in New Zealand schools has a protective impact on young people in the longer term.[7]

WHAT IS ACTUALLY TAUGHT IN SEXUALITY EDUCATION?

The sexuality education guide encourages schools to view sexuality as intrinsically socially and politically located, and suggests that teachers engage students in thinking and learning about sexuality in all its diversity. Indeed, the philosophical orientation to sexuality education as an area of study explicitly encourages the exploration of a diversity of world views. This includes exploring a range of approaches to thinking about knowledge, as well as culturally located values and attitudes, different practices, and a broad spectrum of beliefs.

It does not assume that there is a singular approach, nor does it impose a liberal curriculum per se or assume that individual or collective views of sexuality are consistent. It does assume that schools should support a diversity of sexual identities, and that social justice is an important orientation. Along with other health and physical education curriculum policies in New Zealand, it takes a socio-critical approach.[8] Challenging heteronormativity is a core part of this. The guide, for example, states:

> Sexuality education in New Zealand schools supports and
> acknowledges diversity among students. Schools should work to

question gender stereotypes, and assumptions about sexuality. School programmes and the wider school environment should take opportunities to acknowledge the sexual diversity of New Zealand communities and recognise the rights of those who identify as lesbian, gay, bisexual, transgender, intersex, and other sexual and gender identities.[9]

The sexuality education guide also encourages schools to review uniforms, toilets and other policies and practices that are exclusionary, and which reinforce heteronorms. These moves are a direct response to the significant and long-standing research evidence that schools, both in New Zealand and internationally, are places of exclusion and marginality for non-heterosexual youth.[10] Australian researchers Jones and Hillier note that policies that aim to protect LGBTQI youth can make a positive difference,[11] as can policies that protect teachers.[12] The sexuality education guide thus challenges schools to examine the impact of gender binaries and heteronorms while also exploring diverse views of sexuality. Again, it positions sexuality as an area of learning, not as an intervention. In this, there is space to articulate and explore the complexity of human sexuality, while also naming and exposing inequities and exclusion.

While connecting here with LGBTQI issues and inclusion seems a little tangential to the focus of this book, this is actually extremely important because people who identify as LGBTQI are much more likely to experience abuse, discrimination and harm.[13] And they are much more likely to experience schooling spaces (changing rooms, toilets and so forth) as unsafe. If we truly want schools to be more inclusive places, and we truly want to disrupt patterns of abuse, then we need to ensure that schools are places where issues of sexual and gender diversity are talked about and studied, and we need to ensure that school architectures are welcoming and comfortable.

The New Zealand sexuality education guide, located as it is alongside curriculum policy, takes an explicit approach to social justice in schools. This begins with ensuring that programmes include the study of equity. Some public health agendas, as I argue elsewhere,[14] often directly contravene social justice in schools by imposing particular health-related practices and by viewing health education through an individualistic and medicalised lens. There is a significant body of work on this issue, which is generally referred to as 'healthism'.[15]

WHAT ELSE IS IMPORTANT?

The sexuality education guide explicitly outlines a holistic approach to sexuality, congruent with Māori conceptions of the body, which stress that the physical body is inseparable from the emotional, social, spiritual and mental aspects of sexuality. For example, in the overarching list of learning opportunities, the guide states that students will ideally develop:

- knowledge, understandings, and skills relating to sexual health and development: physical, emotional, mental, social and spiritual; and
- knowledge, understandings, and skills to enhance their sexual and reproductive health, for example, knowledge about the process of conception, contraception, and the skills to make decisions that maintain and enhance their sexual health.[16]

These goals sit alongside statements about developing knowledge and skills to enhance relationships, equity, ethics, rights and so on. The concept of hauora — a Māori philosophy of well-being — is included in the document, in line with previous curriculum policy in health and PE.[17] According to Māori scholar and teacher Sharon Heaton, hauora is 'accepted within the health sector as meaning "a Māori perspective of health and well-being"'.[18] The actual model in the aforementioned New Zealand health and PE curriculum,[19] which also appears in the later *New Zealand Curriculum* and in the sexuality education guide, is Te Whare Tapa Whā ('the four-sided house'). This model was articulated in 1994 by the prominent Māori health academic Sir Mason Durie,[20] and subsequently included in curriculum documents as an expression, or representation, of the concept of hauora.

Within this framework, the physical body is represented in a holistic invocation of physical, mental, emotional, social and spiritual. Māori views of health are in direct contrast with Western biomedical models that tend to privilege the physical body.[21]

The second model is Fonofale — an indigenous model of holistic health from the Pacific.[22]

There is, of course, a long history of the exclusion, erasure and marginalisation of indigenous knowledges in the education systems of Western nations.[23] Part of this erasure is a silent assumption in policy that white populations are the norm, while non-white people are named as culturally 'other'. In writing the sexuality education guide, different ethnicities were named explicitly, including the Pākehā population. The sexuality education guide, for example, states:

> Sexuality can be viewed differently according to people's social and cultural contexts. Teachers can help students to think critically about sexuality and include diverse concepts and content in their teaching. Including knowledge from Pākehā, Māori, Pasifika, Asian, and other world views can enhance the knowledge and understanding of all students.[24]

This statement does several things. It makes it clear that Pākehā are not an unmarked norm; it also positions sexuality as an area of study in which knowledge from a range of cultures and ethnicities can be explored.

WHAT IS NEEDED FOR CHANGE TO HAPPEN?

To sum up some of the points so far, we can say that while sexuality education has a place in the New Zealand curriculum, in most schools there is not enough time given to this area of learning. We can also say that schools have a responsibility to be inclusive and safe places for all students and teachers, including those who identify as gender and sexually diverse. This is important because the more inclusive school environments are, and the more opportunities students have to study human health and sexuality, then the better able they will be to navigate their lives and relationships.

Not only this, but students will also bring knowledge and understanding to their decisions, and to their engagement with health issues in the world. Lastly, if schools are more inclusive spaces, then they will be safer and more welcoming (and we know that people are more likely to succeed and achieve in spaces where they feel welcome). Importantly, sexuality education in schools is about so much more than protecting young people against abuse. It helps them to learn about developing the knowledge and tools to engage in relationships in all their complexity, and it helps them understand human health from a diversity of perspectives.

So, why is this not happening? There are three key reasons. First, teachers have been given no national support in the last 10-plus years to teach sexuality education. The Ministry of Education has put no significant resourcing into helping teachers (primary, intermediate and secondary) to develop knowledge and skills to teach this subject. Given the sensitivity of some of the content, and the difficulty that many people have with talking openly about it, it is an unreasonable expectation for teachers to do this work without support and professional learning. Those who are competent and confident have found their own forms of professional development and professional networks.

In the case of primary and intermediate teachers, who teach across the curriculum, it is not possible for them to develop such skills without significant input and resourcing from the state. New Zealand Family Planning and the association of health education teachers (NZHEA) have done significant work to produce resources and support teachers, but much of this work is with little or no budget from the state-funded education sector. The Ministry of Education has put some funding recently into updating resources, especially for primary schools, but teachers need upskilling to be able to implement these.

The second barrier to schools offering sexuality education is the lack of political will to put this high on the education agenda. Without support — in the form of resources and professional development — this will not happen. But even then, schools need to be given direction to prioritise this learning among the myriad other concerns and accountabilities they have to address. Such direction needs to come from the Ministry of Education, which requires the minister and the government to highlight this as important. Many governments are, however, afraid of taking this kind of action, in my view, because of their fears of resistance from particular groups (often loud, but fringe, activist groups who oppose the teaching of sexuality education in schools). We have got to be more open to this debate, while remembering that sexuality education has been in the curriculum since the 1990s.

The third barrier to schools offering sexuality education is the increasing trend of outside providers offering 'packaged' programmes to schools. There are literally hundreds of programmes available right now for schools to sign up to. Many of them are for sale, but some are funded — ironically — by the government. A few of these programmes work with teachers to upskill them to deliver content, but most offer outsiders to teach lessons to children and young people, without input needed from the teacher.

Space here doesn't allow me to go into depth, but some of these are simply advertising products to children.[25] The five-lesson 'Mates and Dates' is one example of a programme that is delivered by contractors without teacher input. It is operating in secondary schools (years 9, 10 and 11) with significant funding from ACC. This might, at a glance, seem like a tidy solution to the issues addressed above, but there are many problems with this approach.

'Mates and Dates' providers might have no connection to the school, the community or to students, and cannot follow up complaints or student requests. They are not teachers and are not necessarily skilled facilitators (their own evaluation showed uneven delivery skills). Nor can they enable student access to health services if needed, nor give the kind of pastoral care that schools are required to provide. Perhaps the worst thing about 'Mates and Dates' is that it requires huge funding to do a job that should be done by teachers. So, instead of supporting and upskilling teachers, the money is spent on one-off sessions (with no future capacity-building). Programmes like this are well-intentioned but are ultimately a waste of public money. In my view, that money would be better spent resourcing schools and supporting teachers.

A NOTE ABOUT LEARNING, ASSESSMENT AND HEALTH PROMOTION

It is debatable whether sexuality education knowledge should be assessed as part of the curriculum. Depending on one's approach to assessment, this can be seen as important for the subject to be taken seriously, or as impeding learning.[26] If a reductionist approach to assessment is taken wherein the latter is conceptualised as the retrieval of facts, assessment may, indeed, not be very worthwhile. My position on this is that if we are to take sexuality education seriously, and advocate for its inclusion in the school curriculum, then a focus on learning and meaningful assessment is essential. The alternative is, of course, sexuality education as a health intervention, rather than as health education.

The former takes a behaviourist and interventionist approach to sexuality education, positioning schools as health providers, rather than educational institutions. This undermines young people's rights to learn about sexuality and health, and it is also at odds with the intentions of sexuality education in New Zealand curricula. If sexuality education is not about learning, then its place in schools becomes questionable. Rather, as I and others have argued elsewhere,[27] sexuality and health education should be fundamentally concerned with enabling young people to learn *about* health. In this sense, sexuality education might be truly educative in the sense that the intention is to enhance knowledge, understanding and skills, to explore values, and to engage in critiquing social issues and relations of power.[28]

CONCLUSION

Sexuality education in New Zealand has an uneven history. While it has been formally a part of the New Zealand curriculum for all schools since the 1990s, programmes in schools have been irregular and uneven to say the least.[29] This is a result of multiple factors, not least an increasingly neoliberal approach to education and a range of pressures on schools. The current policy of the Ministry of Education is to let schools set their own programmes (across all curriculum areas). While this means schools have flexibility, it also means they can choose to not offer sexuality education at all. In the context of sexuality education — which is almost universally controversial — this approach has led to many schools avoiding this area of study altogether. Some schools have engaged outside providers (at huge cost to the schools or the state), but this approach is short-sighted and not best practice.

In 2015, the New Zealand Ministry of Education released a new curriculum policy document: *Sexuality Education: A guide for boards of trustees, principals and teachers*. This policy is a rare international example of a curriculum document that explicitly values diversity and promotes inclusive school environments, and approaches sexuality education as an area of study rather than as a health promotion intervention. This guide sits alongside *The New Zealand Curriculum* and provides direction for schools to implement sexuality education as a part of the curriculum learning area of health and physical education.

It is the right of every young person in New Zealand to learn about health and sexuality as part of growing up. The place to study these areas of learning is in schools. It is time that adequate time was given to the study of health education in those schools. For this to happen, parents and families need to start asking for it, the government needs to set health as a priority for young people, and teachers need to be given more support and professional development.

ACKNOWLEDGEMENTS

Aspects of this chapter are taken from an article published in the journal *Sex Education*: K. Fitzpatrick, 'Sexuality Education in New Zealand: A policy for social justice?' *Sex Education* 18, no. 5 (2018): 601–09.

This work was made possible by a Rutherford Discovery Fellowship, funded by the Royal Society Te Apārangi.

I grew up in the Hutt Valley during the era of Patricia Bartlett. A former member of the Wellington Sisters of Mercy, Patricia founded and was secretary for 25 years of the Society for the Promotion of Community Standards (SPCS). In 1970 they campaigned against the exposure of bared female breasts, then in 1972 against the stage show Hair, *the film* A Clockwork Orange *and adolescent-oriented sex-education books.*

The New Zealand Film Society was among those who fought back against attempts to stifle freedom of artistic expression, but Patricia Bartlett won sufficient respect for her work to be awarded an OBE in 1977. Then during the mid-eighties, following the decriminalisation of homosexuality, the SPCS and their conservative supporters found themselves hindered by the evidence base that from then on has informed censorship policy. In 1993, various government agencies were brought together to form the Office of Film and Literature Classification.

In the late 1960s, my greatest sources of information about sex had been my friend Andrea, whose older brothers had extended her vocabulary of anatomically correct terms well beyond mine, and my Concise Oxford Dictionary. *Then around 1970 my porn-free run came to an end: my parents bought a dairy, which allowed me sneaked access to* Playboy *and* Penthouse. *The photos of women acting seductively just worried me: Was that how I was meant to look? And act?*

Now, in 2020, the situation for children and young people growing up has changed in ways that Patricia Bartlett could never have imagined, despite her predictions of the dire consequences ahead. Even I, a sex therapist of over 30 years' practice, am shocked by some of the information David Shanks has presented for us here. Having met David and one of his staff, and having had a glimpse into the nature and the quality of work that is now being undertaken at the Office of Film and Literature Classification, I am heartened to see we are in very good hands to face the many challenges of this current era.

8. Technology, new media and child sexual abuse: Time for a change

DAVID SHANKS, CHIEF CENSOR, OFFICE OF FILM AND LITERATURE CLASSIFICATION

ONE OF THE MOST DIFFICULT things I have to do as chief censor is view images or clips showing the sexual abuse of children. It can be incredibly confronting and saddening. How can people want to do such things to a child? And how can there be such a huge market for this material?

Here at the Office of Film and Literature Classification we receive an apparently endless tide of child sexual abuse material from authorities, including the New Zealand Police, Department of Internal Affairs and Customs. These images, videos and text files might have been found on seized laptops or PCs, taken from mobile phones or intercepted from digital messaging sites or forums. The material can encompass almost anything you can think of (and possibly some things you can't). It is our job to determine whether something is banned under New Zealand law. We may have to assess a single photograph, or extended videos of multiple rapes. There might be detailed written instructions on how to locate, groom and abuse children. And on and on it goes.

As you might expect, in this office we need to give serious thought as to how we can provide the right environment, support, guidance and counselling to our staff to manage the potential impacts of this work. And as a consequence there would be few organisations whose staff are more motivated to see an end to child sexual abuse. You don't need to bear witness to this kind of abuse to be convinced that it has to stop.

THE IMPACT OF TECHNOLOGY AND MEDIA ON CHILD ABUSE

This role also puts us in a unique position to see how rapid changes in technology, media and social attitudes are influencing child sexual abuse (CSA). We need to pay attention to this transformation if we are to develop a truly effective strategy to stem the tide. Clearly, CSA is a complex issue which includes socio-economic, cultural, health and legal dimensions, and my view is that the effects of technology and media are additional factors that we simply must incorporate into an integrated strategy. If we disregard these factors, we risk leaving out some significant pieces of the puzzle. We could also miss an opportunity to make a real difference.

One example of what I mean emerges from media reports we are all familiar with. You will have likely seen reports of horrific cases of sexual abuse, often involving an offender in a position of trust (a relative, 'friend' of the family, coach or similar). Offending typically occurs over years, with multiple victims, and grooming is a feature, often involving drugs or alcohol.

This narrative has been depressingly familiar for a long time, but another factor has almost by stealth become a standard part of the story: the recording of the abuse by the offender, who then distributes the recordings to others. This is so common that it scarcely seems to merit a mention any more, but I think it points to a fundamental change in our society, one that is seldom openly talked about. It indicates that our transformed, digital lifestyle is affecting all aspects of our relationships, norms and attitudes. And it is significantly affecting CSA by potentially expanding an 'audience' that is ready and waiting.

The impact of technology is undeniable. The ubiquity of smartphones, an increasingly savvy digital population and the openness of the internet all mean we're now seeing video and audio of child sexual exploitation produced, accessed and shared at a rate we have never experienced before. This same technology also provides the basis for whole new ways to abuse children, for example through 'active, real-time' platforms such as live streaming and webcams.

Potentially even more significant are the rapid shifts in behaviours and norms we now see. The changes in media and technology are enabling ever-increasing levels of sexualisation of children. We know children are often seeing commercial media content intended for adults, and frequently see sexual violence and rape. They can be exposed to graphic pornography, often by accident to start with. They might be confused, even traumatised, by these experiences. Meanwhile, apps that seem to encourage children to present themselves in a sexualised way are increasingly popular. Some young people are sharing nude images they have taken of themselves. Many teenagers view this as quite normal.

Digital technology is a double-edged sword. While it is most certainly being exploited by abusers, and many online behaviours encourage abuse, new technologies also provide fantastic opportunities to inform, educate and connect. Online tools and apps have the potential to dissuade offenders, and to help keep children safe. Are we positioned to get the balance right, in this context?

Not yet, in my view, but with some effort, we could be. I advocate thinking about our approach to these challenges as an interrelated set of three interventions: education, public information and regulation. We can make major gains by updating and coordinating our approach in all three areas. Education has the largest potential for impact in the long term, but providing the public and young people with effective, consistent public information, support and tools will also be key. Regulation and enforcement will be important, but we need to recognise their limitations.

PRE-INTERNET REGULATION? TIME FOR AN UPDATE

As chief censor, I have a role to protect the public (both adults and children) from potentially harmful media. I also need to protect the rights and freedoms we enjoy as New Zealanders, particularly the right to freedom of expression. So, regulation and enforcement is a natural place for me to start thinking about how to make improvements.

My effectiveness as a regulator is closely tied to the effectiveness of the legislation under which I operate, and here we immediately strike a problem. The legislation has been designed for a different era. As its title implies, the Films, Videos and Publications Classification Act 1993 was designed in the early 1990s. It was created partly in response to concerns about the unprecedented access to pornography the New Zealand public was gaining due to the growing popularity of new technologies such as VHS tapes.

Even in the early 1990s, the value of effectively regulating adult sexually explicit material, and in particular preventing its supply to children, was tolerably well understood. The new Act also reinforced the illegality of producing, supplying or possessing material involving the sexual abuse of children.

Besides the issues inherent in recording and promoting such abusive, exploitative and illegal acts, there were real concerns around 'normalising' effects, increasing the risks of further offending, as well as the use of such material for grooming victims. Penalties for producing, distributing or possessing this material were (and are) serious, involving terms of imprisonment of up to 14 years.

This legislation worked pretty well for a 1990s media environment. Commercial adult pornography was regulated with R18 classifications, and vendors and rental stores knew very well that their licence was at stake if they sold or rented such material to children. Adult pornography that featured violent, non-consensual sex (or illegal acts, such as bestiality) could be rejected as 'objectionable' (illegal to sell, hire or possess). A black market in child sexual abuse material certainly existed at this time, but it was largely limited to determined criminals who smuggled physical images, magazines and VHS tapes across the border.

The situation could hardly be more different today. While the 1993 Act remains in force, and CSA material remains highly illegal, virtually everything else has changed.

CURRENT TRENDS IN ONLINE CHILD SEXUAL ABUSE

CSA material has gone high tech and is seldom found in magazines or VHS tapes anymore. We now have smartphones and social media, and increasingly people interact online through a plethora of adult websites, chat rooms and other forums. This has resulted in more CSA material being available than ever before, and it's becoming more extreme. According to a 2018 international study undertaken by ECPAT (End Child Prostitution and Trafficking) International, the trend is to depict abuse of increasingly younger children.[1] Research tells us that material involving younger victims often occurs in a family context and is associated with greater levels of sexual violence.

It's not clear what might be driving the age of abuse victims down. One possible influence is the creation of new forums specifically dedicated to younger children on the Dark Net (a term for parts of the internet that are intentionally hidden from view). Work undertaken by the UK Internet Watch Foundation suggests that around 80 per cent of children depicted on known CSA websites are just 10 years old or even younger.[2]

Meanwhile, brand-new methods of CSA enabled through technology are rapidly gaining popularity. One study to gauge the popularity of 'active' platforms, such as live streaming for CSA material, was undertaken by the European child aid organisation Terre des Hommes in 2013.[3] The study involved four researchers posing as pre-pubescent Filipino girls on 19 English-language public chat rooms, aided by a realistic computer-generated image (CGI) version of a 10-year-old Filipino girl, 'Sweetie'. Over the course of 10 weeks, the researchers encountered 20,172 offenders trying to procure a webcam sex performance from 'Sweetie' after being reminded they were interacting with a pre-pubescent child.

It would be a mistake to imagine all of this happens far away, with foreign paedophiles preying on girls in the developing world. We know that adult New Zealanders are exploiting children overseas and paying for the opportunity to systematically abuse them. Children here in New Zealand are victims of online predators, some of whom live here. Recent cases in this country have involved children being blackmailed into providing more and more intimate and exploitative pictures and video footage, in order to desperately try to prevent the blackmailer from distributing the material they already have. It takes little imagination to picture the dark spiral that this conduct represents to a vulnerable child and the extreme impacts and risks of such abuse.

We continue to build evidence about the level of adult sexual interest in this kind of media. We do know CSA images and clips are often traded on Dark Net boards, with 'preferred' images and material providing the supplier with access to more highly prized libraries of material. This all seems to contribute to the ever more common practice of filming abuse, with all of the horrific aggravation of the harm inflicted on the victims that this implies.

THE ROLE OF BIG TECH

What role do the major internet corporations play in all of this? Unfortunately the report card is mixed. While most major internet search engines have protocols to block and report CSA material, there are some indications that these do not go far enough, and that in some cases search engines might be helping users find this type of content. For example, TechCrunch reports that a recent investigation into the Microsoft Bing search engine revealed that searches for terms such as 'porn kids', 'porn CP' and 'nude family kids' all surfaced illegal child exploitation imagery.[4]

Investigators believe that even when people aren't seeking out this kind of material, they could be led to it by Bing, and they criticise an apparent failure to prevent its suggested searches and images from helping paedophiles. While Google fared better in this particular investigation, searches using Google can certainly generate illegal material, and commentators have noted significant issues with its YouTube platform, which has been reported as showing 'fetish' videos involving 'single mothers' creating sexualised clips with children, even infants, included in the picture.

CHILDREN IN AN AGE OF 24/7 EASY-ACCESS PORN

Technology has driven a massively worrying trend in terms of abuse imagery and forms of abuse by adults — but how have things changed for children and young people themselves? What might the new digital environment represent for them in terms of risky behaviours and vulnerability to abuse? After all, many children in this country are familiar with digital media and devices before they go to school. Many 11-year-olds have their own smartphones. This presents a set of risks and opportunities that bear careful consideration in this context.

One obvious problem is how easy it is for children and young people to access adult pornography. The pre-1990s research underpinning our current legislation suggested that it wasn't a good idea to expose children to sexually explicit material, hence the R18 classification for this type of content that exists both here and in many other countries in the Western world. As we discover more about children's cognitive and sexual development, exposing them to pornography (particularly the sort of material found on porn sites today) seems like an even worse idea than we initially thought. More research is needed, and we can't pretend we know all we need to about the impacts of this material, and how it influences children's attitudes and behaviours. But nobody seriously argues that pornography is a product for children, with evidence suggesting regular use might impair sexual development, reduce empathy, and increase the likelihood of engaging in risky sexual behaviours.

Regardless, our children are looking at porn. A recent major study conducted by my office told us that one in four children in New Zealand first saw porn at the age of 12 or younger, and often by accident.[5] Three-quarters will have seen it by age 17, and by then many are regular users. Even the regular users report having very mixed feelings about viewing porn. They often see things that disturb them, like aggression. Consent is often ignored or ambiguous. Even though they may watch it, most children and young people agree it is just too easy to see this material. Over 70 per cent of the 14- to 17-year-olds in our survey felt that young people's access to online porn should be restricted in some way.

This could be a good idea. We know that our reported rate of sexual assaults on children is concerning enough, but we also know that what's reported is just the tip of the iceberg. There is some evidence suggesting child-on-child sex offences are also an increasingly critical issue for us to pay attention to, as reported by Barnardo's.[6] Might child consumption of porn be a factor in those kinds of offences? Frankly, given current data we can't discount that possibility.

The fact the porn industry is now a multi-billion-dollar marketplace dominated by corporations operating a lot like other 'big data' companies, such as Facebook or Netflix, magnifies the implications for children. There isn't much stopping these companies creating and distributing porn that specifically appeals to kids. This was recently illustrated by news that one of the major porn searches in 2017 was for 'Fortnite porn' (for those who haven't heard of it, Fortnite is a massively popular online game, particularly amongst adolescents and teens). I doubt this particular porn trend was caused only by adult gamers searching for this content. It's possible to do a simple Google search involving a popular game title and get multiple images of a young teen character being raped. It is difficult to avoid the conclusion that many young people are seeing this sort of imagery. I know that at least some young people believe that animated or computer-generated images of child abuse are legal (which is untrue).

It is also well reported that a currently very popular trend in online pornography involves 'step-porn'. This includes sexual video footage that focuses on step-relatives (like stepfather and stepdaughter, or step-siblings). Popular porn directors at the moment tend to specialise in portraying the dynamics of such an encounter (reluctance, shame, manipulation) as realistically as possible. It is difficult to quantify what effect large-volume consumption of this kind of content might have on the likelihood of real sexual abuse within families. It might be assumed that many viewers will be able to separate fantasy from reality. But it is also plausible that some viewers will be less capable of making this clear separation — particularly if the viewer is already prone to offend. Some viewers, including young people, may be less capable of separating porn fantasy from the real world.

Our own research tells us that many children in New Zealand aren't looking for pornographic material when they are first exposed to it. They come across it accidentally, or someone else shows it to them. One consequence of young kids increasingly having their own phones is that children can be confronted with images of explicit porn literally being 'shoved in their faces' by other children displaying clips on their phones anywhere, any time — at school, in the playground or street, or in each other's homes.

That is not OK. The World Health Organization (WHO) defines sexual violence as including unwanted sexual comments or advances. That suggests to me that a child who has an explicit sexual scene shown to them by another child (while asking 'Do you want to do that?' or similar) might be regarded as a victim of sexual violence. If true, that in turn raises the possibility that our technologies and devices are providing platforms for new forms of sexual assault and CSA that would have been hard to imagine not so long ago.

So porn is having an impact on our children's sexual understanding and development, and this presents new and evolving risks. But this is just one part of a much bigger picture about children's sexual development and vulnerability.

THE CHALLENGES OF EXPLORING SEXUALITY ONLINE

Another consequence of providing our kids with pocket supercomputers, with highly advanced video cameras and editing packages built in, is that they are photographing and filming themselves, and sharing the footage. Most parents or guardians of teenagers today will be aware of the phenomenon of 'nudes', in which intimate pictures or clips are shared (this is sometimes referred to as 'sexting' by adults, but young people tend not to use this term themselves). Smartphones make this an easy, almost natural, thing for young people to do. Of course there are obvious risks of this going wrong, which can and does happen, sometimes with shattering consequences for the person concerned. Research undertaken by Netsafe here in New Zealand suggests young people are inclined to believe that this type of behaviour is much more common (and therefore normal) than it actually is.[7] One risk here is that it may not take long for perception to increasingly become reality.

The implications of this are multilayered. Innocent sharing of an image to the wrong person can instantly make a child vulnerable to manipulation by a predator. Any sharing can easily result in the child losing control of their image, and being 'slut-shamed' or ridiculed, or made a victim of 'revenge porn'. While the Harmful Digital Communications Act of 2015 provides some useful remedies in this space, a limiting factor for the effectiveness of this (or any) legislation is the inherent reluctance of any child or young person to come forward and seek help for something about which they feel so much shame.

Meanwhile, many children and young people are forming a whole new perspective on their self-worth based on the number of 'likes' or followers they have on social media. Some are discovering that a sure-fire way to get a large following is to adopt a sexualised persona. Plenty of apps supposedly suitable for kids provide a platform for them to present as adults while lip-syncing explicit song lyrics (as is common on TikTok, for example); or to livestream explicit video (often generating predatory comments from adult watchers, as happens on Bigo Live); or even to have video chats with random strangers (such as Holla, which actually allows users to track a child's location, as does Instagram). While such apps often have terms of use prohibiting sexual content or predatory behaviour, in practice these don't seem to be effectively enforced.

Platforms such as these can present specific and very serious dangers of a child or teen being targeted and tracked by a predator, but the broader risk is a cultural one. What are the risks we face from raising a generation of children and young people who think it entirely normal, desirable even, to present themselves as worldly, adult sexual beings in order to create followers? Where it is 'no big deal' for young people to receive sexually explicit comments from strangers? Conversely, what risks might such apps create by allowing much older users (typically men) to view a parade of young teens and children while making sexual comments, entirely at ease with their anonymity? In other words, what risks exist in a digital world in which behaviour towards children and young people that would be reviled (or be criminal behaviour) in the real world is normalised?

This is the current state of technology and media. Of course, technology is going to keep evolving, and new challenges and issues are certain to arise. We have already seen the rise of deepfake technology, which gives anybody the power to create 'fake' clips by manipulating digital images, for example by combining a target's face onto an actor's or actress's body. This technology is being used to create a new form of digital child sexual abuse product, for example by superimposing a child's face onto a petite porn actress's body involved in a sex scene.

Virtual reality and augmented reality pornography technologies are also experiencing substantial investment and growth, and these technologies might prove to be particularly appealing to gamers and young people. Meanwhile, work is under way to create increasingly advanced sex robots, incorporating artificial intelligence technologies. Hyper-realistic child sex dolls already exist and are creating real concern in the international regulator community.

MOVING FORWARD: TAKING A MULTIFACETED APPROACH TO COMPLEX ISSUES

The major technological and social changes of the past 20 years or more have multiplied the volume of CSA material exponentially and made it easier than ever to access. They have increased incentives for offenders to record and distribute abuse images, and whole new industries have been created that are premised on the abuse of children and young people. Meanwhile, children and young people are commonly seeing explicit material, and are being encouraged to present themselves sexually in a range of problematic ways. Adults with a predilection for this have their choice of platforms on which to engage with young people, and to have their comments and perspectives validated by communities of like-minded people. New technologies in the pipeline appear likely to increase the risks.

This all seems to be an awful mess, but there is also some basis for a cautious optimism, particularly if we can connect these issues with an integrated intervention strategy that will drive down the rate of child sexual abuse.

For example, the rise of risky behaviours by children and young people online seems to have occurred alongside a lowering of traditionally problematic youth behaviours such as smoking, binge-drinking and drug use. A significant multi-year study conducted by the University of Auckland found that there had been 'profound shifts' in youth risk behaviour, possibly away from 'real world' risk-taking in preference to taking risks online.[8] It also suggests that concerted efforts to regulate access and to lead effective regulation public health and social marketing campaigns may all have played a part in reducing traditional risky behaviours. School-based health policies and curriculum changes probably also helped. The same strategies that seem to have worked to reduce 'real world' risks might serve to reduce online risks.

We also need to bear in mind the positive potential of technology. Smartphones, search engines and social media can be powerful forces for good, improving peoples' general understanding, connectedness and autonomy. Even pornography might have its uses, with some of the young people in our studies commenting that it can be helpful in reducing stress, and there is evidence that it may help some members of the LGBTQI+ community feel less isolated.

This can all help inform the way forward. From a regulation and enforcement perspective, there is little doubt that traditional structures have reduced the effectiveness of enforcement. Outdated legislation and international jurisdictional issues have hampered efforts to police what is an increasingly global issue. There have also been issues limiting the effectiveness of cooperation between government watchdogs and private-sector industry, such as internet service providers (ISPs) and global giants such as Google. Often this boils down to a lack of trust, with the private sector often arguing that efforts to limit and regulate CSA material amount to attempts to ultimately censor the internet and establish state surveillance of citizens. And there is little doubt that poorly designed regulatory responses in this area can have unintended consequences, potentially even worsening the issue.[9]

We have to move beyond all this, and I think we will. I see New Zealand as potentially leading some of the thinking in this important area, and demonstrating how the state and the internet industry can work collaboratively on sensible and effective protocols to ensure that illegal CSA material is restricted, that people seeking this material are dissuaded, and that serious offenders are found and prosecuted. I believe this can all be done while protecting our fundamental rights of expression and access to information, maintaining transparency and building public confidence.

Our relatively small size and agility means we have some advantages. We already have in place a 'digital filter' operated by the Department of Internal Affairs in collaboration with key ISPs, which means a large number of websites specialising in child abuse material are not accessible to New Zealanders. This filter has been reported as blocking more than 35 million New Zealand-based attempts to access CSA material sites over a five-year period from 2014 to 2018. That's around 20,000 attempts a day (although it should be noted that one user can generate many 'block' reports). This is a voluntary, opt-in scheme covering 100 per cent of mobile traffic and 92 per cent of residential broadband. The high rate of uptake by domestic ISPs indicates real potential for the development of similar cooperative measures in the future.

Locating and prosecuting serious offenders and blocking extreme sites will help, but this forms only one part of the solution. It is becoming increasingly evident that a key dynamic at play in this space is psychology, in particular the belief on the part of individuals seeking out abuse material that they are anonymous, and that no one cares about their interests (or worse, that their predilections are shared and encouraged by a growing online community). 'Nudge' approaches have been shown in other contexts to be very effective at making it clear to individuals that they are going down a potentially illegal path. Just as an adult making sexual comments to a child in a public space could expect to be immediately rebuked, automated warning notices for those pursuing illegal material could serve as a simple and effective deterrent.

Beyond these simple steps, we are talking about culture change. We can learn from successful enforcement, information and education campaigns that have shifted public attitudes and behaviours in areas as diverse as drink-driving and smoking. There is scope for us to adapt similar techniques to help build healthier societal norms and behaviours. For example, there could be real power in dispelling the shame and self-blame victims often experience, and the tendency for adults to look away from problematic behaviours — things that abusers often rely on to keep their victims silent and evade detection.

This won't be easy, but the time to do it is now. I don't think there has ever been a time when there has been a greater level of attention being paid to sexual violence, and I see a widespread commitment to real change and improvement. The drivers may be the #MeToo movement, the international exposure of systemic abuse in institutions such as the Catholic Church, our own Royal Commission of Inquiry into Historic Abuse in State Care, or any one of a multitude of events occurring here and overseas. These mean we cannot look away any longer; we have never had such a clear mandate to act to improve our systems and culture, and to protect the young and the vulnerable from abuse.

We also need to look to the future. One simplistic answer to the question of how to prevent CSA is that we 'stop raising abusers'. Unpacking what it means to 'stop raising abusers' involves a lot, but one major element would almost certainly be taking care to ensure that children had an opportunity to develop a balanced sense of their own sexuality, at a pace that worked for them developmentally. Working to instil values around sex that are caring, empathetic and relationship-based. Establishing consent as a core value. Having a clear, informed view of how to stay safe, healthy and within the law. Ensuring that our rangatahi have a sound education in these areas, and have access to the right information and support, will inevitably be the most powerful intervention of all.

How this goes next is up to us. All of us. We have real and growing challenges in these areas that we need to address collaboratively and responsibly. There is too much at stake to act in any other way.

RESOURCES FOR ONLINE SAFETY

Advice on safe use of the internet:
netsafe.org.nz/

Office of Film and Literature Classification resources:
Challenging Media: Talking with young people about what they're watching
classificationoffice.govt.nz/news/latest-news/challenging-media/

Information for parents and caregivers:
classificationoffice.govt.nz/public/information-for-parents-and-caregivers/

Make a complaint about online child sexual abuse material:
dia.govt.nz/Censorship-Make-a-Complaint

Child sex offenders are among the most hated members of any community. News that someone newly released from prison or on the child sex offender register is living in their area stirs residents to speak out in angry protest, listing the numbers of children living in the area and the close proximity of primary and pre-schools. Who cannot understand and relate to their genuine concern for child safety?

The writers of the following chapters, however, identify how few child sex abusers are strangers to their victims, how infrequently those who have been through a recognised treatment programme reoffend, how low the reoffending rates are for those on the sex offender register, and how the risk of reoffending is at its greatest when released offenders have no secure home, no job and no sense of belonging.

Confusing, isn't it? Perhaps known, treated, released, housed and employed offenders are not the ones to worry about. The implications of this are a challenge to our natural protective urges, perhaps even too dire to consider. Some people argue, 'Even one individual less to worry about in my community has to be a good thing — doesn't it?' But what say a released child sex offender was your son or someone else you care deeply about? What if they have served their sentence, successfully completed their treatment programme and been assessed as ready to be released? Given that most CSA is perpetrated by first-time offenders, and that the typical perpetrator is known to the child, doesn't that demand a rethink? Finding a way through the maze of emotions in order to best protect our children requires understanding of all points of view.

Here Judy describes her horror, disgust, anger and sense of betrayal on learning that her neighbour had outstanding sexual offending charges for children and adolescents. She is someone I know and respect as a hugely dedicated and skilled mother and grandmother. A wise and intelligent woman with a strong protective radar: who better to represent this piece of the puzzle.

9. Living next door to a sex offender: One woman's viewpoint

JUDY, MOTHER AND GRANDMOTHER

WHEN WE MOVED TO THE home we live in now I was relieved that our new neighbour, John, seemed to be such a lovely person. He was very welcoming, and eventually we enjoyed the occasional drink and meal together. He would look after our garden if we went away on holiday, and vice versa. We would also look after his property for extended periods when he was out of the country visiting his family. We were often invited to his barbecues, but we refused most invitations as we didn't want to get too close or too involved.

As pleasant as he was, I could not shake the feeling that something wasn't quite right. This was due in part, probably, to the odd lifestyle he led. John became a 'couch surfer' provider, which was strange as he was in his sixties and the couch surfers were young men (and only rarely young women). He said they provided company as he lived on his own and often got lonely. He also rented out his second bedroom to mature male tenants, apparently to help with the mortgage.

So his life was different from ours, but we knew him for a long time and he became our friend. He became particularly friendly with my husband, Peter, who was the chairperson of the body corporate and helped John with minor repairs to his property. On one occasion, while John was overseas, Peter supervised renovations to his kitchen and bathroom.

Meanwhile, I was responsible for our numerous grandchildren, most of whom were of pre-school age. They came to our place at least twice a week (all day) and would play in the front of our place and John's property. As they were so young the supervision was constant and fairly intense, so they were almost never on their own.

Once again, John had gone overseas for a number of months to spend time with his family. His plan was to return for summer, get his house ready to sell and then move overseas permanently to be with his children and grandchildren. During his time away, another neighbour came to tell us she had some terrible news about him. Our immediate thought was that he'd been in a car accident, but as it transpired it was nothing like that. Rather, he had been caught in a 'sting' for paedophiles and was in court awaiting sentence.

The shock was immense. It was literally unbelievable. This man whom we thought of as a friend obviously wasn't the person we thought we knew; he was someone entirely different. I was upset and angry, but more than that I was ashamed. I couldn't bring myself to tell my friends about the man next door. Somehow I felt that I should have known. This nice ordinary man, a father and a grandfather, was a paedophile and I felt utterly contaminated.* There were other concerns, too, in particular for my grandchildren, some of whom were young boys. I reassured myself that they had been safe as their supervision was so intense and they had never spent any time with John. Nonetheless, the thought of them being next door to a paedophile was more than upsetting.

My other big concern was my husband's attitude. While John was in jail awaiting sentencing he emailed us and asked us to ready his house for sale as, of course, he would not be returning. My immediate reaction was not to help. Peter thought otherwise. He still felt that John was his friend and needed our help. I pointed out he was not the man we thought he was and therefore could not really be our friend. We agreed finally that he would do only what was required by law as the chairperson of the body corporate.

We heard some weeks later that John had been sentenced to six months in jail. All this information about him was in the media, and as a result several

---

* In preserving Judy's voice, we have retained her use of the term 'paedophile', even though it may or may not have been applicable in this instance. The term's precise meaning is given in the introduction to this book.

men came forward to complain that John had sexually interfered with them when they were children in his care. He was again charged and went to trial, but I'm unaware of the outcome.

John's house was eventually sold, and it was a huge relief when our new neighbour was a middle-aged woman with five children and three grandchildren! My sense now is of being scarred by this experience but not permanently damaged.

———

About a year later I asked Judy to reflect again on what she had written. I also asked her to consider how she might react if one of her adult children or someone else she loved had carried out sexually harmful behaviour by using a child. She replied: 'I have rarely thought about our ex-neighbour, though when I do I still feel nauseated and disappointed and very, very relieved he's no longer our neighbour. I must say I have never thought about a loved one being a paedophile, only the horror of a loved one suffering at the hands of one. I'll leave you to decide what to do next!'

It was a clear 'I'm not going to go there' message from Judy, and therein lies the 'too dire to consider' challenge I identified earlier. The pathway towards stopping child sexual abuse asks that strong, loving, protective members of the community such as Judy open themselves to consider all of the avenues identified in this book.

It is in the best interests of all who care about protecting children from sexual abuse, and who want to take effective strategic action to this end, that we become well informed about what is known and what is provided by the professionals who work in our prisons with convicted child sex offenders.

It takes a special kind of person to work effectively in a prison, and even more so with child sex offenders. Alexandra Green, manager of psychological services at Kia Marama special treatment unit, describes for us why she chose to do this work and the impact of that on her as a mother. She outlines how the idea of a specialist treatment unit for male child sex offenders came about and details just what happens inside such a unit.

It's valuable for us to know that every step taken in the ongoing development of prison-based assessment and treatment processes is backed by sound research evidence. Also, that staff hold offenders accountable for the harm they have done, while working to reduce the risk of reoffending. As will be further explained in a later chapter on measuring risk, Alexandra has interesting things to say about the necessity of differentiating between the severity of harm done and the risk of reoffending, along with targeting treatment to this risk level in order to produce the best results. This is a matter that can be overlooked by members of the public in the desire to punish.

As she explains, it is far easier for us to view strangers as a threat than someone we know and love. Yet the risk is more often close to home. Knowing this, we need to resist the urge to vilify released sex offenders, because doing so can create a situation where offenders on parole become increasingly isolated, increasing the risk and thus compromising children's safety. Vigilance is needed for sure, and for that to happen the public needs Corrections, allied agencies and all the individual support people associated with released offenders to be carrying out their duties.

10. Kia Marama: Providing child sex offender treatment in prison

ALEXANDRA GREEN, MANAGER
PSYCHOLOGICAL SERVICES, KIA MARAMA

> The critically important factor is the simultaneous capacity of the therapist to extend respect to people as human beings, to empathise with their pain, and to believe in their capacity to do better in the future, whilst not colluding with sexual abuse one single inch.
> — Anna Salter, *Treating Child Sex Offenders and Victims* (1988)

I STARTED WORKING AT KIA MARAMA in 2002, following two years working in the Child, Adolescent and Family Mental Health Service (CAFS) at Southland District Health Board. Before moving to Southland I had worked for the Department of Child, Youth and Family Services (CYFS, now known as Oranga Tamariki) at Kingslea Residential Facility in Christchurch.

When I first said that I wanted to work at Kia Marama, colleagues questioned why I would want to work with 'those offenders', who, by nature of their offending, were generally seen as the lowest of the low, even among their fellow prisoners. My rationale for this was clear to me: I wanted to work in an area where I could take a role in preventing the sexual exploitation of children, rather than deal solely with the aftermath of the abuse. I believe my earlier experiences with CYFS and CAFS helped prepare me for my work at Kia Marama, and through this exposure to children who had often been victimised I learned about the impact of sexual abuse on children, adolescents and families.

When the Kia Marama special treatment unit opened in October 1989 at Rolleston Prison on the outskirts of Christchurch, it was the first such prison-based rehabilitation programme in New Zealand. It came about due to independent pieces of work being carried out by the New Zealand Law Society, which recognised that increasing numbers of their members' clients had repeat child sex offences, and a joint initiative by the Department of Corrections and University of Canterbury, which had developed a proposal for a psychological cognitive behavioural therapy (CBT) and social learning-based group treatment programme in response to findings of the Roper Commission (Ministerial Committee of Inquiry into the Prisons System, 1989).[1]

Supported by research, it was proposed that the delivery of treatment should occur in a stand-alone prison unit that would reduce the extent to which mainstream prison culture influenced the treatment environment. It was noted that the pioneer CBT group programme for treating men with child sex offences developed in Canada by Dr Bill Marshall was showing some encouraging, albeit provisional, initial results in reducing recidivism for this group, despite being delivered in standard mainstream prison facilities.

Unsurprisingly, concerns were raised about the plan to establish a national child sex offender treatment unit. Some related to a concern that the unit at Rolleston might result in increased numbers of men convicted of sex offences being released into the Christchurch area. Meetings involving a range of stakeholders, including the Department of Corrections and the Christchurch City Council, led to a commitment that the prisoners transferred into the region from other areas would be returned to their places of origin and not be released to Christchurch. Corrections has continued to adhere to this commitment.

While a number of men convicted for sexual offences who transfer to Christchurch for the purpose of undertaking treatment may express their desire to stay in the area on release, research supports offenders returning to their home areas, where they have natural support systems, rather than starting afresh where no one knows them. Returning home offers better outcomes in terms of managing future risk.

In 17 years I have seen many changes at Kia Marama. I believe we have become more sophisticated in the assessment of risk to ensure that men who have offended receive the right 'dose' of treatment. We have added to the child sex offence programmes available, identifying men who are assessed as at a lower risk of reoffending and offering them a programme commensurate with this assessment. We have on several occasions reviewed the programme to ensure that it stays up to date, and we have added a targeted programme for men who are assessed as having low cognitive functioning. This has involved modifying the treatment programme to ensure that it can be adequately understood by those who may otherwise struggle to comprehend and actively participate.

The Psychology of Criminal Conduct, first published in 1994,[2] is a seminal piece of literature which underpins the Department of Corrections' work. The risk–need–responsivity (RNR) model set out in this book outlines the optimal framework of principles for working with offenders, specifying that our approach should always be based on risk (that is, we should spend more treatment time with high-risk offenders than with low-risk offenders), that treatment work should be focused on the needs that have the greatest influence on criminal behaviour, and that offenders who start treatment but do not complete are at a higher risk of reoffending. The model also highlights the importance of building motivation and accurate assessment of treatment readiness to ensure that those who start treatment will be more likely to complete the whole course.

The principles associated with the model highlight the importance of not confusing the seriousness of the current offence with the overall risk level of the individual. This is a difficult concept to grasp, and I think that over 20 years later this understanding of 'harm done' versus 'future risk' is still not well understood by the public at large or by many professionals working in this area. While there is often a belief that the more treatment offenders receive the better the outcome will be in terms of reducing their risk, the opposite can also be true.

The perception that men who have committed child sex offences are all the same and are all equally dangerous is a common myth, unfortunately often unhelpfully promulgated in the media. There are certainly some men who by nature of a repetitive pattern of engagement in abusive behaviour need to remain in prison, probably for a significant period of time, as they have demonstrated the proclivity to sexually offend against children despite previous sanctions and treatment. However, in contrast to what is generally believed about men who have sexually offended against children, the majority of men who undertake treatment will not reoffend and can go on to have productive lives and healthy adult relationships. Positively, research from New Zealand and internationally indicates that the base rates of child sexual reoffences are decreasing everywhere.

Unfortunately this information, alongside the positive outcomes of treatment programmes such as Kia Marama, seldom makes the media headlines, nor is it used to reassure the public or counter the attention-grabbing stories of sex offenders being released back into the community.

Further, there will always be some instances of reoffending, despite our best attempts to assist some men to lower their risk of reoffending and to understand the impact of their abusive behaviour on others. It is important to remember that by far the most common scenario for child sexual abuse is that which is perpetrated against victims who know their abusers, either through a family connection or a trusted relationship. The unwillingness to focus closer to home when we are assessing the risk to our own children is likely due to our innate distaste about viewing our trusted relationships through this lens. It is far easier for us to view strangers as more of a threat than someone we know and love.

ASSESSMENT AND TREATMENT IN A NEW ZEALAND PRISON CONTEXT

Subsequent to the opening of the Kia Marama special treatment unit (STU) at Rolleston Prison in 1989, Te Piriti STU at Auckland Prison opened in 1994. These two programmes remain the only two specialised group treatment facilities for sex offences against children across the suite of STUs operated by the Department of Corrections. Four other STUs based in prisons around the country offer specialised treatment for men assessed at high risk of violent and sexual offending against adults.

Research has proven that programmes, activities and therapy are most effective when matched with a prisoner's rehabilitative needs, characteristics and demographics, including their cultural background. The therapeutic approach in the Kia Marama and Te Piriti programmes considers the physical, psychological and emotional well-being of each prisoner. The treatment programme delivered by both STUs is structured into different modules which collectively address the risk factors for reoffending that have been identified by international research. The programme focuses on participants gaining insight into their offence process and understanding how they came to offend.

Once men have identified the problematic areas inherent in their lives at the time they offended, the next phase of treatment is to help them address the deficits identified. These deficits are addressed through the development of skills, in areas such as emotional regulation, adult relationships and interpersonal competence, which enable individuals to perspective-take and have empathy for others. Finally, programme content is also directed at addressing sexuality issues, and specialist interventions designed to extinguish sexual attraction towards children.

The STU therapy programme is group-based, as research has shown that this is a more cost-effective allocation of resources, as well as delivering better outcomes. Each treatment group has 10 participants, who meet for three-hour sessions three to four times a week for approximately 33 weeks. The entire programme takes nine months, as it includes an intensive pre- and post-treatment assessment period. Each treatment group is facilitated by a psychologist with oversight from a senior psychologist, whose predominant role is to ensure the integrity of the programme.

The STU therapy team is led by a manager psychological services, who has overall clinical responsibility for the treatment programme. Although sexual offences against children are not exclusively carried out by men, men do make up the overwhelming majority of perpetrators. Where women are convicted of sexual offences against a child, either as a co-offender with a male partner or on their own, individual psychological intervention is made available to assist them.

The prison unit in which the programme is delivered is operated as a 'Community of Change' environment. The focus of a Community of Change is social learning, so that all the day-to-day experiences of participants can potentially be utilised to foster change in offence-supportive attitudes and behaviours. This special social context provides opportunity to cognitively and emotionally process new information, often through discussion with peers, as well as to practise new behaviours; this 'treatment generalisation' effect means that the knowledge and skills learned in the group room can be reinforced and developed in the wider environment.[3] Research has found the therapeutic environment to be a critical factor in determining treatment outcome, as many of the treatment gains are actually made outside of the core therapy groups.[4] A further benefit of a Community of Change environment is that it is a context that is more culturally akin to a kaupapa Māori approach.

Over time, Kia Marama STU has developed a set of overarching principles which serve to guide and moderate behaviour. The goal for men to learn to live their lives in accordance with the principles of respect, personal responsibility, openness, collaboration and support means that abuse cannot continue to take place, and adult relationships are enhanced.

Despite the Community of Change context, the unit operates within a prison, and as such standard prison rules and regulations apply, including regular cell inspections, the wearing of prison clothing, standard food and regular work routines. Rolleston Prison also operates under a 'working prison' model, which means that outside of their participation in treatment participants are expected to engage in meaningful employment to benefit not only themselves but also the prison and the wider community. Currently this means that men are also working in the prison's plant nursery and gardens to supply food for local volunteer services, and in the prison's construction yard, which is working to build and repair social housing damaged in the Christchurch earthquakes.

Education and recreation programmes are also available and may include working towards unit standards in the area in which they are currently employed. After completing the core part of the treatment programme, men go on to the 'graduates' or maintenance phase of treatment to consolidate the changes they have made, and take on roles in the Community of Change that enable them to practise the skills they have learnt through the core programme, as well as to assist the new men coming into the unit.

To be eligible for treatment, prisoners must be convicted of, or have admitted to, one or more sexual offences against someone under the age of 16. The treatment programme is voluntary, but realistically an individual's motivation to enlist may have been 'extrinsically' encouraged to a degree. Many are subject to the New Zealand Parole Board's decision-making around their release date; being granted release on parole is contingent upon having satisfactorily completed treatment and demonstrating that they are able to manage their future risk. The motivation for others may be the outcome of encouragement by family members to make the best use of their time in prison.

In order to meet the entry criteria to undertake treatment, men must admit to their offending; this need not be an admission to the entirety of their offences, but rather some acknowledgement that through their actions they have taken sexual advantage of a child. In order to benefit from the treatment programme, which is intensive in nature, any mental health difficulties must be effectively managed; as mentioned above, we also complete cognitive assessments to ensure that those with intellectual deficits, which would limit the benefits of programme participation, are identified.

ASSESSING THE RISK OF REOFFENDING

Treatment recommendations are based on the person's assessed risk of reoffending. In the same way that GPs are cautious about not 'over-treating' people by prescribing excessive medication, as it can make someone more unwell, research indicates that over-treating low-risk men convicted of child sexual offences can inadvertently increase their risk of reoffending. In 2012, the Short Intervention Programme (SIP) was designed to offer an alternative group-based intervention for those men whose level of risk did not warrant participation in the high-intensity STU programmes. The SIP is run by psychologists from both Kia Marama and Te Piriti for men who are assessed at low and medium-low risk of reoffending.

Both child sex offence programmes help men who have offended to look at the patterns of their offending and identify high-risk situations that should be avoided in the future. Every person completes the programme with a reintegration plan that identifies approved support people, follow-up sessions with probation officers and, for the higher-risk offenders, attendance at maintenance groups as conditions of parole. Every man who completes the treatment programme is also monitored by probation officers for a period of at least six months following release from prison.

Over the years, the process of identifying the different pathways to offending, and of assessing someone's likelihood of reoffending, has become increasingly sophisticated. Risk assessment research has continued to evolve, and as psychologists we are bound by the New Zealand Psychologists Board Code of Ethics to ensure that we stay abreast of relevant research and utilise assessment instruments that offer the best possible efficacy. Assessment of risk is probably best understood by viewing an offender's past behaviour alongside their more recent behaviour. In risk terms, aspects of past behaviour are referred to as indicators of static risk, while current behaviour may be referred to as dynamic risk. The combination and weighting of both are important.

In terms of static risk, the Department of Corrections uses the Automated Sexual Recidivism Scale — Revised (ASRS-R) as a brief actuarial screening instrument to estimate the likelihood of sexual reoffending among men already sentenced for a sexual offence. This is a computerised statistical model that looks at an offender's criminal history; research has shown that sexual recidivism risk increases as the ASRS-R score increases.

The ASRS-R calculation utilises the following variables:
- total number of prior sentencing dates;
- convictions for non-contact sexual offences;
- prior sentences for non-sexual violence;
- index offence of non-sexual violence;
- number of unique prior sentencing dates for sexual offences;
- any convictions for male sexual victims; and
- current age.

Where dynamic risk is concerned, the Violence Risk Scale — Sexual Offender version (VRS-SO), developed by Professor Mark Olver and his colleagues, offers the most detailed assessment measure. This risk instrument utilises those factors that research has found to be associated with recidivism. These are grouped into three main areas: sexual deviance, criminality and responsivity concerns. The added benefit of this instrument is that the factors identified also enable the determination of treatment targets and provide a means of objectively measuring the change made during treatment.

DO THESE PROGRAMMES REALLY WORK?

It is to the mutual advantage of Kia Marama and the University of Canterbury that postgraduate psychology students are able to pursue research under their respective academic supervisors using the data produced by the STU. One of these pieces of research, by Lucy Moore, looked at all offenders who had committed a sexual offence against a child and who were released between 1998 and 2010.[5]

The study examined the criminal history and post-release outcomes for 428 men convicted of sexual offences against children who had attended Kia Marama and were followed up for an average of 6.36 years. They were compared with a cohort of 1956 men who were also incarcerated for sexual offences against children but did not attend Kia Marama or a similar STU and were followed up for an average of 6.81 years.

Results showed that attending Kia Marama was associated with a 29 per cent reduction in sexual reoffending, and the reduction was statistically significant. They revealed, too, that treatment significantly reduced the rates of both violent reoffending (from 18.4 per cent to 10.3 per cent) and general reoffending (from 40.2 per cent to 32.7 per cent). Notably, the research highlighted that the treated offenders showed a lower risk of violent and general recidivism, as sexual offences are sometimes reduced to violent or general convictions as a result of plea-bargaining, and therefore a reduction in violent and general recidivism may also suggest further reductions in sexual recidivism.

This research study included programme dropouts and non-completers, who have been previously identified as typically presenting the highest risk of recidivism post-release. Overall, the results show that programmes such as Kia Marama are worthwhile investments to protect the potential victims of sexual offending and to reduce the social and economic costs associated with reoffending.

It must be acknowledged that there are men — often those undergoing indeterminate sentences — whose lack of responsiveness to treatment means that they ultimately make minimal progress. An open-ended sentence such as preventive detention is usually the result of having a persistent pattern of abusive behaviour despite previous sanction and even treatment. For these individuals, the need to keep the public safe means an open-ended sentence of imprisonment has been determined as the only viable means of managing risk.

The threshold for considering whether parole should be granted to such individuals by the New Zealand Parole Board is understandably high. As a result, some men serving preventive detention sentences will likely spend the rest of their lives in prison. Advancing age does serve as a protective factor for future sexual offences for most men, but there is a small subgroup who will not demonstrate a significant decrease in their risk profile, despite their increasing age, and in order to ensure the ongoing safety of the community there will likely be no other option but to keep them imprisoned for the foreseeable future.

'NOT IN MY BACK YARD': REINTEGRATION AND ITS CHALLENGES

Most of us have strong opinions about what should happen to men who have committed sexual offences against children, how these individuals should be treated when they are released from prison, and indeed whether they should be released at all. However, the reality is that the vast majority of men who serve prison time for such an offence do return to the community on the completion of their sentences, or when they are granted parole.

Although many men express a wish to start anew in an area where no one knows them, the research tells us quite clearly that they are best to return to the areas where they have existing support. Support in this context should not be regarded as 'unconditionally positive': the most useful form of support comes from people who are able to hold someone with child sex offences to account for their behaviour, and provide constructive feedback about any unsafe behaviour they observe.

However, the nature of child sex offences, which may often have occurred within a family system, may result in the offender no longer having the support of family members. The individual will often be known to professional services such as police, probation services and community support agencies such as the Salvation Army and Prisoners Aid and Rehabilitation Society, which may provide a starting point to build the social support needed.

If sexual offending is conceptualised as a highly dysfunctional and misguided attempt by an individual to meet a need for intimacy and acceptance, then interfering with their reintegration plan and ability to connect appropriately within adult relationships can increase risk. It is an unfortunate reality, however, that communities may at times be reluctant to accept a person known to have committed child sex offences back into the area, and may be motivated to make their displeasure widely known. This can in turn create a situation where safety becomes compromised: offenders on parole may feel increasingly isolated and fearful, as a result of which their risk of reoffending is actually increased. Research indicates that poor release planning has been associated with a shorter time to reoffending.

There is no easy solution to this issue. The Department of Corrections makes extensive efforts to ensure that accommodation for men convicted of sexual offences is assessed as suitable in terms of safety to the public. From a psychological viewpoint it is clear that not all men with these convictions present the same risk profile, but this is generally not a concept that is well understood or accepted by the public at large.

CONCLUSION

As mother to a 10-year-old, I can readily understand the natural concerns parents have about their children's safety; the nature of my professional role, and my experience in this field, means that I sometimes have to work hard to avoid becoming excessively cautious as a parent. Intellectually I know that the vast majority of men would never cause harm to a child, but I also accept that the lens through which I view behaviour is skewed towards risk and potential danger. I also accept that my child will likely have less encouragement to stay at her friends' houses; that I'm likely to be more comfortable with her friends staying with us. I know that if she is at a sleepover and rings to say she wants to come home I'm not going to question that or suggest she stay the distance. That's because I know that an offence is more likely to be committed against a child who knows their abuser rather than the stranger on the street.

Over the past 17 years I've been privileged to work with a dedicated team of psychologists, social workers, custodial staff and probation officers who focus their energies on reducing offenders' risk of reoffending. We have seen men make significant change to their lives. They have taken responsibility for the abuse they have committed, beyond just a guilty plea in court, and they have developed an empathic appreciation of the harm they have caused.

They are not inherently evil, as some would believe, but they certainly have behavioural difficulties and have acted in a way that has caused widespread harm and pain for their victims, their victims' families and their own families, who also bear the consequences of the choices they made. We have also heard their own stories of childhood experiences which they have disclosed in treatment; stories of abuse that no child should ever endure. If that has been offered as a distorted rationale for why they have gone on to hurt others, we have pointed out the inconsistency in this, given that the majority of victims of sexual abuse never go on to harm anyone else.

We have done our best to ensure that men who have committed child sexual offences have the best reintegration plans possible — not because we think that their transition from prison back into the community should be easy, but rather because we know that developing a robust reintegration plan is in everyone's best interest. We continue to encourage men to try to see the world from their victim's viewpoint, in order for them to appreciate the consequences of their offences, and we have been clear that the relationships and opportunities that are no longer there for them are natural consequences of the choices they made.

It can at times be a challenging environment in which to work. It certainly highlights the importance of high-quality supervision and a cohesive and supportive context in which to work, which we are fortunate to have. Belief in the capacity of the individual to make change is also essential. In the course of our work we sometimes have bad days, but even on the worst days we take comfort in knowing that programmes like Kia Marama do make a difference in keeping our children safe.

I first met Hinewirangi Kohu Morgan some years ago when we were both keynote presenters at a psychotherapy hui. Reading her chapter will make it clear why I remembered the depth of her wisdom and chose to ask her to write about her therapeutic work with Māori child sex offenders in Waikeria Prison.

She of course cannot tell us the confidential stories of individual offenders' journeys into healing. Instead, by way of identifying the healing process, Hinewirangi has gifted us with details of her lifelong personal journey to becoming someone who now works powerfully with both victims and perpetrators of child sexual abuse.

In doing so she draws compelling parallels between the devastating harm done to children by sexual abuse and to Māori by colonisation. She also draws parallels between the process for victims to heal themselves, the process for perpetrators to heal themselves in order to no longer be destructive, and the process for Māori to heal from colonisation. For Hinewirangi, being able to connect with the vulnerable human being in her abuser was an essential part of her personal healing process.

Hinewirangi also illustrates for us how Māori healing processes may be quite different from those of Pākehā: neither is right or wrong, but rather each individual needs to find what works for them. On reading her chapter I was particularly saddened by the arrogance she has encountered in having the system she works within call her Māori approach 'alternative'.

Mokori anō kia mihi a koe e Hinewirangi. Kua horahia ngā kai, nāu anō i takoha mai. Kikī ana ngā pātaka kai o ngā kaipānui i a koe. E kore rawa te puna aroha e mimiti.

11. Singing my soul back into being

HINEWIRANGI KOHU MORGAN
PSYCHOTHERAPIST, WAIKERIA PRISON

Rimu, rimu	Seaweed
Tere, tere	To ebb and flow
E haere ana ki Te Pō	I go to the realm of darkness
Kei reira koe e Hine	There you are Hinenuitepō
E tatari ana mai e	Waiting...

THE ABOVE SONG WAS TAUGHT to me by my nan when I was a little girl. She explained that I would need to sing this song throughout my life, and if I ever needed her, she would be 'across the river'. I never really knew what this song was about; only that it pacified me when my heart was heavy and my mind was clouded. I could not have known that this song was going to save my life... over and over again.

This chapter is a presentation of my life and the events and experiences that have contributed to who I am today. My early journey through life has been one of chaos and strife, sadness and unrest. This chapter may be hard for any reader to comprehend or appreciate, but who I am today cannot truly be understood without exploring the journey I took to get here.

My story is one of incest, drug addiction, prostitution, attempted suicide and obesity, yet through it all I found forgiveness, empathy and even love. It is a journey that saw a frightened little girl emerge as a courageous woman.

The purpose of this chapter is to assist in identifying key learnings that have made me the practitioner I am today. How I make sense of the world and how I conduct myself can be attributed to everything I have experienced; the good, the bad, and the downright ugly.

AT SIX YEARS OLD I was raped by an uncle. I tried to tell other adults but they didn't believe me, all except my mother. Even though she never admitted it, I know she believed me. Unfortunately, this news triggered memories of her own abuse and she continuously cried. I blamed myself for hurting my mother and I was determined to never make her cry again. This decision meant allowing the abuse to continue until I was 15 years old. I never talked to another adult for the longest time. In my mind I sang my nan's song over and over again; it helped ease my pain. I would whisper to my nan, 'You were right, this song does make me feel better.'

Eventually, I had had enough. I missed my nan and longed to 'cross the river' to see her. I climbed to the top of a three-storey building and leapt. Mid-air my nan came to me and carried me down. I cried and screamed at her to let me cross the river, but she told me it wasn't my time. I landed with a thud and only hurt my wrist.

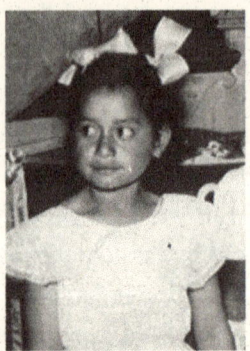

Me at the age of 7

When I reached high-school age I was sent to a boarding school. Most mornings the cooks would come to work and catch me in my pyjamas arguing with my nan, only they couldn't see her. They saw only me, screaming into vacant spaces. Eventually, I was admitted to Tokaanui Psychiatric Hospital. 'I am singing my song, Nan, I am.'

Time went by and I was finally released. I went headfirst into a world of drugs. Heroin, LSD and cocaine: you name it, I had it. I found a special place, a tree in a grove of bushes, that no one frequented. I would sit there and indulge in a near-lethal cocktail of drugs. One day I awoke in hospital after having my stomach pumped. I was told that hunters had found me, but I knew better: my nan had intervened once again. 'OK, Nan, I will continue to sing my song.'

I later moved to Wellington and entered the world of prostitution. I was practising S&M, punishing men for what they did to me and being paid for it. One day, as I stood at the traffic lights on the way to The Balcony to pay Carmen her cut from the night's work,[1] I heard two men in front of me making derogatory comments about a woman across the street. 'Fancy fucking that!' I followed their gaze and saw an obese Island woman. They were disgusted by how she looked, and in my mind I had just discovered a way for men to find me unattractive. I became 250 kilos. I hoped that this move would also ensure that I inherited all the illnesses that came from being obese. My nan couldn't stop me now.

Me at the age of 18

Obese at the age of 46

In the course of this journey I lost the ability to give birth. I had three babies who were all stillborn. My cervix had been damaged from being penetrated as a six-year-old. Eventually, I became pregnant again. A girlfriend once told me that I would never be a real woman if I did not have a child, and so I longed to have this child; to be a 'real' woman. I went home to my mum because the doctors wanted me to abort my baby. She took me to her doctor, who told me I could give birth but I would have to agree to be admitted into hospital that day. I was two and a half months into my pregnancy. My son was eventually delivered through caesarean section, and he changed my life completely.

LIBRA TĀNENUIĀRANGI KOHU: THE JOY OF MY LIFE

My son was my world, my lifeline. He loved me unconditionally, but I was still hooked on drugs.

At three years old, my beautiful son looked at me and said, 'I don't like you, Mama, when you fly away.' My heart broke. He was the only person other than my nan, koro, mum and dad that I truly loved. I had to change; I couldn't lose this child. I cried for weeks but I kept singing my song to help me. I knew I had to get rid of the drugs.

Libra Tānenuiārangi Kohu

I sought the help of a local district nurse and her husband, the local policeman. They helped me to go cold turkey. My son went to live with the husband while the nurse came to live with me. She boarded up the windows and emptied my room of everything bar a mattress on the floor. She watched over me as I went through the process of withdrawing from my addictions. When I could take no more and wanted to give up, she would bring my son to me and let him spend an hour or so with me. I was an absolute mess but he loved me anyway. He held me and told me he loved me in his tiny little voice. 'I'm still singing my song, Nan.'

During three months of pain and anguish this nurse stayed by my side. She had whānau come in and feed me, help me wash and go to the toilet. The hardest part was the cravings. I wanted drugs so much that every inch of my body ached. One day, it was over. I had made it to a place of being able to care for me and my son. I will always be indebted to the nurse and her policeman husband. The journey towards the healing of my mind, my body and my soul could now begin.

In 2000, I had built up the courage to confront the abuser I had protected for so long. I cursed and screamed at him, releasing all the pain and anger I had experienced and harboured over the years. I told him how he was responsible for the death of my babies because of the mess he had made of my cervix. I let him have it.

He stood there fearful and motionless, and in my state of aggression glimpses of my childhood began to flash through my mind. There was a time when I had loved and respected this man. As a master carver he had taught me much and fostered a love for the arts within me. My anger began to subside and I just wept, mostly in pity for him. I was staring at a very vulnerable man who had probably spent his life in turmoil, too. Only then did I begin to see a magnificent tohunga whakairo (master carver) standing before me. I had sung my soul back into being. I have only been truly alive for 17 years.

HAVING ADDRESSED THE TRAUMA IN my life, I could finally sit back and acknowledge life's positive experiences — and, more importantly, the people connected to those positive experiences.

Hinewīrangi Whareware Brown

Te Ratu Mataira

Ko Hinewīrangi Whakaware Brown tōku kuia	Ko Te Ratu Mataira tōku koroua
Ko Tangitū ki te moana	Ko Moumoukai tōna maunga
Ko Maungaharuru ki uta	Ko Nūhaka te awa
Ko Mōhaka te awa	Ko Ngāti Rākaipāka te iwi
Ko Ngāti Pāhauwera te iwi	Ko Tākitimu te waka

I was raised by my kuia Hinewirangi and my koro Te Ratu for the first five to six years of my life. During this time I was loved and spoilt rotten. My nan dressed me in lace dresses and bobby socks before I went out to play mud pies with my cousins. Unimpressed, she would drag me back into the bath and put me in a new dress. I always felt pretty.

My nan was elegant in every way, especially in the way she recorded stories, articulating and retelling them using varied forms of language such as classical and metaphorical language. My love for stories came from this woman.

The world of my koro Te Ratu was one of a prolific gardener whose garden fed us with vegetables of the season. He also farmed cows, horses and chickens. He milked his cows by hand, and taught me all I know about the gathering and harvesting of food.

Everyone in the village of Nūhaka had gardens to help sustain their families. We were also sea people, so everyone went fishing. When I was a child, there was one garden that captured my interests: that of my uncle, Teddy Whaanga. He planted hue (gourds) by his fence line and I watched them grow over the season. I was fascinated with their shapes and sizes. I watched him hand-pollinate, explaining how the bees didn't visit with the girl flowers so he would have to take a boy flower (the long flower at the top of the vine) and touch the girl, allowing her to give birth to fertilised children: little hue.

Ki te taha o tōku whare tangata/whaea
Ko Moumoukai te maunga
Ko Nūhaka te awa
Ko Ngāti Rākaipāka te iwi
Ko Kahungunu te tangata
Ko Rongomaiwahine te arikinui
Ko Tākitimu te waka

Helen Nelly Hineatarau Mataira Kohu   Anaru Kohu

My mother believed that every animate and inanimate thing had life, therefore they had a whakapapa (genealogy). According to her, whakapapa without story is lifeless. In order to breathe life into whakapapa one must first find the stories attached to it. She had in her possession journals written by my father; he had documented his learning over the years.

My mother parted from my father while still carrying me in her womb. Eventually, she entered into a relationship with my first stepfather, Wiremu Morgan. During that time, a travelling haka troupe from Te Waipounamu came through Gisborne. My parents joined this group and we all headed south, ending up in Motueka picking hops.

After exiting the relationship with Wiremu Morgan, my mother married Anaru Kohu. He was the only father I knew. He was my father in every way.

Like my nan, Anaru Kohu was a storyteller who regularly narrated these around an open fire at night. He was also a master carver. Pūrākau (stories) were important to him in his profession; he carved many of his stories on the whare whakairo (carved house) at his marae, Hūria. He believed that carvings helped him to capture the essence of stories for future generations.

ALL OF MY LIVED EXPERIENCES have contributed to who, how, and what I am today: a woman, mother, artist, advisor, student, teacher and friend. I have learned to focus on, and appreciate, the small teachings throughout my life; the moments that brought me joy. I have managed to weave these thin strands together, creating an enduring lashing.

I understand the relevance of whakapapa and how it can be brought to life through appropriate stories, much in the same way an ancestral house embodies an ancestor. These stories must also be nurtured and cared for, then handed down. The best way for me to describe it is through the life of a hue.

Hue seeds

A seed must first be sown. This seed is carried by the tāne (male) and has a whakapapa that contributes to determining the shape and size of this hue. According to traditional lore, Tāne Mahuta, in his search for te ira tangata (human essence), mated with Hinepūtehue, and from them came the hue.

Hue plant

The plant that grows from these celestial seeds connects the realms of tangata (human) and atua (God). They bring forth stories of old; of creation. The vine covers the ground and spreads out in search of the best place to grow. At this stage the plant is a hermaphrodite, with both male and female parts.

Hue gourds

Once harvested, the hue requires six months to dry out before it can be shaped into a useful vessel. It is first washed and cleaned, then placed in a warm place to dry. The drying-out process also allows for the skin to harden.

My life is much like that of the hue. He kākano ahau i ruia mai i Rangiātea (I am a seed sown from an ancient place). I am connected to the traditional stories that have brought me into being. As I grew I continuously sought out what I thought were safe spaces for me. Many times I failed, but I never gave up. Perseverance brought me my son, my safe space, and like the hue I was cleaned, hardened and carved.

'Thank you for your song, Nan.'

This is the framework that I worked through. If you want to heal me, then you need to use this framework.

WE SPEAK ABOUT 'HISTORICAL RAPE OF MY PEOPLE', colonisation and its impact on Māori and its long-term effects. Understanding it requires you to study colonisation and its impact on indigenous nations. Great Britain could boast that the 'sun never set on the British colonies'. Aotearoa was one, and the impact was devastating on Māori.

First, it raped us physically, emotionally, spiritually and tribally of our whenu (land); of our ability to access our natural resources in order to live; of our goddesses/gods that were a part of our natural world; of our papakāinga (tribal home) where there were full whānau support systems; of our language. Colonisation rewrote our histories, took us away from the feet of our kuia/koroua (elders), and wiped out our whakapapa. Our women were used as sexual objects by the many travellers to our shores; they used their sexual prowess to obtain guns as payment during the wars, then killed themselves because they felt impure. Through patriarchy our men became dominant, and forgot their roles as protectors and hunter-gatherers.

I use this frame of colonisation when working with men in prison who have sexually offended against children and others. To begin the process of decolonisation, I work through what was in place before the invasion of Aotearoa and what happened between the seventeenth and twentieth centuries. They have to learn. Often the end result of the study for many is emotional hurt, anger, hate, dislike, amazement: many different emotions.

My job then is to help them close their doors on all the hurting and open the door to their internal healer. They will have learnt many things, such as:

- They are colonised and live like Pākehā and want to change.
- What opens up for them is the need to find their Māori identity, to find their whakapapa (genealogies), to find their pūrākau (stories).
- They want to work once again with their whānau (families) to learn their tribal tikanga and kawa (protocols and customs).
- Men are looking for whaikōrero (as a healing process it has an ancient format for inner healing) in all the roles of a man on the marae; women are looking for their roles: karanga (the first voice call), manaakitanga (the ability to host and take care of whānau and manuhiri/visitors).
- They are looking for the special places to learn the esoteric knowledge of the gods and goddesses, and their role in each realm of the natural world.
- They are looking for the healer within, to help them design their own healing processes.
- Men and women who joined gangs know it as their only whānau after having been disenfranchised from their own whānau.

Our role is to be there, to open the door to the soul, to help with tools so they can discover themselves. From there they can design a plan that they have full control over in order to heal themselves.

Our role is to continue to decolonise, replacing and reclaiming our tupuna (ancestor) knowledge, which is not found in a monocultural learning school; rather, it is with our ancient ones that lie dormant within. Māori believe that the intrinsic knowledge is passed to the child through the waiū (breastmilk) of the mother. The Māori scholar Dr Hirini Moko Mead alludes to this in his book *Tikanga and Kawa*.

USING THE FRAMEWORK OF Te Whare Tapa Whā ('the four posts of the house'), gifted by our tīpuna and further developed by Sir Mason Durie, I began the process of healing each part. I found the healer within, and I needed to find the tools that would help me see the process.

It took me many years to perfect the processes and work with Māori to put them into practice. I opened the first Māori Women's Centre for sexually abused women, children and men, and we used Māori processes to heal. I started the first Māori Women's Refuge, Te Whakaruruhau, named by my father Anaru Kohu, to be able to practise our own tikanga and kawa.

I currently work at Waikeria Prison. I cannot talk about particular cases, but my lived experience and practice over the years will help our men, who have been disenfranchised from being hunter-gatherers and protectors by the processes of colonisation.

I will continue to fight to heal our people, by constantly opening the door to their healer within, and throwing them tools that they can use to heal. I will stand by their sides until they can stand fully in their own mana.

THE WORK WITH CONVICTED OFFENDERS is immense and I use the many frameworks that I have built out of my own lived experience to work with our people. I have encountered some who cannot make themselves safe to be in the community, and I use another part of my Māori intuition to identify them. Most of the men at risk of reoffending are in prison because it is the safest place for them; some are currently being housed outside the wire but close to the prison, but I have had no counselling contact with them.

Unfortunately there are two fronts that I have to work from: a Pākehā front and a Māori front.

Pākehā front

It's a big fight, with Pākehā experts (psychologists, psychotherapists, counsellors and so on) believing their way of healing our people is the only way. They are not open to other healers, and they call us the alternative. In fact, we are tangata whenua and have been here way before they came; *they* are the alternatives.

Most Māori who have trained in this area of work have followed that Pākehā learning and find it hard to look at a Māori healing practice that heals our people better. It takes more than a single person to heal another Māori: it takes the whole whānau, but this is not done in a Pākehā practice. I am not putting down the Pākehā practice; some of our people choose to go there, and if that is what they want, I want that for them also. But it is not reciprocal on the Pākehā side to refer them to us. In fact it's unheard of. I know we could heal our people as well as they can.

Māori front

It is a big fight also with our people, who are so afraid to be decolonised that we have to work in small groups to encourage them. We simply begin with:

- pepeha (stories or sayings) — it is not about the mountains, rivers, etc., it's the stories that are most important in this research: maunga (mountain), awa (river), waka (canoe), marae/papakāinga (tribal base or land), tangata/tūpuna (ancestors), whakapapa (genealogy), ingoa (name);
- whakapapa/pūrākau (stories or research) of each person;
- karakia tuturu (ancient chants);
- ngā atua (the gods and goddesses);
- te reo (language);
- ko wai koe (who are you), creatively writing your story;
- karanga for wāhine;
- whaikōrero for tāne; and
- waiata for everyone.

We slowly move through each of these as a healing programme left to us by tūpuna. No one owns this knowledge and we can't copyright it; it is not ours to do so. That is also the difference between Māori and Pākehā.

Mauri ora.

Most readers will at least have heard of the prison specialist treatment units whose work is described in the previous two chapters and further developed in the following two chapters. Many may not know of, or be well informed about, the work of community-based treatment agencies for anyone experiencing harmful sexual interests. There are three such agencies, with branches throughout Aotearoa New Zealand: SAFE, WellStop and STOP. All do excellent work and lead the way internationally in preventing sexually harmful behaviour.

The staff at WellStop Central (covering Manawatū, Horowhenua, Whanganui and Tararua) agreed to meet with me to discuss this book, and the breadth and depth of their expertise and knowledge quickly became evident. Their manager, Deanna Hollis, offered to write this chapter for us about the work of a community treatment agency.

Some who attend this service are mandated to come by Corrections, some are self-referred, and others come via referral from allied agencies. Some have sexually abused children; others fear they will. You may be shocked to learn who these people are, what their behaviour can involve, and what is known about why so many children and young people have developed harmful sexual behaviour.

We will also learn about what effective treatment involves, and read Deanna's recommendations for how we as a society can work alongside such important treatment agencies to help prevent child sexual abuse.

12. Hurt people hurt people

DEANNA HOLLIS
MANAGER, WELLSTOP CENTRAL

WHEN WE CONSIDER HOW TO stem the tide of sexual harm it is common to think of how we work with victims and how we work to prevent sexual abuse, but few people consider the importance of the work that is done with those who have developed harmful sexual behaviour (HSB). New Zealand is at the forefront in community treatment of HSB internationally, with three agencies constituting the HSB sector. These are SAFE, which covers the upper half of the North Island, WellStop (lower and central North Island) and STOP (South Island). These agencies, while separate, work together to provide consistent services across the country.

WHO ARE THE SEXUAL HARM PERPETRATORS?

When considering those who present with HSB, most people imagine the stereotypical 'dirty old man'. The reality could not be further from the truth. In terms of age, offenders can range from children as young as three years of age with concerning sexualised behaviour, through to young people and of course adults. Not only are they not all old, but also they are not all male. The behaviours may range from concerning through to harmful or abusive, which is determined primarily by the age and developmental stage of the person and the person who is being harmed. Behaviours are considered harmful if those who manifest them begin to engage other children and youth in sexual behaviour, often with coercion or force as a feature. Sexualised behaviour in children is generally considered abusive when there is an age difference, or some other power differential, such as size, or where the person who is harmed is vulnerable in some other way. While referrals for adult female offenders are not common, disclosures of having been sexually abused by a female are. The research has recorded an entire group of adults in treatment who had all been sexually abused by an adult female when they were children.

Australian researchers McKibbin, Humphreys and Hamilton reported that 'harmful sexual behaviour carried out by children and young people accounts for about half of all child abuse perpetration'.[1] At WellStop, approximately 80 per cent of referrals are for children and youth, but this does not take into account incidents that, for a variety of reasons, are not referred. Referrals also include some children who may not have sexually harmed other children but nonetheless have presented with concerning sexual behaviours, such as persistent masturbation, or have appeared to have more sexual knowledge than is developmentally normal. People are generally shocked to hear that children and youth are by far our biggest cohort.

The focus of interventions with children and youth is on breaking the cycles of abuse and violence. Intervention consists of a comprehensive assessment, which informs holistic treatment plans that will always include family, whānau or caregivers.

HOW CAN CHILDREN BE SEXUALLY HARMFUL?

In order to support appropriate referrals, as an agency we reference Dr Toni Cavanagh Johnson, recognised internationally as an expert in the area of children's sexual development.[2] One of her many publications is *Children's Sexual Behaviours: A parent's guide*, which explains what sexual behaviours are developmentally normal, and when to be concerned (see the Appendix of this book). It is not intended as a guide to determine whether a child has been sexually abused, as it is important to consider all factors that have precipitated the behaviour.

When discussing HSB it is important to understand that this is an umbrella term for a continuum of behaviours, as mentioned above. It is developmentally normal for children to explore sexual behaviour and experience sexual learning in childhood, at differing ages and stages, such as playing 'mummies and daddies', and 'I'll show you mine if you show me yours'. Children engage in this behaviour out of curiosity and the need to explore and make sense of their environment, and parents can usually manage it with age-appropriate information and boundary setting.

It is recognised that childhood sexuality should not be totally repressed or considered to be indicative of sexual abuse. However, any adult who observes sexual behaviours in a child should intervene, and use this as a teachable moment to help him or her understand what is appropriate and safe behaviour, including body safety, while making it clear what behaviour is not OK. Even if the behaviour is developmentally normal, the child should still receive some correction as to appropriate behaviour. When considering whether the behaviour is harmful, factors such as consent, equality and coercion also need to be considered. In children this means considering that:

- both children (assuming two are involved) understood what was being proposed and one did not trick the other;
- both children had similar knowledge;
- both children had a similar understanding of the consequences; and
- there were no repercussions for either agreeing or disagreeing.

Equality relates to the balance of power and control. With children, some aspects of this (for example age, size, developmental level) are obvious, while others are more subtle. One child may be stronger or have established dominance in a fight prior to the sexual interaction. Other children are the 'leader' or 'boss' within a group of children. Sometimes power differentials are established in fantasy play such as 'king and slaves' or 'doctor and patient', and even 'mummies and daddies'. Coercion relates to the pressures applied to gain compliance, and may range from manipulation to threats or force.

The most common reasons children engage in sexual behaviours that are not considered developmentally normal are when family violence is normalised and/or they have been exposed to adult sexual behaviours, including having been sexually abused and/or having witnessed adults having sex, whether in reality or in media. This does not mean that all children who experience these events will go on to develop harmful sexual behaviours, but it is important that those who do are given help and support to make sense of their experiences and to develop positive strategies for coping with adverse experiences. It is important to note that almost all individuals who are referred for assessment and treatment have some trauma history, which informs this writer's hypothesis that complex trauma is the most common precipitating factor for HSB in children.

YOUTH AND CHILD OFFENDERS

It has been noted that there has been an increase in HSB in youth where the use of pornography is the primary precipitating factor. Not everyone who accesses pornography is going to go on to sexually offend; practice-based evidence indicates that offending behaviour is more likely in those who have poor coping skills, a history of trauma, and a lack of safe, supportive adults to whom they can talk about sex and sexuality.

In the past decade there has been an exponential increase in the number of children and young people accessing pornography, largely due to the proliferation of smartphones and other such devices. Another contributing factor is that today's mainstream porn depicts violence and sexual domination as common themes; what was mainstream porn a decade ago can now be seen on prime-time television. As a society we have become desensitised to the increasing levels of sexual material in all media, with children being exposed to and affected by this at a much younger age.

Research shows that adolescents with HSB have more in common with other youth offenders than they do with adults who sexually offend. As indicated earlier, more adolescents who sexually abuse have been the victim of or witness to family violence than have been sexually abused (though there are still high rates of sexual abuse in their histories). As with all those with HSB, adolescents who sexually harm are not one homogenous group, although poor impulse control is a common factor in young people's offending. There is, however, a school of thought that impulsiveness may simply contribute to their being discovered, rather than having a causal effect.[3] Other common variables in youth with HSB include:

- They are usually male.
- 30–60 per cent have learning disabilities or problems with academic work.

- Up to 80 per cent have a diagnosable psychiatric disorder (for example ADHD, conduct disorder, depression, anxiety, bipolar disorder).
- Many have difficulties with impulse control and judgement.
- 20–50 per cent have histories of physical abuse.
- About 90 per cent have witnessed violence (physical, sexual and/or verbal).
- 40–80 per cent have histories of sexual abuse.

Young people who sexually abuse generally target either younger children or their peers, although some young people also target adults. A recent report by an Australian service provider found that:
- 84.5 per cent of the victims of referred adolescents were aged six to 11 years;
- 94.3 per cent of the adolescents knew their victims; and
- 45.9 per cent abused someone within their immediate family.[4]

The above statistics are consistent with practice-based evidence, which indicates that a significant number of children who present with HSB have been sexually harmed by an adolescent sibling, cousin or step-sibling. These situations still commonly occur in the context of the normalisation of family violence, mental health issues and substance abuse issues.

Very few young people present with premeditated behaviours; rather, they are usually impulsive, opportunistic and curious. They often lack understanding regarding consent, either because of their own experiences of being abused or through a lack of knowledge or misleading sources of information, such as pornography. A recent survey of schools conducted in our region by the Public Health Sexual Health Promoter revealed that only 25 per cent of schools were delivering sex education programmes, and for those that were there was a lack of consistency regarding content. And yet anecdotally it seems that many parents rely on schools to provide sex education. Recent research informs us that many youth are relying on pornography for sex education.[5]

A number of variables are recognised as contributing to an ongoing risk of further HSB. A review of studies of sexual reoffending by young people identified four categories of the factors implicated in increasing the risk of further sexual offending:[6]

- Supported (found in at least two published studies):
  - Sexual interest in children or interest in sexual violence
  - Prior criminal charges for sexual assault
  - Past sexual offences against two or more victims
  - Choosing a stranger as a victim
  - Lack of a close peer relationship/social isolation
  - Not completing sex offender treatment programmes
- Promising (found in at least one published study):
  - Attitudes that support sexual offending — blaming the victim or believing there was no harm
  - Difficult relationship with parents/being rejected by parents
- Possible (identified as potential risk factors but no clear evidence found yet):
  - Being obsessed or preoccupied with sex
  - Being highly impulsive
  - Choosing a male victim
  - Influence of antisocial peer group
  - Environment that provides or supports opportunities to reoffend
  - Having sexually abused a child in the past
  - Using or threatening to use violence or weapons during the sexual offence
  - Being unwilling to change deviant sexual interests or attitudes that support abuse
  - Behaving in an aggressive manner
  - History of antisocial behavior
  - Highly stressful family environment
  - Indiscriminate choice of victims — either gender, any age, in and outside family
  - Recent increase in anger or negative emotions
- Unlikely (should *not* be used for determining risk at present — no evidence found yet):
  - Denial of the sexual offence
  - Lack of victim empathy
  - History of non-sexual crimes
  - Sexual offences involving penetration
  - History of being sexually abused themselves

These variables need to be considered in the context of the young person's environment, psychosocial history and offending history, and the risk should not be assessed by someone who does not have experience and knowledge in this domain.

How do we help?

Treatment for children and youth with HSB generally includes individual therapy, family therapy and group therapy (for youth), as well as social work interventions, multi-systems work, and collaborative work with other services such as mental health services and Oranga Tamariki. Research carried out by Associate Professor Ian Lambie at the University of Auckland and clinical psychologist Dr Malcolm Stewart found that 98 per cent of adolescents with HSB who completed community treatment with an HSB treatment agency, such as WellStop, SAFE or STOP, did not engage in any further HSB.[7]

As an agency WellStop promotes best practice and the use of evidence-based models, including the Good Way Model,[8] developed by Lesley Ayland (CEO, WellStop) and Bill West; this was originally developed for working with youth and adults with intellectual disability, but it has evolved to be used across ages and learning abilities, and is now recognised internationally. The Good Lives Model is also utilised for youth and adults,[9] along with other recognised talking therapies, as well as trauma interventions including narrative therapy and cognitive behavioural therapy-informed models.

ADULT OFFENDERS

Adults who come to our service may be mandated through Corrections, as the result of being convicted of a sex offence against a child or young person, or they may self-refer (non-mandated). For a number of reasons people do not always get charged, and it is important to be able to offer help to those who are worried about offending. More recently, the Ministry of Social Development has recognised the need to provide services to men who are at risk of offending, or have some offending-related thoughts and fantasies, and it has increased funding to the sector to address this.

A common stereotype to address is that not every adult who sexually offends against a child or young person is a paedophile. As noted earlier in this book, paedophilia is a specific diagnosis, for which most adult sex offenders do not meet the diagnostic criteria. The majority of men referred to community treatment programmes also do not meet the criteria for paedophilia. There is a mix of sexual orientation; they come from diverse backgrounds, but are often in adult relationships with partners or wives, and have families. What is common is a history of childhood trauma and a lack of emotional coping skills. Often offending is precipitated by some form of stressor or crisis.

Internet offending (the viewing of child abuse images or other objectionable material online) is increasingly prevalent, with an increase in referrals for men who have committed this crime, and whose primary sexual attraction is not children. This is attributed to the addictive nature of pornography, which is now understood to stimulate the same neural pathways as a Class A drug does, making viewing and/or masturbating to pornography an extremely reinforcing behaviour.

Some will quickly become desensitised to mainstream pornography and seek more shocking and deviant material to gain the same 'buzz', much like a drug addict seeking a different drug to increase their reward response. As a result, they begin watching material that does not align with their dominant sexual orientation, but nonetheless they may find themselves being aroused by it, which in turn often creates significant cognitive conflict, especially in a brain made more vulnerable by insecure attachment.

The seeking of more deviant material often leads individuals to watching objectionable material. 'Objectionable' is defined under the Films, Videos and Publications Classification Act 1993 as 'a publication ... [that] describes, depicts, expresses, or otherwise deals with matters such as sex, horror, crime, cruelty, or violence in such a manner that the availability of the publication is likely to be injurious to the public good'. All objectionable material is banned and thus illegal to access.

It is not uncommon for those referred as a result of charges such as these to present with a significant amount of shame and confusion over how they had put themselves in such a situation. Often they are 'groomed' by others on pornography sites, who begin chatting to them and offering to send material that gradually depicts younger and younger people. By the time the individual realises what is happening, it is usually too late; in the eyes of the law, they have committed an offence.

There is no evidence to suggest that all those who watch child abuse images online will go on to 'hands-on' offending. In fact, the opposite is commonly observed: they make a psychological justification that they are not harming anyone by 'just' looking at pictures or videos. Part of their treatment includes the realisation that there are children being harmed in the material that they are viewing, and that they are therefore just as culpable as those who are doing the 'hands-on' offending.

A number of psychological factors contribute to individuals justifying their offending behaviours, including (but not limited to) the belief that it is not harmful to the child; that the child/young person won't remember; or that the child/young person wanted it or instigated it. Anecdotally many have developed the insight to understand that for a number of reasons they had objectified their victim and disassociated from them as a family member. It is also common for some to completely deny the behaviours despite overwhelming evidence to the contrary.

Research informs us that denial does not contribute to the risk of further offending, but is more likely associated with shame and fear of consequences. Many present to our agency with significant remorse and shame on entering treatment, and with high motivation to learn the skills necessary to support them to remain safe in their communities. The following chapter describes how the Good Lives Model informs treatment, with a focus on 10 recognised domains that need to be fulfilled to have a 'good life'. Each person is individually assessed to understand which domains present with limitations, and it is those limitations that will inform treatment.

PRECIPITATING FACTORS

While pornography has become increasingly common as a primary precipitating factor of HSB, the most common precipitating factor remains complex trauma caused by exposure to family violence, neglect and/or dysfunctional attachment styles. Having been exposed to adult sexual behaviours, whether by having been sexually abused or through witnessing adult behaviours, is recognised as the next most common factor.

Complex trauma or developmental trauma disorder describes how children's exposure to multiple or prolonged traumatic events impacts their ongoing development. Typically, complex trauma exposure involves the simultaneous or sequential occurrence of child maltreatment, and may include psychological maltreatment, neglect, physical and/or sexual abuse, and witnessing family violence. Almost all clients who are referred to our service have experienced some form of complex trauma, and a significant number of children and youth are in Oranga Tamariki care.

Traumatised children may act out sexually for a range of reasons, including (but not limited to) self-soothing behaviours, seeking to connect with others, seeking control over their environment, or acting out what they have seen or experienced as a means of making sense of the experience. The majority of adults who present with child sex offending or ideation have experienced their own sexual abuse as a child. This does not excuse the behaviour, but it does help to put things into context, as it is recognised that it can be difficult for an individual to face their own accountability, particularly if no one was held accountable for what happened to them. Addressing their own trauma does have significance when treating those with sexually harmful or offending behaviours, and it contributes to sustainable positive behaviour changes.

MOVING FORWARD

To reduce the prevalence of CSA, a multi-systemic approach, delivered as a community-wide collaboration, is essential. McKibbin et al. recommend three opportunities for prevention, including the reform of sexuality education, redressing victimisation experiences, and help with the management of pornography. Practice-based evidence in the HSB sector would support this, along with the need to address childhood trauma at the earliest possible point.

As a community agency specialising in the intervention and prevention of harmful sexual behaviours we are not resourced to tackle this issue alone, therefore it is important to work with other agencies to address sexual harm across the domains of prevention and intervention, along with increasing the level of expertise in this area. Focusing interventions on victims alone will not break cycles of abuse, and until those who perpetrate abuse have the right help, including working on their own trauma, we run the risk of further people being harmed and cycles of abuse being perpetuated. Resourcing agencies with the knowledge and capacity to address concerning sexual behaviours appropriately will contribute to a significant decrease in the numbers of individuals who present as victims of harmful and abusive sexual behaviours.

Ideally, if children were not exposed to trauma of any type a huge number of HSB incidents would be eliminated. Additionally, if those traumatised had early access to trauma interventions, coping mechanisms would improve and the likelihood of developing negative coping strategies, including harmful sexual behaviours, would decrease. An increased range of prevention education programmes, along with better access to these programmes, will be an important component of a holistic approach to eliminating CSA.

Not only should these programmes address body safety, but they should also address how to manage exposure to pornography, how to understand what healthy relationships look like, how to combat bullying, and how to develop positive coping skills, to name a few. Some recent research on the impact of pornography has prompted the need for change at a government level. If this is implemented it will help alleviate the impact of exposure to pornography on children and youth.

Agencies such as WellStop take pride in working in what is recognised as a challenging and difficult area, offering services to individuals who are able to come for help without fear of judgement or persecution. Until society learns to better understand HSB and how it occurs, there will always be stigma attached to it. It is ironic that we have become desensitised to the levels of sex and sexuality to which we and our children are exposed by a media that often normalises violence, yet we are unwilling to accept the real-life consequences.

So far we have been given significant insight into what happens in specialist child sex offender treatment within prisons and within a community agency working with those with problematic sexual behaviours involving children. One model on which such treatment programmes are based was developed here in Aotearoa New Zealand by Tony Ward, now a professor of psychology at Victoria University of Wellington. In this chapter he and his colleague Mayumi Purvis provide crucial understanding into some antecedents of harmful behaviours and the essential skills-building required to enable a pro-social life and thus stop offending.

Tony believes anyone can change, but only under three conditions: they need to want to change, they need the skills to do it, and they need an environment that allows it — a job, a social group and support. A rehabilitation programme that focuses on stopping unacceptable behaviours but doesn't provide a compelling alternative or the resources to live differently is, in his view, likely to fail. The Good Lives Model (GLM) recognises the wide range of individual differences in child sex offenders. From the understanding that these are human beings who have sought universal human needs through very unacceptable means, the model identifies for each person the things that matter the most to them and helps them find a socially acceptable way to achieve them.

This model is used in many countries, including England, Scotland, Ireland, Wales, Belgium, France, Germany, Norway, the United States, Canada, Japan, Hong Kong, Australia and New Zealand, in prison treatment units, community treatment agencies and probation services. Important research projects continue to evaluate outcomes and expand the knowledge in the field of the rehabilitation of child sex offenders and those with problematic sexual interests.

Tony's previous experience includes psychiatric nursing, drug and alcohol counselling, and working with eating-disordered women. After training as a clinical psychologist he eventually took on a role in 1989 as the first director of Christchurch Prison's Kia Marama special treatment unit. While understanding the public's anger at child sex offenders, he also realised that once offenders have served their sentence for punishment they will be released, hence the essential need to ensure they develop the skills to make them much less likely to reoffend and harm others.

Dr Mayumi Purvis is a criminologist, independent consultant and researcher, and an honorary fellow at the University of Melbourne. Along with coordinating and teaching in a post-graduate course in sexual offender management, she delivers ongoing training to correctional staff in areas such as sexual offender management, best practice in case management and the GLM. Recently she has added death literacy to her skill set, looking at how we transform end-of-life care and the de-medicalisation of death.

Together Mayumi and Tony have pioneered the development of the GLM case management approach, which is applied in a number of jurisdictions. Mayumi is the lead author of a 2013 guide to applying the GLM.[1]

13. The Good Lives Model of rehabilitation

DR MAYUMI PURVIS
UNIVERSITY OF MELBOURNE

PROFESSOR TONY WARD
VICTORIA UNIVERSITY OF WELLINGTON

THE GOOD LIVES MODEL (GLM) is a strengths-based approach to working with individuals who have committed offences. It is premised on the idea that in order for long-term change to be achievable, individuals need the opportunity to lead better lives; lives that are both personally meaningful and socially responsible, not simply lives that are less harmful to other people.[2] Furthermore, the best way to achieve these long-term prospects is via capability building.

Simply put, if individuals are to have any real chance at giving up their harmful behaviours and living healthy, pro-social, meaningful lives, then they need to be equipped to live differently. Merely teaching them how to identify their own risk factors and avoid situations where they are likely to engage in harmful behaviours is unlikely to work.

While the central aim of the GLM is to build psychological and social capacities that help men and women to live more fulfilling lives, it also sets out to reduce the risk of further offending. Thus it has two goals:
- Monitoring: manage the risk posed by clients to the community (risk management); and
- Engaging: enhance well-being by increasing clients' strengths and

capabilities so that they are better equipped to live a pro-social and personally meaningful life (goods promotion).

It is important to understand that the GLM is not a comprehensive theory of offending behaviour or a treatment model. It does not aim to explain *why* individuals commit crimes, nor does it detail a specific treatment for a particular problem, such as aggressive behaviour. Rather, it is a model of healthy human functioning. In line with positive psychology, it provides practitioners with a map of what constitutes a healthy, pro-social adult life, and what kinds of internal and external resources individuals need to get there.

THE GLM'S CONCEPTUALISATION OF OFFENDING BEHAVIOUR

The GLM views offending behaviour in completely natural and humanistic terms. Human beings are goal-directed, and human behaviour, therefore, is meaningful, purposeful and directed by one or more legitimate goals. As such, the GLM explains that all meaningful human actions represent attempts to secure primary human goods (PHGs). PHGs are explained later, but for now it is helpful to know that they essentially represent overarching life pursuits or ultimate concerns, and are expressed in the many and varied goals that we set for ourselves. PHGs are such powerful human motivators that we are naturally predisposed to seek them for the sake of their impact on our overall psychological, physical and social well-being.

Even offending behaviour has an underlying legitimate goal and, as such, it can be viewed in terms of the (problematic) pursuit of PHGs. Take, for example, a young man drinking in a bar. He is pushed from behind and spills his drink and is superficially injured in the process. He turns and confronts his perceived aggressor, and although it is clear that it was an accident, the person responsible is unapologetic and unsympathetic and tersely tells the young man to 'get over it' and insults him by engaging in some name calling. The young man feels enraged by this injustice and, due to an absence of adaptive coping skills, an inability to control his impulsivity, poor consequential thinking and the presence of social supports for violence as a means for resolution, he physically assaults the other party, leaving them seriously injured. This results in criminal charges and formal sanctions.

So, one might ask, what was the legitimate goal? Some might say that his goal was to hurt another person, and this is surely not OK. In fact, causing physical harm to another was actually a dysfunctional means or strategy for achieving an otherwise legitimate end. The actual goal is likely to be the need for control or agency, to regain some perceived loss of power, and/or perhaps to feel respected and admired by others. These are normal states for adults to pursue; however, in the above example it is the *way* in which these goals are achieved that is problematic. Therefore, the strategy or means is the target for intervention, not the goal itself.

THE CAUSES OF CRIME ACCORDING TO THE GLM

An important question is: why do some people offend? That is, why do people use a problematic means for an otherwise legitimate goal? According to the GLM, it is often a lack of skills, knowledge and pro-social opportunities; deficits or problematic characteristics in place of adaptive ones. These deficits or weaknesses can be internal or external. Internal factors refer to the person's skills, attitudes, beliefs, psychological characteristics, physical health, educational background and so on. External factors refer to environmental, social, cultural and interpersonal opportunities and circumstances.

As clients often lack the strengths, positive attributes and environments to overcome their lives' challenges pro-socially, they act in problematic, harmful or antisocial ways that are symptomatic and reflective of their unique profile of deficits and obstacles. Those internal and external deficits, which drive offending behaviour in the pursuit of PHGs, arguably represent an individual's unique set of dynamic risk factors.

USING THE GLM TO PROMOTE OFFENDER COLLABORATION WITH WORKERS

If we understand what the client was or is seeking in terms of PHGs when they offended, then we understand something key about what motivates this person and what they value and desire for themselves. Identifying the legitimate goal in offending behaviour enables us to link this to, and understand, the PHG the person was seeking. Thus, we can tailor our intervention and rehabilitative efforts at helping them to build capacity in precisely those areas that are under-resourced. By helping people to acquire the necessary conditions (internal and external capacities) for fulfilling their needs and pursuing their PHGs in adaptive, pro-social ways, they will be less likely to harm others and themselves.

Furthermore, the enhancement of client well-being reduces risk and protects the community in two ways. Firstly, learning certain capacities involved in successfully implementing the GLM will reduce the risk of any antisocial behaviour (for example through improved emotional control). Secondly, individuals are likely to be more motivated to engage in programmes and thus make gains if they see them as a means to achieve valued goals. This in turn is more likely to make it easier to engage them in the difficult process of change.

GLM CORE CONCEPTS: PRIMARY HUMAN GOODS

Primary human goods (PHGs) are actions, states of affairs, characteristics, experiences and states of mind that are intrinsically beneficial to us and are sought for their own sake. They represent our ultimate concerns, and they sit across multiple life domains. Based on past and current cross-cultural and cross-discipline research, Tony Ward and his colleagues have identified 11 classes of PHGs.[3] There is no 'right' order to these PHGs; they can be subjectively ordered only according to individuals' personal priorities and values. The definition for each PHG is provided below, along with some examples of pro-social seeking and problematic seeking. The examples provided refer to the functional or dysfunctional ways in which people may attempt to secure the PHG in their lives; that is, the means by which they seek it, not necessarily the form the PHG takes.

Life

Life essentially incorporates all the physical needs and factors that are important for healthy living and physical functioning: food, water, shelter, a physically healthy body, and so on. The good of Life also requires that the person's living circumstances are adequate and suited to their needs. Ideal fulfilment of this good would produce a physically healthy person whose physical functioning and living circumstances are optimal. Examples of pro-social seeking would include securing stable accommodation, exercise, financial management to meet basic needs, and properly managing health problems. Examples of problematic seeking might include squatting, couch surfing, self-medicating and theft.

Knowledge

People are inherently curious and seek to understand aspects of themselves, their natural environments and other people. The good of Knowledge satisfies this need and includes acquiring wisdom or information, such as facts, theories and ideas, which we can use to answer a number of questions: What does this mean? What is valuable? Why did this happen? How do things work? And so on. This good is not concerned with IQ or how smart someone is; instead, Knowledge acquisition should be assessed according to how well informed individuals feel about things that are important to them. Examples of pro-social seeking could include studying, taking lessons and asking questions. Examples of problematic seeking might be extortion and stand-over tactics.

Excellence in Play

Human beings seek to enjoy and be good at a range of recreational tasks that may or may not be structured into games or events. This good refers to the desire to engage in leisure or fun activities that promote a sense of pride, achievement and satisfaction, or skill development. This good is likely to have both an intrinsic value (accomplishment for the sake of it, that is, for personal enjoyment) and an instrumental value (accomplishment for a specific purpose; for example to win a competition, move up to the next grade/level or achieve greater physical fitness). It must be matched to an individual's personal set of skills, interests, preferences and desires. Examples of pro-social seeking could be participating in team sports or competitive online gaming. Examples of problematic seeking could include acts like cheating and sabotaging others in order to get ahead.

Excellence in Work

Being meaningfully employed in a role that provides mastery experiences and challenges which are matched to the person's level of functioning is important. This good includes the desire to engage in work, which provides the person with a sense of pride, achievement, satisfaction and/or skill development. Meaningful employment will have both an intrinsic value (for example, for personal fulfilment) and an instrumental value (for example, a promotion, greater responsibility or salary increase) and must be matched to an individual's personal set of skills, interests, preferences and desires. Examples of pro-social seeking would be paid or volunteer work, self-employment and apprenticeships. Examples of problematic seeking could be organised crime, white-collar crime, and taking credit for other people's work and achievements.

Excellence in Agency

Our desire to formulate our own goals and seek ways to realise them in actions and activities of our own choice accommodates our adult need for autonomy, self-directedness, personal power, control and mastery. This good concerns our individual ability to act in a way that produces an intended outcome: to stand on our own two feet, to be able to pursue what we value most, and to shape our life in ways that are consistent with our deepest values and concerns. Examples of pro-social seeking would be acting assertively, upskilling and achieving financial independence. Examples of problematic seeking could include aggression, violence and manipulation in order to dominate others.

Inner Peace

Inner Peace refers to emotional self-regulation (control) and our ability to achieve a state of emotional balance. It also refers to the need for emotional competence, encompassing skills such as awareness and understanding of our own emotional state, the ability to express how we feel, the capacity to identify other people's emotions, the capacity to respond empathically to others, and the ability to manage aversive emotions through a range of adaptive strategies. Examples of pro-social seeking might include meditation, counselling and exercise. Examples of problematic seeking could be self-harm, avoidance, and the use of drugs or alcohol to manage aversive emotions.

Relatedness

Human beings naturally desire warm, affectionate bonds with other people, ranging from romantic relationships to intimate family relationships and platonic yet close friendships. As such, this PHG refers to the close, caring, mutual relationships that adults establish with an intimate partner, family members and close friends. The activities that constitute the good of Relatedness include disclosure, support, sexual activity, physical contact, honesty, spending time together, sharing interests, mutual emotional caring, equality and so on. Examples of pro-social seeking could be adult romantic relationships, close family relationships and very close friends. Examples of problematic seeking are promiscuity and stalking.

Community

Human beings desire to belong to social groups, to feel connected to groups that reflect their interests, concerns and values. Being part of a wider social and/or cultural network helps us feel we are contributing to a larger social unit, and can rely on this larger group to meet our own needs. Examples of pro-social seeking could include volunteer work, membership in special-interest groups and religious affiliation. Examples of problematic seeking could be cult association, membership with anti-social/hate groups and criminal gangs.

Spirituality

A sense of meaning and purpose is an important need, along with the overall experience of being content and satisfied with one's life. This could involve seeking religious truths and involvement, a spiritual connection with a transcendent being or reality, or simply the experience of being part of a wider whole. In short, this good refers to a variety of activities in which participation provides a broad sense of purpose and direction to life and relates to the overall feeling of happiness and contentedness that emerges from understanding one's involvement with the wider world. Examples of pro-social seeking include belonging to a church or religious group, living one's life according to a spiritual belief system, or a connection to an environmental association. An example of problematic seeking could be cult association or living life according to fanatical religious ideology.

Pleasure

Pleasure involves both a state of being in the here and now and pleasure-seeking: essentially healthy self-indulgence and gratification. It is often implicated in activities that bring about feelings of enjoyment, deep satisfaction and excitement. Examples of pro-social seeking could include massage, food, sex and thrill-seeking activities. Examples of problematic seeking might include drug-taking, overeating, self-harm and risky sexual encounters.

Creativity

The novelty, innovation and individuality of creativity may be reflected in the experience of doing things differently, being engaged in an activity that results in an artistic output, or perhaps producing a novel product of some kind. Creativity does not require that an individual be artistic in a traditional sense, as it may be implicated in a range of everyday activities. Creativity is essentially the expression of oneself through alternative forms. Examples of pro-social seeking could be gardening, solving problems, playing a musical instrument and interior decorating. An example of problematic seeking is illegal graffiti art.

PRIMARY HUMAN GOODS COMPARED TO GOALS

Often, PHGs are mistakenly referred to as life goals, and while it is true that people inherently aspire to acquire PHGs for the sake of their overall well-being, PHGs are fundamentally different to goals. Goals are a way of achieving PHGs, which are ultimate ends and essentially underpin the goals. A comparison can be drawn to assist in the differentiation, as set out on the opposite page.

FOUR KEY PROBLEMS THAT DIMINISH HUMAN WELL-BEING

According to Ward and his colleagues, there are four primary types of problem that undermine human well-being and lead to unhappy, disconnected lives. These have been identified as capacity, means, conflict and scope, and they interconnect in an ongoing way. Although they have

Fig. 13.1: Comparison table of primary human goods (PHGs) and goals.

Primary human goods	Goals
Objective	**Subjective**
PHGs are objectively defined, capture cross-discipline and cross-cultural ideals, and are not bound by age, class, culture or gender.	Goals are the subjective means by which people pursue PHGs and are shaped by age, class, gender, culture, personal preference, and all other human attributes.
Finite	**Infinite**
There are 11 PHGs and the number of PHGs is representative of and bound by research and discoveries about human strivings.	The number and type of goals that people can set for themselves in reference to any one PHG are bound only by social and cultural norms (at best) and are potentially unlimited.
Static	**Dynamic**
Although PHGs have the potential to evolve on the basis of research and discovery, they are essentially unchanging due to their objective nature.	The potential for goals to change and develop is ongoing. Goals will change as a result of achievements, failures, financial status, age, religion, relationship status, education, and a wide range of other factors.
Universal	**Individual**
Due to their objective nature and wide research base, PHGs are said to be universally relevant to human beings.	Goals are constructed in an entirely individual way and essentially represent a person's unique identity.

been set out in detail elsewhere,[4] the following summary is provided.

Poor capacity refers to a lack of the internal and external resources required to successfully secure PHGs in pro-social and personally meaningful ways. When internal and external resources are ample and available, the person is considered to have good capacity and therefore is able to engage in behaviours and strategies that are enabling and productive, thus promoting the attainment of PHGs. However, when capacity is lacking, the individual is likely to have a range of internal and external obstacles (deficits and weaknesses) that hinder the pro-social and healthy pursuit of PHGs.

As a result the person pursues PHGs in a way that is problematic, harmful or illegal. The earlier example of the young man in the bar who seeks to gain respect or justice via violence and aggression is an example of how poor capacity (internal: poor emotional coping, impulsivity, lack of consequential thinking; and external: social supports for violence as a means for resolution) drives problematic behaviour. Therefore, in order to intervene with behaviour, we must first understand its purpose (the goal/s and PHG/s) and then identify the capacity issues that fuel the strategies chosen, with the aim of bolstering capacity in order to promote alternative means.

When PHGs are sought via problematic means (which are driven by capacity issues) they cause conflict in other areas of functioning. For example, someone who seeks freedom from emotional distress (PHG Inner Peace) by abusing drugs or alcohol (problematic means) due to poor emotional regulation skills (problems in internal capacity) and a lack of social supports (problems with external capacity) is going to experience problems and dysfunction in other areas of their life due to the problematic means used; this is referred to as conflict. Specifically, seeking Inner Peace via substance misuse might undermine (conflict with) the person's health (PHG Life); produce relationship strain (PHG Relatedness); and incite poor work performance or job loss (PHG Excellence in Work), which in turn will only increase the person's psychological turmoil (compounding problems with PHG Inner Peace).

The final problem is referred to as a lack of scope. Within the GLM, healthy functioning and optimal well-being are considered to be achieved when all 11 PHGs are accounted for to varying degrees in a person's life (full scope). However, when not all PHGs are present (poor scope), this may lead to a neglect or absence of one or more of the three components of human well-being: social, physical and psychological. A neglect of one such cluster could lead to physiological dysfunction, psychological distress leading to mental health problems, or social maladjustment, all of which will invariably lead to poor overall life satisfaction and therefore emotional distress.

In summary, we can see how problems with internal and external resources cause problematic behaviours for otherwise legitimate goals, which leads to a thwarting of other PHGs, which, in turn, disables full access of all 11 PHGs. Each of these problems builds on the other in a linear way, but also creates circular traps that hold the person in a perpetual cycle of an endless lack of fulfilment and resultant problem behaviours. The aim of rehabilitation, therefore, is to build and add to individual's social and psychological resources. In this way, we increase and improve the person's capacity, choice, opportunity, well-being and outcomes. This building up of the person then allows the individual to access goods in pro-social ways that are also intrinsically beneficial and meaningful.

GLM EMPIRICAL RESEARCH

The GLM has been developed based on an extensive and ongoing review of interdisciplinary theory and research, and its construction therefore emerges from strong, established and widely accepted theoretical and empirical foundations. Yet it is important that the GLM has its own research base, and, as a result, empirical studies on the GLM are beginning to build, as are the associated positive findings. A number of studies, for example, have been published which highlight the positive implications associated with implementing GLM-consistent ideas into treatment programmes.[5]

One of the pivotal empirical studies into the application of the GLM compared the outcomes of those participants who received GLM-consistent management and treatment to those who received the traditional relapse prevention approach.[6] The study found that GLM participants were more motivated and more likely to complete treatment. Furthermore, those who did not complete treatment stayed in treatment longer than the comparison group. In addition, GLM participants were identified as being more likely to have a social support group in place upon completion of treatment. A more recent study noted that the GLM improved client and therapist satisfaction with treatment experiences,[7] and another found that a group of offenders with complex mental health needs were able to engage well in a GLM treatment programme, in spite of their significant challenges.[8]

CONCLUSION

Services and practitioners who are serious about promoting the rehabilitation of clients will know that punitive responses not only trap individuals in feelings of helplessness and cycles of offending behaviour, but they also undermine the health and well-being of communities as a whole. Given this awareness, the GLM has experienced notable popularity in offender rehabilitation programmes and has undergone continued theoretical development.

Even in light of its limited but growing empirical research base, the GLM's humanistic and logical approach to problem behaviours makes it a useful and comprehensive rehabilitation framework for working with people. It advocates for a practice that is deeply respectful and yet highly targeted and meaningful. Within GLM-consistent programmes, clients are able to realise a genuinely attainable alternative to their previous way of living; that is, a life that is not just pro-social, but also personally meaningful and deservedly fulfilling.

Sarah Beggs Christofferson, researcher, clinical psychologist and mother of three, brings substantial scientific research expertise and experience in the field of child sexual offending to our understanding of the work of child sexual abuse prevention. Her rigorous research continues to provide crucially important information.

With those who have sexually offended against children, the ability to measure the severity of risk and identify the types of risk factors guides the type of treatment programme that will be most effective for each individual, thus reducing the risk of reoffending. Further, such measures — completed from professionals' trained observations, not by the offenders themselves — show progress during and after treatment, which can inform release decisions. Sarah has been working on the development and evaluation of such assessment tools for many years now.

Some who offend are sentenced to community-based treatment, and some individuals with harmful sexual behaviours are referred to or voluntarily seek community-based treatment. Having recognised that the tool used to assess the risk factors had not as yet been proven useful and accurate outside of prison-based treatment programmes, Sarah, with the help of others working in community treatment agencies, has launched a research project to evaluate this measure in such agencies. It is clear that this will make another important contribution to the goal of preventing child sexual abuse.

Eighty-four per cent of those convicted of child sexual offences each year are being caught for the first time. As Sarah makes clear, this means we cannot focus on only those currently identified. Read on to learn what her research suggests is the best way to identify and effectively treat all those who are at risk of sexually abusing children.

14. Assessing risk and treatment change, and the shift towards prevention

SARAH BEGGS CHRISTOFFERSON
UNIVERSITY OF CANTERBURY

THE FIELD OF RESEARCH INTO child sexual abuse is vast and varied, with hundreds of new studies carried out each year and research methods continuously being refined. These efforts aim to increase our knowledge on a huge range of relevant and important concerns — everything from how often these harmful kinds of behaviour happen, the impact on those affected, what causes people to act in this way and how likely they are to do so again to, and most importantly perhaps, what changes we can strive towards to protect children.

Despite the size and breadth of the field, all this research has one common goal: to better inform the work of practitioners and policy-makers in order to ultimately eliminate this highly destructive behaviour from our communities. I have been involved in this field for the past 15 years, as both a researcher and a clinical psychologist.

One thing that stands out when I reflect on this time, the work I have seen and the people I have met, is the dedication of all those working in this area in their many different roles to achieve the same key goal: eradicating sexual abuse and the harm and suffering it causes. Whether this can ever be achieved is unknown, but it is heartening to know that so much effort is being put in by so many.

In this chapter, I will introduce two areas of child sexual abuse research I am involved in at the time of writing, both of which are being carried out in New Zealand. The first involves the questions of how we can estimate the likelihood of a person who has been convicted of sexually abusing a child doing so again (risk), and how, should they receive treatment to reduce this risk, we can evaluate whether it has been successful, and the effect this might have had on their risk of further offending (change).

The second area of research is quite different, as it is not about people who have actually engaged in sexually abusive behaviour. Rather, it focuses on how we might be able to help people who have not yet committed an abusive act, but who may be at risk of doing so due to their thoughts, urges or fantasies. This second area of research relates to *prevention* — treatment not to prevent *re*offending but rather to prevent initial offending, a much newer concept in the field.

RESEARCH PROJECT 1: ASSESSING RISK AND CHANGE USING THE VIOLENCE RISK SCALE — SEXUAL OFFENDER VERSION (VRS-SO)

One thing that has been made very clear from research is just how varied the group of people who have perpetrated child sexual abuse is. Each person will have come to the point of committing their harmful acts along their own individual pathway, with different patterns of contributing factors. This variation has obviously complicated attempts to develop effective treatment approaches — how much easier it would be if there were a single, straightforward, known and treatable basis behind all instances of sexually abusive behaviour! But this is not the case, and what we know is that individuals who attend this kind of treatment have vast differences in their psychological make-up and functioning relevant to their offending.

For example, some but not all (around 50 per cent) will meet criteria for paedophilia.[1] Others, despite being primarily interested in adults, may be hampered somehow in their ability to initiate and maintain intimate relationships. Some are sexually preoccupied, with an abnormally high and difficult-to-manage sex drive. The offending of others may be most likely to happen at times of severe emotional distress, perhaps as an inappropriate attempt to make themselves feel better.

Some may have developed skewed thinking in relation to sexual behaviour with children, such as justifications, rationalisations or a minimised view of the harm that offending causes to victims. Others, in contrast, may have a clear understanding of the wrongness of sexual contact with children, but simply lack the ability or will to self-manage their behaviour. They may view their offending as having 'just happened', with themselves being passive and powerless to stop the course of events that led to it.

Each of the above examples describes a risk factor, or an aspect of an individual that has been linked with reoffending likelihood. The first step in treating someone in order to reduce the chances they will offend again is an assessment to uncover which risk factors in particular apply to them, and how many. This process is known as risk assessment. Generally speaking, the more risk factors that apply to a person, the higher the likelihood, or risk, that they will commit further offences in the future.[2]

The risk of reoffending is therefore something else in which individuals who have sexually abused children differ greatly. Overall, rates of reoffending among those convicted of sexual abuse against children are actually much lower than many assume; a New Zealand study that followed over 1500 people released from prison sentences found that the re-conviction rate after an average of 15 years was 12.8 per cent.[3] This is similar to rates found internationally. It is acknowledged, however, that official rates such as these may underestimate the true rates as there is likely to be some proportion of offending that goes unreported and/or unprosecuted for a variety of reasons.

However, importantly, the same study also found quite different rates amongst smaller groups within the sample. For example, around 6 per cent of those classified as 'low risk' reoffended (less than half of the overall average of 12.8 per cent), compared to 37 per cent of the 'high risk' cohort (almost three times the overall average). It is very clear, therefore, that reoffending risk varies between individuals.

Risk is, in fact, a hugely important concept in the field. A large body of research accumulated over a number of decades and compiled into a highly influential text by leading Canadian forensic psychology researchers Don Andrews and James Bonta taught us that in order for treatment services to be effective at reducing reoffending rates, treatment intensity (frequency of sessions, programme duration and so on) needs to be matched to risk level.[4] So, those with the highest risk need to undertake the most intensive treatment, those around the average risk level require more moderate-intensity programmes, while those who are low risk should have only minimal or even no treatment. This is known as the risk principle.

Research has also told us that to reduce reoffending, treatment needs to focus specifically on changing aspects of the person that have been shown to be linked with the likelihood of reoffending — in other words, risk factors. As outlined above, some examples of risk factors for sexual reoffending are sexual preoccupation, limited skills for adult relationships and difficulties in coping with negative emotions.

The Violence Risk Scale — Sexual Offender version (VRS-SO) is a tool developed by a team of Canadian researchers led by Mark Olver at the University of Saskatchewan.[5] Designed to assist professionals to carry out reoffending risk assessments of people who have committed sexual offences, this is one of several such tools available. The VRS-SO was specifically designed to accomplish the important tasks highlighted above: identifying the person's risk level and therefore what intensity of treatment programme they need, and identifying the key risk factors that need to be targeted for change in their case.

The tool includes 17 items corresponding to potential treatment needs, which are rated by the assessing clinician; for example, deviant sexual preference, cognitive distortions, emotional functioning and intimacy deficits. But, further, the VRS-SO was also specifically designed to track changes in risk made across treatment. This is vital, given that we know that treatment can reduce reoffending but not necessarily to the same degree for everyone.[6]

Just as in other learning environments, how well someone does in sexual offending treatment depends on factors such as how motivated or ready they are to change, how responsive the programme and staff are to their particular needs, how much effort the individual puts in, and how much they take treatment concepts on board and choose to put newly learnt skills into practice. Without a valid, structured guide, determining how much change has occurred and what this might mean for someone's risk level is challenging.

Doing so objectively can be particularly fraught for a therapist, who may (for example) be very invested in seeing their clients do well, creating an unintended potential bias. As a key advantage over other risk tools, the VRS-SO includes objective guidelines for the clinician to use when evaluating change at an individual level across every risk factor. Therefore, as well as identifying baseline risk level and key treatment needs, the VRS-SO can also assess how much change a person has achieved on each of those needs by the end of treatment, and how much, if at all, their risk has reduced.

Assessment tools need to be valid. This means they need to measure accurately what they are intending to measure. For risk assessment tools, the key criterion for the validity of a test is whether high scores are in fact predictive of increased reoffending, as intended. In the case of the VRS-SO, its accuracy in predicting reoffending risk among men incarcerated for sexual offending was first shown in a study by the developers of the tool.[7] They also found that those who achieved more treatment change as measured by the tool were indeed less likely to reoffend than those who did less well in treatment. Later research,[8] carried out by myself and Randolph Grace at the University of Canterbury, confirmed the accuracy of VRS-SO risk and change scores for the New Zealand population, contributing to it being the current tool of choice for local prison-based treatment programmes for those who have sexually offended against children.

However, such treatment is not always undertaken in prison. Some offenders receive community-based sentences, such as intensive supervision or home detention, while others receive short sentences of imprisonment within which there is insufficient time to complete one of the programmes available. What hadn't been investigated to date anywhere in the world was whether the VRS-SO would produce similar levels of accuracy and usefulness among those participating in community-based sexual offending treatment programmes.

Therefore, in 2015 the New Zealand community-based VRS-SO validation study was launched. This is a project in which I am excited to be involved, alongside collaborators from community treatment services based at several sites around the country. After receiving training on the VRS-SO, clinical staff at these services began to rate the measure with their clients and compile the scores into an anonymised data set. In due course, once longer-term outcomes become available, re-conviction information for this group will be gathered and anonymously analysed alongside the VRS-SO scores to determine whether, similarly to the prior prison-based research, those with higher risk scores and those who made less change in treatment were indeed more likely to have committed further offences.

This is important research because treatment settings in the community equally require accurate tools given the important decisions that risk assessments inform, such as what treatment intensity is required. Although it is too early to know what the findings of this study will show, early analyses of VRS-SO scoring carried out in the participating community treatment settings found good consistency of ratings,[9] indicating that the treatment staff were using the tool correctly.

This bodes well for later findings ideally showing that the VRS-SO is valid for community use. It is my hope that such a finding would be helpful for harmful sexual behaviour clinicians in community-based treatment settings not only in New Zealand but also elsewhere. However, if the study were to show that the VRS-SO is not valid for community use, this would be an equally important finding and would indicate that further work is required to develop suitable alternatives.

RESEARCH PROJECT 2: PREVENTION — HELPING THEM BEFORE THEY HARM

Research work to improve risk assessment and risk-reducing treatment for those who have sexually offended is clearly a worthwhile and necessary pursuit. As mentioned, the ultimate goal is always to work towards eradicating this harmful behaviour altogether from society. However, an important point to consider is that if we focus only on those who have already committed offences, we are drastically limiting our ability to make a true dent in the rates of abuse. This is because New Zealand figures show that in the course of a year, only around 16 per cent of those convicted for sexual offences against children are reoffending.[10]

The other 84 per cent are previously unknown to authorities at all in terms of posing a sexual risk. Efforts and investment aimed at reducing reoffending, though vital, are therefore not enough. They have no effect on preventing the bulk of new offences each year. Research exploring prevention is therefore well justified, and could have important implications for reducing overall rates of child sexual victimisation. For these reasons, I have been working in recent years to expand my research focus into the area of child sexual abuse prevention.

Prevention efforts can be generally understood as occurring at three levels: primary, secondary and tertiary. In terms of child sexual abuse prevention, the most common and well-researched model to date is tertiary prevention, which involves providing treatment to known (that is, convicted) offenders in order to remove or reduce the likelihood of repeat offending behaviour. Such services are widely available in New Zealand (for example, the Kia Marama special treatment unit run at Rolleston Prison), and have been shown through research undertaken at the University of Canterbury to be effective.[11]

Primary prevention refers to the earliest interventions aimed at the whole population: for example, sexual violence education, awareness-raising activities and social norms campaigns. These types of initiative are also common in New Zealand.[12] Secondary prevention involves targeting individuals who are potentially at risk of engaging in the problematic behaviour, but before they have done so, with the aim of assisting them not to, as opposed to offering help only after they have abused someone. The overarching aim is again, of course, to reduce victimisation rates. Systemic secondary prevention initiatives have to date been lacking in New Zealand, so this is where my current focus lies.

Primary and secondary prevention efforts in the fight against sexual abuse are well-justified, given the very high percentage of convictions for those without a history of such behaviour. Further justification comes from considering the well-known 'ambulance at the bottom of a cliff' metaphor. We know from research in Germany, where secondary prevention treatment services do operate, that the need and demand for such treatment exists in communities.[13]

Why then would we as a society choose to withhold help until the individual is in the criminal justice system, after a child or children have been harmed, with all the fallout and costs that entails? Secondary prevention could be the 'fence' at the top of the cliff: a relatively small investment with large potential pay-off, both in financial terms and, arguably more importantly, in terms of social cost savings.

Despite the clear rationale, several challenges face the implementation of a secondary preventative service in the area of child sexual abuse, and researching these challenges has been a first step in my prevention research focus. Since the people in need of preventative treatment have not yet done anything to bring themselves to the attention of authorities or services, to participate in such a programme they would need to self-refer; in other words, front up of their own accord and willingly open up to a therapist about their troubling thoughts and fantasies. Understandably, for many this would not be an easy thing to do.

Despite growing understanding among researchers in the field that sexual interest in children is not a choice that someone makes (rather, it seems to be something that one discovers about oneself, similar to gender orientation),[14] there is nonetheless a great deal of stigma surrounding this issue.[15] For those affected, this may have been something they have grappled with in secret for a long time, and they may be fearful of what might happen if they share this with another person — even a therapist. And this concern is not necessarily unfounded. While confidentiality of client information is a basic tenet of settings such as counselling and therapy with a psychologist, in many places there are limits to this.

Across all states of the USA[16] and Australia,[17] for example, mandated reporting laws exist requiring certain professionals to report beliefs or suspicions they have about harm to a child based on information their clients have told them. In New Zealand, professionals are not mandated to report but they are permitted to in certain circumstances,[18] including if they believe there is a risk of future serious harm happening as opposed to harm that has already happened. Therefore, although a therapist may legitimately choose not to make a report to authorities in order to provide preventative treatment to their client, they could choose to.

This results in a lack of certainty for people in need of help; and since, as noted, such help generally requires self-referral, this presents a clear potential barrier to a preventative service being viable. However, as mentioned, an exception exists in Germany, where there are no mandated reporting laws and where, moreover, therapists are firmly prohibited from breaching client confidentiality. A prevention service for people seeking treatment in relation to experiencing sexual interest in children, Prevention Programme Dunkelfeld has been in operation in Germany since 2005.[19] Importantly, in this context of guaranteed full client confidentiality, hundreds of people per year approach the service to seek help, and evaluation has shown that the programme is successful in reducing a number of key risk factors linked with child sexual abuse perpetration.[20]

Although it is indeed difficult to see how a secondary prevention service like Dunkelfeld could operate in places where there are mandated reporting laws, I have been working to explore whether it may be possible in New Zealand. Recently, I surveyed over 100 New Zealand health professionals about how comfortable and confident they would feel if a client were to disclose sexual interest in children to them as a means of seeking help; how knowledgeable they were about the legal and ethical duties that would come into play in such a scenario (for example, the fact that reporting of risk is permitted in some circumstances, but not mandated); and what their thresholds were for deciding to breach client confidentiality for risk management purposes.[21]

The key findings that emerged included that while practitioners tend towards feeling comfortable and confident in dealing with a client scenario of this nature, misconceptions regarding their duties under the law were prevalent. Specifically, 75 per cent of those surveyed wrongly believed that reporting of risk to authorities was mandated in New Zealand. Although most of those surveyed reported that their general tendency when given the option would be to maintain client confidentiality, it was clear that issues of professional liability (that is, the potential for they themselves to come under fire for choosing not to make a disclosure, even though the law does not mandate it) weighed heavily on their minds. Accurate knowledge of the law was associated with having a higher threshold for breaching client confidentiality. This study has therefore identified a key training priority for professionals, which could assist to reduce barriers to self-referral for those in need of preventative treatment services.

Public support, or the lack of it, is another potential barrier to implementing a secondary prevention service in New Zealand, not least because it touches on the issue of funding. A student member of my research group recently conducted a survey of over 700 New Zealanders that revealed high public support (over 80 per cent) for the idea of establishing such a service in this country.[22]

Survey participants were also asked for their views on what the likely benefits of such a service would be, as well as about any concerns. The most commonly endorsed benefits were that it may reduce rates of child sexual abuse, and that it could improve the quality of life for the people who would be the intended targets for the service. In terms of concerns, many participants considered that the individuals who were most in need might not actually come forward to utilise the service and that this kind of programme may not be successful in reducing child sexual abuse. Such findings are helpful to inform future directions. For example, public awareness campaigns highlighting the high utilisation rates and positive effects of existing services such as Prevention Programme Dunkelfeld could prove useful in further increasing and strengthening support.

IN TERMS OF FUTURE DIRECTIONS for child sexual abuse prevention research, I believe there is much work to do and I remain excited about being involved. I am currently working with a team of experts to design a secondary prevention programme for the New Zealand context that we hope could be piloted as a joint research and treatment facility for the benefit of those who currently have few options to seek help, and those whom they may be at risk of harming. It is vital that we continue to learn more about the population who experience sexual interest in children, so that we can learn how to more effectively help them and, in turn, reduce the victimisation of children.

Meanwhile, existing tertiary and primary approaches to prevention also need our continued support for the excellent work they do across the country. Working together is undoubtedly the best way to eliminate the scourge that is child sexual abuse in our society.

I first heard about Project Restore NZ from a police detective who spoke in glowing terms about the gains she had seen being made by a victim and her family. It can take a bit to impress detectives experienced in the field of child protection, so I was curious to know more.

I made contact and grilled Lisa Markwick, its executive director: How do you make sure the offenders don't manipulate the child victim? What do you do with intra-family child sexual abuse by a male partner when the mother sides with her partner, and who supports the child through the process? How do you know a child is ready to do this? Won't there be pressure from the court system or the offender's lawyer to push a restorative justice process through in time for it to look good in court? Some readers will recognise and identify with my cynicism!

Lisa handled my questions thoroughly and with ease, leaving me reassured that this agency has been set up with immense care, a deep understanding of both the different and the shared cultural values that make up our society, and equally extensive knowledge of all the dynamics that can occur with child sexual abuse. Project Restore serves the survivors, both when they are children and also years or decades later when they are adults, and it also serves the whānau/families and the perpetrators. It is heartening to know that restorative justice, which demands huge courage on the part of survivor, perpetrator and whānau/families to be effective, can be part of a way forward for individuals and families who have experienced sexual harm.

Most chapters in this section finish with some suggestions for how we can improve the situation in the future. This entire chapter is a model of what is already providing both significant support to victims of child sexual abuse and significant prevention interventions.

15. Restorative justice: Enabling a new 'normal' after sexual violence

DR SHIRLEY JÜLICH, JENNIFER ANNAN
AND LISA MARKWICK, PROJECT RESTORE NZ

THE GOAL OF RESTORATIVE JUSTICE in the field of sexual abuse is to provide survivors with an opportunity to experience a sense of justice that will hopefully enable them to move forward with their lives. Restorative justice provides the opportunity for people harmed and those causing harm to come together and talk about what happened, the context in which it happened, the harm caused, and the ripple effects on their wider families and communities. The aim of restorative justice is not to restore an abusive relationship. Rather, it offers an opportunity for restoration of relationships among the often far-reaching number of people affected by an incidence of harm caused by sexual violence.

Established in 2005 in response to the dissatisfaction and frustrations of survivors of sexual violence, Project Restore NZ is one of a small number of programmes worldwide that focuses on addressing harm caused by sexual violence. Project Restore delivers services nationally, using a modified version of the New Zealand model of restorative justice conferencing, and specifically aims to meet the needs of survivors of sexual violence. In addition, offenders are held accountable for their actions. While our work is survivor-centred, participation by both the survivor and the offender is entirely voluntary and either party may withdraw their participation at any time. All those who participate are supported throughout by a survivor specialist, an offender specialist and a restorative justice facilitator. This team has in-depth experience of restorative justice and the complex dynamics of sexual violence.

Unfortunately, a significant proportion of our work relates to children who have experienced sexual violence and who have disclosed relatively soon after the abuse. This is an ideal time to support them in their healing and recovery with clear statements from the perpetrator that 'it's not your fault and I'm not angry that you told'. A supportive caregiver is essential to support children, and most are represented by a protective adult.

When we are working with adults who have experienced childhood sexual abuse, restorative justice processes offer the opportunity to gain an understanding of why the sexual abuse occurred through their adult eyes, thereby enabling healing and recovery to occur with their wounded 'inner child'. Survivors regularly comment that they feel lighter, and that a weight has been lifted from their shoulders at the end of a restorative conference.

In the case of intergenerational abuse, early intervention is optimal in order to prevent further harm and trauma. Neuropsychological research has shown that the impact of trauma can mean that people are less able to identify danger or act on it, sometimes perpetuating the cycle of abuse. Restorative justice may be one way of highlighting some of the harm done to, or by, those who are blind to the effects of that harm, which has the potential to reduce the risk of further intergenerational abuse.

WHO CAN ACCESS RESTORATIVE JUSTICE?

Restorative justice through Project Restore NZ is available to anyone who has experienced harm caused by sexual violence in New Zealand. Some cases are referred directly from the community. Most, however, are referred to us by the New Zealand court system. Project Restore sources funds for this work — some from government and some from trusts and philanthropic organisations. Restorative processes serve a different function from the mainstream criminal justice system and can work alongside or as an alternative to criminal proceedings in some cases. In New Zealand, restorative justice is an additional layer of justice for those who are referred by the courts.

Following the Sentencing Amendment Act 2014, New Zealand courts are now mandated to refer restorative justice in all cases of sexual harm where there has been a guilty plea; that is, an acknowledgement of causing harm. The judge will take into account how the restorative justice conference went and is keen to know if the survivor's needs were met by the person causing the harm. There may be a reduction in the offender's sentence if it is perceived that they have shown genuine remorse and demonstrated that they are no longer a danger to others.

Alternatively, community referrals to Project Restore can take place without a formal report to a criminal-justice agency. A referral may come from a variety of sources: victims/survivors, their family/whānau, anyone who has caused harm through sexual violence, independent therapists or community agencies. Police may also refer directly to Project Restore in some situations. In all these circumstances we liaise closely with multiple third parties to ensure no further victimisation, that public risk is considered and minimised, that the legal rights of all parties are clear, and that there is agreement over what happened. In the absence of a clear guilty plea (which would occur in the criminal system), we need to be clear as to exactly what harm is being addressed.

WHAT DOES RESTORATIVE JUSTICE DO?

While the role of the law is predominantly punitive and requires little agency by those harmed, the role of restorative justice attends to the needs of those harmed in a relational way that allows healing and recovery. Restorative justice may also be seen as preventative as it supports harm-doers getting help so they don't continue their harmful sexual behaviour.

A sense of justice can be experienced by the survivor via conversations that are genuinely meaningful to them personally and to their whānau or extended family. The process gives the survivor a voice: the opportunity to ask questions of the offender and to clarify what happened. They can experience an offender taking responsibility for their actions, demonstrating accountability, and may receive an apology from the offender.

A key question that might be asked of the survivor is: What does justice look like to you? Often the survivor wants the impacts to be acknowledged and validated and to be reassured that the offending will not happen again.

All this is said in a restorative conference between the parties, which is audio recorded so those involved can have a record of the process. A transcript of the recording is the basis of the report to the court.

In a court of law, the victim impact statement is read out by the survivor or their representative. Such a delivery can never truly represent the depth of emotions experienced by a survivor of sexual violence. In a restorative justice process, this statement is delivered by the survivors themselves or someone they choose to do so on their behalf. The delivery is usually much more emotive and powerful given that it is spoken directly to the person who harmed them. Some survivors have been disappointed when the offender has not agreed to meet as they really want to be able to tell them directly that what they did was not okay.

Having an offender answer a victim's questions is a key part of restorative justice that also makes it distinct from the criminal-justice proceedings. It is not uncommon for survivors to have experienced or witnessed other forms of abuse and to have concerns about a number of connected issues. In these cases, if the offender is open to meeting and can provide the survivor with answers and clarity, the survivor is able to move forward with some sense of peace.

It is common for young people and children to be scared that the person who harmed them will be angry with them for revealing the abuse. Hearing directly from the perpetrator that this is not the case can be reassuring and can lift the burden of guilt they often feel.

Common outcomes for the survivor include:
- A deep, genuine understanding that the sexual harm they experienced is not their fault.
- An understanding of the context in which the offending took place from the perspective of the offender. This is often very humanising — which also helps in moving forward.
- A sense of having been heard and supported through the process by those close to them.
- The development of a support network moving forward into the future so they are not carrying the burden of harm alone.
- Strengthened relationships with significant non-offending family members, such as parents, siblings, etc.

And for the offender:
- A greater understanding of the full impact of their offending.
- Often because of the above, a determination not to reoffend, and a deeper understanding of themselves and their behaviour.
- The opportunity to extend an apology. This is a sensitive issue that calls on Project Restore's specialists to be extremely vigilant. If the child is in the room (which mostly they are not, as they are represented by a guardian/adult), then there could ordinarily be issues around imbalances of power. It is the natural tendency for a child to want to please (and feel pressured to 'forgive'), and potentially the offender could reapply manipulative practices. For this reason, any face-to-face interactions between a child and an offender tend to be brief. The specialists can call breaks, and closely facilitate this dialogue.

It should be noted that while Project Restore offers a systemic solution unique to New Zealand in its particular form, many Māori are also engaging in their own restorative processes on the marae.

We have worked together with Māori to tailor processes that meet the specific needs of individual cases so that restorative conferences can take place on the marae. In these cases, tikanga is followed to support whānau to heal and move forward. It is vital to have a cultural guide to avoid imposing Western processes and value systems.

THE RESTORATIVE JUSTICE PROCESS

At least seven people will be present at a restorative justice conference: the survivor, the survivor's support person, the survivor specialist, the offender, the offender's support person, the offender specialist and the specialist conference facilitator. It is critical to the success of the conference that there is a significant level of trust between the practitioners — the survivor specialist, the offender specialist and the restorative justice facilitator — to support a safe process where the survivor's needs are held as the foremost priority.

The venue for the restorative conference will depend on where the survivor or offender is located. However, if the offender is imprisoned, a special room within the prison is made available. The room is generally set up with the chairs in a circle, with the survivor contributing to seating arrangements of participants, as this gives them control to find the best place to sit in relation to the offender. A no-surprises approach is vital to ensure the safety of all present, hence there may be some information shared with the parties before the meeting. For example, the offender may not remember all the details described by the survivor; this will be shared with the survivor.

When young children are survivors they may attend only part of the conference to ask questions of the offender and hear the response. In such situations, the Project Restore survivor specialist or their therapist will have helped them formulate their questions. Young survivors typically might say: 'If you do this again, you're going to jail.' Importantly, when young survivors are participating, the conference room is organised in such a way that they feel emotionally safe and protected from direct contact with the offender.

The conference process usually begins with the offender acknowledging the offending, and explaining why they offended, in as much detail as they can at this stage, and how they now feel about what they have done. Then the survivor is able to ask any questions of the offender; again, because of a no-surprises approach, these have been shared with the offender at an earlier date. The survivor is able to then share the impact of the offending. The decision about who speaks first is negotiated prior to the conference so that everyone is comfortable with the process.

The final part of the conference is determining outcomes. This is not just about moving on, but also about how to mitigate future risk. Desired outcomes of the conference are discussed in advance with both the survivor and the perpetrator but final agreements are made in the conference. This may include encouraging the offender to seek treatment. Although this can't be mandated, Project Restore follows up the post-conference actions of the offender.

Safety planning, future contact, name suppression, survivor needs, and establishing who has access to the restorative justice report are generally discussed. Reparation may be negotiated in the form of financial compensation, although this can be complex, given that it is not legally binding. A survivor may wish to be informed of the offender's treatment progress, and this can be facilitated by Project Restore if requested.

The whole process can be very powerful, as the full impact of the offending is acknowledged and this is witnessed by everyone present. For some offenders, there is a 'lightbulb' moment in which they suddenly experience real remorse and empathy. Changes are often clearly visible in the faces and bodies of the survivor and the offender as well as their support people. Various participants have described a feeling of lightness; when the offender takes responsibility, it is as if a burden has been lifted.

While the restorative justice process utilises therapeutic interventions, it is not a substitute for therapy or counselling. The survivor specialist works alongside the therapist/counsellor in a collaborative way. Many of the staff at Project Restore have had experience in working with the agencies that offer therapy/counselling to assist both survivors and offenders. Project Restore is unique in that it is based on research and has drawn on the expertise of many of the survivor-helping agencies and offender-specialist support agencies, as well as independent therapists working with sex offenders.[1]

RESTORATIVE JUSTICE PROCESSES FOR CHILDREN

The documentation covering restorative justice standards for sexual offending requires that consultation with a child specialist occurs whenever there are children present at a conference.[2] This is one reason why Project Restore ensures only highly experienced people work in this field. It is especially important that children have a protective caregiver, are matched with a suitable counsellor and given access to ongoing therapy outside of the restorative justice process.

The appropriateness of having children at a restorative justice conference is given much consideration. Even the act of asking a child whether they would like to attend a conference can result in re-traumatisation. Each case is unique and requires specialised assessment to know how to proceed. Our team is experienced in this evolving and dynamic risk-assessment process. It is not at all unusual for siblings to be sexually abused over a prolonged period of time by a close relative. In such cases, it could be possible that it is considered appropriate for one sibling to participate in a restorative process but inappropriate for the other. The Project Restore team designs a process that suits everyone's needs and minimises risk for all potential participants. Progressing slowly could enable both siblings to participate to a level that ensures no further harm occurs to either of them.

The age and, more importantly, the mental and emotional capacity of the child is also important. Generally, if the child is over 16 years of age they are likely to be able to give informed consent. If they are younger then it is not appropriate. However, the survivor specialist will work with the child in collaboration with their guardian and therapist. If the survivor has been selected (or groomed) based on their perceived vulnerability, due to possible family dysfunction or neglect, then it is even more critical that the child's needs are protected.

When children who are survivors of harm caused by sexual violence decide not to attend or are assessed as not ready for a restorative justice conference, a protective parent or caregiver may attend in their place. This can still be validating for the child. In such cases, young persons know that their parents not only believe them but also are prepared to 'go in to bat' for them. If survivors are not able to attend a restorative process, the offender can write personal letters taking responsibility for his or her offending that young survivors can read at a later time when the protective caregiver assesses they are ready.

The inclusion or exclusion of children is not without controversy. There are always certain risks present when only the parents or caregivers are involved. Questions must always be asked and satisfactorily answered around whether a parent or caregiver can comprehensively represent the needs of the child in each and every case. Also, the needs of the parents must be taken into account and could influence how restorative processes proceed.

CHALLENGING DYNAMICS FOR CHILDREN AFFECTED BY SEXUAL VIOLENCE

One of the more challenging dynamics that can arise when sexual violence has occurred in the family, particularly when the victim is a child or young person, is where the mother supports the offender. The resulting breakdown in the relationship between the mother and her child can be as damaging as that caused by the sexual abuse itself.

This is where an understanding of the family violence context is essential. Non-offending parents are in difficult positions. Their circumstances are not always understood by the professionals in their lives and they may feel blamed. Such parents may well be victims of the perpetrator or are being manipulated. This can be quite subtle and not always evident to outsiders.

Family dynamics can serve to perpetuate sexual abuse. When children do not feel supported by parents, they can often feel as though they carry the primary responsibility to keep the family together. The burden of responsibility makes the child much less likely to disclose any abuse due to the impact it may have on others; that is, their parent/s and/or caregiver/s along with wider whānau/family.

This situation requires empathy rather than judgement and presents a very real challenge for Project Restore's specialists. The dynamic needs to be acknowledged prior to a restorative justice conference to help both the non-offending parent and child understand what is happening. Where it is assessed to be suitable for the child to attend the restorative justice conference, the primary support people may include a counsellor and close family member who is protective and can hold the relationship with the non-offending parent. If it is not possible to navigate this issue then it would not be safe to proceed with the restorative justice conference. Project Restore specialists are aware of different cultural contexts which can have an impact on how survivors, offenders, their families and communities contextualise sexual violence and the harm it causes. Culture can also have an impact on the desired outcomes of restorative processes. In such situations, cultural guides are invaluable as they can maximise the benefits of restorative justice and minimise the risks to all those concerned.

WHEN AN ORGANISATION IS INVOLVED WITH THE PERSON RESPONSIBLE FOR SEXUAL HARM

There are two layers to be addressed when a child has been abused by someone in a position of power that stems from their role in an institution, religious order or organisation. The first layer is the offender in person, and the second is the institution or organisation that either failed to protect the survivor or colluded with the offending. When the offender has been lauded as a great person in the community, survivors are often left feeling even more distressed by the harm they have endured.

In instances where the offender is no longer alive, an acknowledgement and apology from the institution, religious order or organisation can help the survivor to feel vindicated. Financial reparation may also be sought as part of the restorative justice process with the institution. However, this can be more challenging if the offender has not been convicted for this particular crime.

BRINGING FAMILIES BACK TOGETHER

One of the compelling reasons to offer restorative justice is to support families impacted by sexual harm to move into the future free from sexual violence. In many situations much work must be undertaken to repair relationships between the survivor and non-offending family members. The preparation for a restorative process must address these relationships and develop capacity in the non-offending family members or intending participants to maximise the opportunity for the survivor to experience a sense of justice and move forward with his or her life.

If a family has been separated because of sexual violence, it is not at all unusual that survivors want their family to be reunited. For this to happen, the safety of the survivor must be assured. The opportunity for restorative justice in such situations is to ensure all participants can access support programmes to help address their particular needs, including an opportunity for the offender to hear and acknowledge the impact of their offending. Over a period of time, through collaboration between the family and the professionals involved in the process, it is possible that a family can be reunited.

Ongoing oversight would be required to ensure that the survivor is recovering from the offence and is kept emotionally, physically and sexually safe from any further harm. Work also would need to continue with the offender to ensure that even though he or she is a loved and valued part of the family, he or she remains accountable for the harm caused. However, it should be noted that it is not always possible to reunite families.

Project Restore offers a unique specialist restorative justice service for people affected by sexual harm that is survivor-centred and culturally appropriate in the New Zealand context.[3] We are deliberate in ensuring that this service continues to fill a gap when criminal proceedings are seen to be inappropriate (and not desired), or when it is appropriate in parallel with the criminal justice system, and that it works with the wider system to focus on the needs of those impacted by harm caused by sexual violence. In particular, Project Restore works to provide trauma-informed best-practice methods that are based on research and specifically designed for children, parents and families. New Zealand children, like children everywhere, must be protected from harm caused by sexual violence and from the lifelong impacts of this type of abuse.

16. The development of constructive sexual behaviours

ROBYN SALISBURY, CLINICAL PSYCHOLOGIST

SEX IS FOR FUN, EXCITEMENT, pleasure, release, reproduction; it is for closeness or for stretching your boundaries. Deconstructing sex psychologically, as I'm about to do, does not make it sound sexy at all, but please keep in mind that my close examination is for a good cause. From a physiological perspective arousal and sex have been described as 'a neurovascular event in a hormonal environment'.[1] While all the organic contributions from conception until the end of life play their role in the development of human sexual behaviours, the exploration of those is largely outside the scope of this book.

Psychologically, what shapes your sex life? How did any of us come to be turned on by the things that turn us on, and to what extent can we change that? You might read this section of the book with an interest in learning more about yourself or exclusively to understand how an individual can develop harmful sexual behaviours involving children. Either way, this is important for your consideration.

Anyone daring to define healthy or constructive versus destructive expressions of sexuality treads on shaky ground. It is easy for one person to impose their personal values onto another. It took a while for past generations of sex therapists to identify and then challenge the unspoken rule-of-thumb diagnostic criterion of compulsive masturbation as 'anyone who masturbates more often than I do'. That said, this book focuses on child sexual abuse in New Zealand, which is illegal and thus clearly designated as destructive for both victim and perpetrator. It makes clear that the impingement of adult sexual needs onto children is injurious. A model of the developmental milestones of sexuality further illustrates the significant disruption caused by child sexual abuse.

Sexuality is complex and even paradoxical, as you will see. Many of us have components of healthy and destructive sexual behaviours; the frequency of affairs affirms that. However, most of us are not at risk of child sexual offending; things have to go seriously awry in the development of sexuality for this risk to arise. I will first examine the 'good enough' development of sexuality, then in the following chapter move on to identifying the factors that can build destructive sexual behaviours.

WHERE DO WE ACQUIRE OUR SEXUAL BEHAVIOURS?

Definitions of healthy sex generally require sexual activities to be consensual (without strings attached or more overt forms of coercion), pleasurable for each person involved, engaged in with awareness and presence and providing a way to connect with partner and/or self. Where do we learn how to do this?

My entrée to working as a therapist was training as a marriage guidance counsellor, where I was fortunate to have the supervision of a sex therapist. It was in working with couples grappling with their relationship problems that I first began to see the impact of our early years on adult behaviour. At first I fought this, telling myself it was such a cliché and it blamed parents. These were adults I was working with. But the many hundreds of couples and individuals I have subsequently seen through my ongoing training and work as a psychotherapist, then as a clinical psychologist, have all undeniably confirmed that the early years play a crucial shaping role.

I do not blame parents; most of us do the best job we know how of raising our children, and of course all children are born with their genetic inheritance of temperament and sensitivity along with physiological components of well-being. The fact remains, however, that anyone raised without enough of the vital input that I now go on to describe misses out on some fundamental life skills. They are also likely to develop an internal working model involving negative beliefs about themselves and important others, and about what they can expect from the world. This means that as children reach the age where they engage with peers and teachers, encountering other valuable learning opportunities, they view these experiences through their internal working model. If this is negative, it skews their ongoing learning.

It is certainly possible to change this by addressing an essential task of adulthood: stop, reflect and take responsibility to heal any hurts; challenge any destructive behaviours; and fill in any gaps. This allows any insecurely attached person to earn a secure attachment for themselves, which opens the door to constructive loving and sexual behaviours. If that task is not completed, the risk is living, parenting and partnering far from optimally.

It's not uncommon to come across jokes and disparaging references about counsellors, therapists and psychologists assuming that it's all the parents' fault or it's all about what happened when you were a child. I can unequivocally state that the fundamental requirement for human well-being, a part of which is the capacity for life-enhancing intimate interpersonal relating, is a range of early life experiences that are pretty well summed up by the concept of secure attachment.[2] This concept is sometimes rejected because many research projects have chosen to focus on the biological mother as the central attachment figure, even though British psychologist John Bowlby, the originator, acknowledged that others could equally be attachment figures. Research currently under way on an updated multidisciplinary theory and parenting support approach which fits cross-culturally has been selected to be the recipient of the income from sales of this book. (See the end of this book for details.)

ATTACHMENT

Wellington clinical psychologist Dr Karen Faisandier has described well what this is and how it is achieved: below is a summary.[3]

> Humans and all other mammals are born with the need to bond with others. We attach to the immediate caregivers who are responsible for feeding, sheltering and supporting us, whether this be a parent or parents, extended family/grandparents/older siblings or others. All attachment experiences, secure and insecure, shape

the nervous system. Secure attachment also optimises learning, growing and developing essential life skills. Important processes that develop during attachment include emotional regulation (the ability to soothe yourself during times of stress and distress), behavioural impulse control (how well you can resist urges and desires) and empathy and compassion (how well you learn to hear the emotional distress in others and respond appropriately).

Your attachment experience as a child is found to persist into adolescence and adulthood unless you improve your attachment status in therapy or other healthy adult relationships, in order to achieve an 'earned secure attachment'. A 'good enough' secure attachment forms the foundation for adult relationships including the ability to seek out and maintain intimacy, closeness and sexual behaviour that is unlikely to cause distress and impairment. It sets someone up for optimal mental health and optimal relationships and also impacts on physical health including a strong immune system.

The children whose caregiver/s respond appropriately enough to their needs often enough learn they are loved and worthwhile; that there are others it is safe to seek comfort from and that the world is mostly a safe place. This set of beliefs about self and other is called a 'working template'. Securely attached children have a template that allows them over time to cope with the initial stress of being away from their primary caregiver/s and then later all other stresses. They have the ability to interact productively with others and to effectively self-soothe.

While meeting a child's physical and cognitive needs is valuable, the crux of a secure attachment is related to emotional distress and how it's handled. A response which accurately resonates with what the child is feeling, like 'Oh I can see you're really disappointed about that; you were hoping to . . .' is far better than caregivers who tell a child to stop crying or that they are 'alright' when they are clearly distressed. This secure attachment approach in no way indulges a child, it simply recognises their feelings and provides a compassionate, soothing response. Around 50 per cent of a population achieve secure attachment, depending on the country/

cultural practice and research study. Infants rub their mouths and genitals when they're trying to soothe themselves and reduce their distress/arousal. Secure infants will stop this behaviour as they learn alternative ways of soothing themselves, first by receiving timely and appropriate comforting from their parents then learning to emotionally self-soothe with the support and encouragement of the parents.

The remaining 50 per cent of the population fall into three adaptive insecure attachment categories (preoccupied, avoidant or disorganised), meaning that the brain develops clever strategies to manage the attachment needs not being met. These shortcomings are not usually the result of any destructive intention from the caregiver/s but rather a child/caregiver temperament mismatch, the caregiver's own attachment style influencing their parenting style and adverse life events such as losses, illness or mental health problems.

It is the insecurely attached who are at risk of developing sexual behaviours that are destructive to self and other. They have a core relational problem in that they do not have the prerequisites for getting their own needs met or for responsible sexual behaviour: these include attuned communication, emotional balance, response flexibility and empathy.

There is more on the impacts of insecure attachment in the next chapter, but before we move on, here's some advice for parents: helping your child achieve secure attachment does not have to mean understanding and responding accurately every time, being with them constantly and never letting them get distressed. Unfortunately, some interpretations of attachment parenting set the bar well beyond what is realistic, necessary or even helpful. Also, be clear that in order to be securely attached children require boundaries, along with opportunities to strive and encouragement to do so. Secure attachment does not make fragile, demanding children; it makes them tougher, more resilient and healthier. Who would not want that for their children?

OPTIMAL SEXUALITY

You don't have to have had a secure attachment to want, give and get non-destructive, very enjoyable sex; but if your fundamental orientation to the world is to mistrust closeness or you don't know how to achieve it, you're not likely to find deep and lasting sexual satisfaction until you address this problem. US sex therapist Sylvia Rosenfeld found the following core themes in her unpublished research on couples who were deeply satisfied with their sexual relationships: contentment, closeness, connection, conscious intention to create romance, commitment, initiation of sexual opportunities, creativity and variety, good humour and communication. Canadian clinical professor, psychologist and sexologist Peggy Kleinplatz later published research that found exactly the same themes.[4] She further identified three key factors that take satisfying sex into the extraordinary: authenticity, being present and vulnerability. Secure attachment, in creating the capacity for all these factors, is a vital ingredient in constructive, deeply satisfying, life-enhancing sexuality.

MILESTONES IN SEXUAL DEVELOPMENT

Erik Erikson's developmental model, shown earlier, describes psychosocial stages achieved (or not) from infancy onwards, throughout the lifespan. In her 1998 book *Sex Smart* Aline Zoldbrod proposes the developmental milestones of sexuality, each of which has to be achieved and passed through in order to move to the next.[5] The field of neuroscience has progressed significantly since Zoldbrod created this model, allowing greater understanding of how the brain works and, in doing so, affirming the validity of this model.

The state known as secure attachment, which develops relationally, can be seen in this model to facilitate children passing through the vital early developmental milestones. Children get to develop their sexuality at their own pace when loving, informed adults provide the right conditions.

Intimacy is just one aspect of sexuality which may or may not be present in any sexual experience; there is much more to explore in understanding sexuality. The concept of intimacy doesn't explain, for example, what turns people on and why erotic turn-ons and turn-offs are so different for different people. Nor does it tell us if sexual preferences are able to be changed and what that requires.

Fig. 16.1: Milestones in sexual development. From Aline Zoldbrod, *SexSmart: How your childhood shaped your sexual life and what to do about it* (1998).

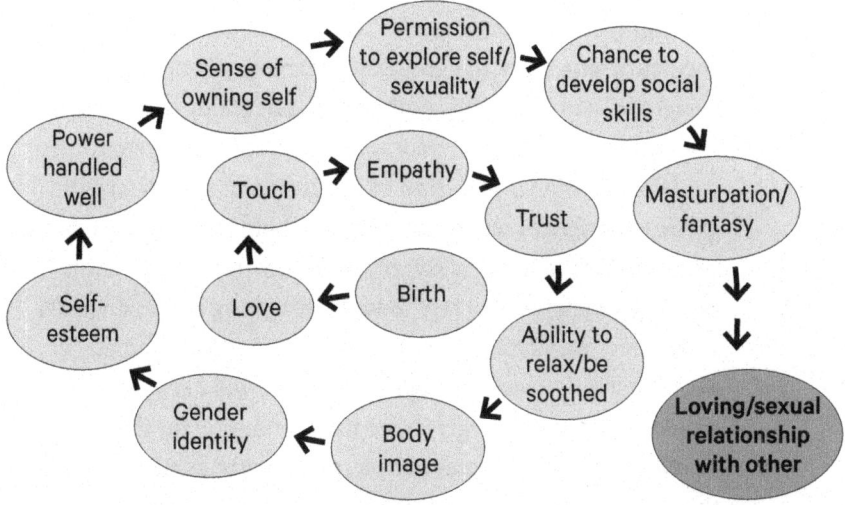

EROTICISM

American psychologist and best-selling author Bernie Zilbergeld identified that 'arousal is the spark to drive good sex'.[6] Does attachment also play a role in arousal? It seems it does, but at times in the opposite way to what may be expected. Recognised as an international authority on eroticism, American sex therapist Jack Morin identified the complex connection between the erotic and our search for emotional closeness and the hopes and fears that accompany that.[7] He says that 'eroticism is the interplay of sexual arousal with the challenges of loving and living', which can also be described as *attraction + obstacles = excitement.*

Morin describes four psychological cornerstones of eroticism, which are expressed uniquely for each individual. These are the often unidentified basic components of turn-ons:

1. Longing and anticipation: Longing directs its attention to what is missing or in short supply. As adults we transfer old feelings of longing towards whomever we desire now. Intermittent partial reinforcement, that is, only very occasionally getting what you long for, increases desire.

2. Violating prohibitions: All societies try to shape sexual behaviour. While this can be a well-intentioned aim to enforce cultural ideals, it has an additional unintended effect of providing readymade obstacles that anyone can use to enhance their turn-ons. This 'naughtiness factor' is most pronounced in societies that try to repress expressions of childhood sexuality (most Western societies). Morin suggests this cornerstone also explains the higher inclusion of naughtiness factors in peak erotic experiences reported by gays, lesbians and Catholics, and why the forbidden nature of affairs makes them all the more exciting. (Society's progress towards accepting sexual diversity, albeit slow, may reduce this naughtiness factor for some.)
3. Searching for power: Inevitable clashes of will between children and their caregivers set the foundation for the development of strategies to overcome powerlessness. Whether those strategies be direct or indirect, the search for power involves overcoming obstacles and establishes some degree of dominance and submission themes as unfailing turn-ons. Both these roles are powerful as they require interaction with the other for their erotic energy. Societal attempts to restrict sexual power imbalances can actually result in increasing the erotic tension by adding in the naughtiness factor. Of course, for the constructive enjoyment of dominant–submissive power struggles, safety and consent have to be established.
4. Overcoming ambivalence: As Morin puts it, 'Everyone is hurt in some way by loving, yet we still long for love. The need to reach out versus the imperative of self-protection is such a fundamental human conflict that it affects all areas of life, including our eroticism.' Ambivalence and its underlying fear becomes one of the obstacles that some find exciting.

Not all people have all four psychological cornerstones operating in their eroticism. Those that are most consistently a part of our early arousal feature most often and most powerfully. While these four cornerstones are the building blocks of eroticism, emotions themselves can be seen as the energisers, our most powerful aphrodisiacs. A degree of pleasure and tension release can be obtained by emotionless sex, but the most powerful encounters need emotion. The emotions that most commonly result from highly arousing sex are satisfaction and exuberance.

There are three main emotional aphrodisiacs or drivers of arousal. Closeness, the first, is not available when it's an obligation or demand and when couples are not differentiated (see below), resulting in merger. Anxiety, the second, can occur in response to perceived potential dangers, and while for some it is a dampener of arousal, for others the risk-taking that results in anxiety enhances arousal. Guilt, the third emotion, learned from around the age of two in response to looks or words of disapproval, evolves into a form of self-policing which, with good parenting, gets integrated as the emotional part of your conscience.

Without those optimal circumstances described in the secure attachment experience that allow the individual to develop a positive sense of self, guilt can become harsh self-condemnation and shame, where the individual thinks they are a bad person. An example of this arises for some children when they are criticised or threatened for masturbating. Guilt can inhibit arousal, but it can also enhance it and energise some people. When guilt is an aphrodisiac, it is usually a self-protective emotional component of violating prohibitions and overcoming guilt and anger. To continue with the above example, masturbation can then become more frequent and more intense for some who are using sexual arousal to overcome shame, anger or fear.

Morin sums this all up succinctly: 'High states of arousal flow from the tension between persistent problems and triumphant solutions.' In this way core erotic themes reflect the search for wholeness. Does this mean a 'problem' is always part of arousal? I would suggest replacing the word 'problem' with 'need'. Attachment experiences during the developmental years of childhood and adolescence play a fundamental role in shaping arousal and eroticism. Then in adulthood the next psychological developmental process required for constructive sexual relating is differentiation.

No one has written better about differentiation than American psychologist and sex therapist David Schnarch.[8] This lifelong developmental process, also described as individuation, involves delving deeply to claim your core solid self while maintaining a relationship with someone you love.

As a form of connecting, differentiation is very different from emotional fusion, which involves losing yourself, either becoming submerged into someone else's character or jointly forming a couple character while not retaining individual selves. Differentiation involves balancing autonomy and connection by balancing two life forces: the drive for individuality and the drive for togetherness (attachment). Giving up one to achieve the other leads to being less of a person with less of a relationship, which is obviously undesirable.

Differentiation involves mutuality: moving forward with your own self-development while being concerned about your partner's happiness and well-being. You can choose to be guided by your partner's best interests, even at the price of your own individual agenda, but that doesn't leave you feeling like you're being ruled by the other's needs. Holding on to yourself allows mutuality — that is, considering your partner's needs and goals and sometimes forgoing immediate gratification in order to go with your deepest values.

Taking care of your own feelings, an integral part of maintaining a relationship, fuels attachment and self-direction. As a differentiated adult you do not expect your partner to take care of your needs, but rather are willing to self-confront and deal with the resulting 'clean pain'. In other words, you acknowledge, name and take responsibility to deal with and release whatever emotion you are experiencing, rather than create 'dirty pain' by defending, denying or deflecting to keep from seeing or doing something. This work of adulthood achieves earned secure attachment in yourself, with all its benefits for well-being and optimal sexuality, regardless of what your growing-up experiences have been.

SOCIETAL IMPACT

All of the above occurs in a larger context: society. How does society shape sexuality, and are those influences positive or negative? To some extent that depends on how much your sexuality reflects what the social order of your country and your era imposes as the 'norm'. You may grow up with optimal secure attachment, allowing you to have good self-esteem and positive expectations from those in your close circle and from the world. But if, for example, you are gay, or your gender does not fit a binary model, you will not fail to observe times when there are negative reactions to women who are deemed, for example, not 'feminine enough' and to men deemed not 'masculine enough', making the task of claiming your own sexual identity and feeling good about yourself all the more challenging. This significant work of leaving the responsibility for oppression with the oppressors and refusing to be shamed is faced by a lot of people, given that nature creates many variations in sexuality.

Societal influence is, of course, even more complex if your sexual orientation involves attraction to minors and thus is illegal and harmful to act on. There is not, nor should there be, the opportunity to make sex with children acceptable. However, as I will go on to explore, society can play important roles in supporting constructive sexuality and in protecting children from child sexual abuse, hence the inclusion of this section in this chapter. Societal shaming pushes people underground, rids them of social support and places them more at risk of destructive sexual behaviour, as described further below.

A society that can be well informed about such things can hold separate the total unacceptability of sexual behaviours of any sort involving children, from compassion for those unfortunate enough to have sexual desires they cannot legally act on. There is, as yet, no certainty about whether some may be born with minor attraction as a sexual orientation or whether post-birth developmental experiences exclusively shape attraction to minors.[9]

Of great relevance to this book, Morin identifies that as eroticism is paradoxical (that is, the impact of any factor could inhibit *or* arouse an individual, according to the circumstances), there is a danger that societal negativity can drive eroticism into the shadows where it's actually most likely to form the shape we fear. Morin suggests we can keep society safer by accepting the paradox and becoming well informed about eroticism, because anything we try to banish from awareness festers in the shadows, eventually breaking into consciousness often in 'bizarre or perverted sexual fantasies that flagrantly disregard both cultural norms and personal values'. And of equal concern, 'shadow fantasies commonly involve manipulation, exploitation, coercion, and a host of other violations, both large and small'. Carl Jung made a similar observation: 'One does not become enlightened by imagining figures of light, but by making the darkness conscious.'[10] Although this procedure is emotionally challenging and therefore not popular, I argue that facing the shadow, at individual and societal levels, is an important aspect of developing constructive sexual behaviour and thus keeping children safe.

American sex therapist, author and blogger Dr Marty Klein highlights another potential destructive result of shaming.[11] He describes shame as leading to sexual secrets, acting out, violence, and what he calls 'sexual exceptionalism', where sex gets treated differently from other aspects of life, in ways that don't serve you or your sexual partners well at all. 'You go to Mary's house for dinner, you tell her how you like your chicken cooked. You go to bed with Mary, you don't tell her you'd like less fingernails on your back. You go hiking with John and you tell him to slow down a bit. You go to bed with John and you don't tell him you wish he'd slow down a bit.' Hence he argues one appeal of the internet for some: there you can anonymously be yourself, own and express your preferences and get your needs met without being shamed.

It seems to have long been a challenge for our New Zealand culture (and we're certainly not alone in the world) to have an open, joyful and accepting, matter-of-fact attitude towards things sexual. Often there are mixed messages: superficially a celebration of the body and all things sensual and sexual, but underneath that an objectification that leaves many women and some men feeling unsafe or that their imperfect bodies are deeply unacceptable and trying to shape them into something currently deemed desirable. Sex is also used to sell products.

Further complicating the development of constructive sexual behaviour, too many parents seem to avoid discussing the whole uncomfortable and admittedly complex topic with their children, who are actually very interested in bodies and how they work and generally will have found their own genitals at an early age and learned how to generate pleasurable feelings from that. Adults comfortable with their own and their children's sexuality can generally avoid shaming children for their natural sensuality and curiousness.

NEXT I WILL EXPLORE A little the impact of the digital world; but first let's acknowledge that, along with the direct societal impacts on sexuality described above, there are also gender-based shaping factors. The enormity of the #MeToo response during the time of writing this book suggests that, as much as we may like to think we are enlightened and have moved well beyond gender stereotypes, boys and girls are still socialised differently. Boys seem to still be taught at some point in their development to not express their feelings, leaving too many with sex as their only means of seeking closeness. The objectification of women and children is still occurring, and too many men still have both a sense of responsibility for and a sense of ownership of women and children. While women are now increasingly speaking up about objectification and harassment, some are still being taught aspects of passivity and are subjecting their bodies to efforts to 'improve' at much greater rates than men do. (This is indicated by such factors as the prevalence of eating disorders and amounts spent on cosmetic products and surgery.) Many individuals of all genders have moved beyond such stereotypes, but too many have yet to do so.

THE IMPACT OF INTERNET-SOURCED SEXUALLY EXPLICIT MATERIAL (SEM)

This is currently such a contentious issue that the research literature overflows with arguments on the potential destructive effects, many of which I see as valid concerns. So why is this piece here in the chapter on how healthy sexual behaviour develops? The internet can and does provide some very helpful, empowering sources of information on all aspects of sexuality. Further, it provides potentially arousing images which have been around in one form or another for centuries and always will be. Some people use erotica destructively, as will be seen in the next chapter; some simply use it as one source of stimulation for individual or partnered sexual activity.

The use of pornography can certainly cause some strain between couples if it is occurring to a degree that reduces couple sex or if there has been no mutually respectful, successful communication about such use. Sometimes frequent masturbation to pornography can result in an individual desensitising themselves to real, partnered sex. They have become so accustomed to high-intensity novel stimulation that engaging with another human being seems distracting or boring in comparison. Sometimes, pornography is blamed for what is actually inconsiderate behaviour or a distancing in a relationship.

Unfortunately the research about SEM/pornography has many shortcomings: it often demonstrates correlations but not causation, and there is no agreement about what constitutes pornography. There is very little done in New Zealand representing our culture/s, and some projects making negative claims are laboratory-based only, so we don't know if the findings can be generalised to society as a whole. What's more, positive outcomes, such as individuals and couples feeling well informed or warmed up to constructive sexual relating by reading or viewing erotica, fail to get reported. Negative findings have often failed to materialise across different bodies of research. There are powerful forces both lobbying against and promoting pornography. The potential for the destructive impact of SEM is explored further in the next chapter.

CONCLUSION

The development of the key life skills that are essential for optimal sexual relating, and for the larger tasks of achieving well-being and being able to successfully live life on life's terms, begin with parenting that is well informed about and helps infants achieve secure attachment. Then through adolescence and adulthood, individuals have the task of achieving differentiation: becoming fully functioning, independent beings. This task is most effectively achieved in relationships: both peer and partner. It is in all of our interests for society to become well informed and able to be matter of fact about issues of eroticism, including the range of expressions of sexuality which nature and nurture manage to produce. All informed efforts to support the development of constructive sexuality will aid a goal of reducing the prevalence of child sexual abuse.

17. The development of destructive sexual behaviours

ROBYN SALISBURY

HAVING ESTABLISHED HOW CONSTRUCTIVE, LIFE-ENHANCING sexuality is formed, turning to the development of destructive sexual behaviours follows quite logically, with some additional twists. We human beings have an almost infinite number of ways of using our sexuality destructively: affairs that breach a loved one's trust, sex with a stranger that is regretted the next morning, and humiliating sexual acts carried out to please or retain a lover, to name a few. But the focus of this chapter is specifically on how some come to extend that destructive sexual behaviour to being sexual abusers of children.

To clarify a side issue: an increasing number of people are recognising that their sexual behaviour is 'out of control' (sometimes referred to as sex or porn addiction). Regardless of the descriptor used, the individual is still responsible for their behaviour. Any such compulsive sexual behaviour can certainly be destructive; however, sexual compulsivity does not necessarily involve attraction to children, and conversely not all child sexual abuse is compulsive. But compulsivity in those attracted to children certainly increases the risk of acting on that attraction.

THE IMPACT OF INSECURE ATTACHMENT ON SEXUALITY

Just as secure attachment is a useful overview concept to illustrate the development of life-enhancing sexual and intimacy capacity, so insecure attachment is equally useful in identifying what can be central to the development of destructive sexual behaviours. Glyn Hudson-Allez, a British psychologist and psychosexual therapist, shows how secure attachment and its insecure counterpart have significant implications both for observable behaviours and for the chemicals found in the bloodstream.[1] Secure attachment orients the infant to repeat behaviours found to be effective at getting their needs met, thus releasing calming, feel-good hormones into the bloodstream. Insecure attachment puts the individual in the position of often, if not always, experiencing all the discomfort of stress hormones. This discomfort then drives the search for pleasure and a state of calm to external sources, often with destructive consequences, as further described below.

Fig. 17.1: A secure attachment bond produces endogenous opiates in the brain and peptides that stimulate the pleasure centres. The insecure attachment template produces only stress hormones, so people search for pleasurable feelings externally. From Glyn Hudson-Allez, *Infant Losses* (2011).

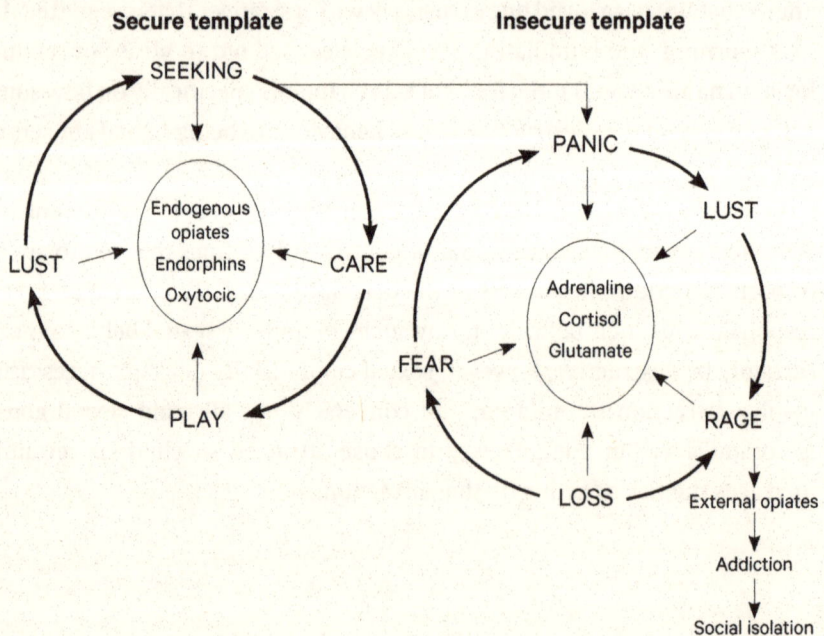

This diagram highlights the role sexual lust can play in driving that external search for feel-good hormones to provide comfort in response to fear and even panic. The insecurely attached individual is unable to achieve calmness in constructive, internal ways until taught to do so. As American psychologist and researcher in the field of neuropsychology Alan Schore has shown, for the insecurely attached, the infant's first spontaneous emotion learned outside of the mother is the fear of loss from rejection or abandonment.[2] Constantly searching for a secure base, this sense of fear is so great for the insecure child (and, later, adult) that it's a struggle to tolerate the extreme emotions triggered by the amygdala, the alarm centre in the brain. Instead, as life progresses, various substances or behaviours — food, drugs, alcohol, sex, work, shopping, online gaming or other activities, gambling or religion — are desperately used to stimulate the dopamine pathways to provide soothing of a kind.

Alternatively, some individuals restrict and control their access to any pleasure or comfort in endeavouring to create a sense of strength and security. Insecure attachment does not necessarily create destructive sexual behaviours, but this adapted drive to achieve self-soothing can create a range of self-destructive and potentially other-destructive behaviours. This process can feel addictive precisely because it provides a soothing that can't be accessed from internal sources, so there is always a drive to find more. The sense of compulsivity is of great concern as it involves the continued use of a substance or activity, despite the resulting harm.

Bruce Perry, a psychiatrist and international child trauma expert, summed this up in a training workshop by describing how the pull to any 'drug' is determined by the pleasure it delivers in comparison to the pleasure you get from everything else.[3] Insecurely attached people will get greater pleasure and anxiety relief from their 'drug' of choice than they are currently capable of getting from meaningful contact with self and other. Such adaptations bring only very temporary relief and often lead to social isolation, thus increasing vulnerability. This can result in relationally deprived adults with reduced opportunities to alter their attachment status from insecure to earned-secure. In contrast, the opiates available from the interpersonal interaction of the securely attached, as shown above, calm the individual, contribute to warmth and security, and further enhance social bonding.

A fundamental problem for those missing out on the 'good enough' attunement and responsiveness that results in secure attachment, is that the primary caregiving relationship/s that infants are reliant on become a source of threat rather than comfort. Attachment research has demonstrated that insecurely attached children have to develop a range of adaptive behaviours, often problematic as described above, in order to cope. It is definitely possible to later make changes and achieve secure attachment with the help of quality input from a loving other and/or a skilled professional, but without that input insecure attachment and its accompanying behaviours tend to remain into adulthood and throughout a person's lifespan. The variety of behaviours associated with insecure attachment has led to the description of three primary categories, referred to internationally by various names but basically:

- Avoidant attachment: These children shut down visible signs of distress and detach from their own internal signals. In the face of neglect or abuse they have learned this is their best way to deal with the pain of longing. Emotions and closeness are experienced as overwhelming and to be avoided.
- Preoccupied attachment: Children in this category tend to experience their needs and emotions as overwhelming. They cannot trust that anyone will ever be there for them, they are often clingy, they tend to amplify their distress, and should anyone offer appropriate responses they are not able to take it in and be comforted by it.
- Disorganised attachment: This category is associated with severe abuse, neglect or other trauma. These children learn that life is unpredictable as the biological drive to seek comfort is countered by the biological drive to escape danger. They have a high degree of emotional arousal and swing between the two strategies above, experiencing neither as helpful.

Some people relate to aspects of each of these categories. It's evident from these behavioural descriptions why those who are insecurely attached will struggle to find and give satisfaction in intimate relationships, with all the potential consequences previously outlined.

We have seen how the omission of fundamental emotional attunement and responsiveness (secure attachment requirements) and/or the occurrence of traumatic experiences lead to reduced emotional regulation skills and the need to seek external sources of pleasure and calming. International child trauma expert John Briere sums up these harmful circumstances as 'acts of omission or commission'.[4] Briere has developed a Reactive Avoidance Model to add to this explanation. He differentiates explicit memories (memories you can consciously remember) from implicit memories (which come from pre-verbal years, or which may have been stored away without description because of the overwhelm of trauma). He has demonstrated that early childhood maltreatment or mis-attunement can create painful implicit memories and attachment disturbance. This then leads to reduced emotional regulation skills and a set of triggers, the most distressing of which are interpersonal.

When the implicit memory system is triggered, this leads to re-enactment. The individual experiences no choice to remember or not remember. It's hard to differentiate in the moment between a justified reaction to a here-and-now event, and a re-enacted implicit memory (the intrusion of early feelings and 'primitive' thoughts). The individual develops distress reduction behaviours, as shown on the secure–insecure attachment template diagram, one of which can be sexual offending. In heightened activation circumstances the hippocampus and explicit memory system shuts down and the amygdala and implicit memory ramps up. These changes make a person more reactive and less rational. Along with the dysfunctional behaviour comes the source–attribution–error problem. This is where activated distress is relived as a new event and beliefs formed from this new event are also dysfunctional — for example the individual blames the other, rather than recognising they have been triggered.

More generally, the society an individual lives within has been suggested to have a potential negative impact on sexual behaviour, increasingly so with the insecurely attached. American author and trainer Phil Rich argues that given the way in which contemporary Western society uses sex as a commodity, it's not surprising that so many individuals with insecure attachments develop maladaptive sexual strategies as a way of coping with their inability to regulate the extremes of their emotions. 'Sex is desirable and endows special properties onto those who engage in and control it, including power, adulthood, masculinity, special knowledge, pleasure and prestige.'[5] Sex is also, of course, used as a powerful marketing tool. This can contribute to insecure, lonely, stressed or depressed individuals using sex as a way of trying to change how they feel about themselves.

WE HAVE SEEN HOW INSECURE attachment can put an individual at risk of destructive behaviours, including sexual behaviour. Now we need to begin addressing the shaping of the erotic template or internal working model: What determines the 'who' and the 'how' of sexual attraction? What is known about the determinants of children being the focus of sexual behaviour?

From an early study of sex offenders, psychologist Professor Tony Ward, who is a contributor to this book, and his colleagues found that different insecure attachment styles can be related to different forms of sexual offending.[6] Again, keep in mind that not all insecurely attached adolescents or adults sexually offend — there has to be the lining up of the multitude of variables outlined in this chapter — but for the minority who do, this research found that learnt preferences, skills deficits and the resulting chemical/hormonal differences described previously did appear to shape offending.

THE IMPACT OF CHILD SEXUAL ABUSE ON SEXUALITY

Being sexually abused yourself in no way necessarily makes you into a sexual abuser, but it is another risk and shaping factor for destructive sexual behaviour, particularly for the insecurely attached. Child sexual abuse is harmful, often deeply so. With help and/or great internal fortitude survivors can become resilient, constructive and fulfilled in their lives. For those with secure attachment, the process of recovery from trauma, while still significant, is more straightforward as they already possess the emotional regulation, basic trust and other capacities and skills that trauma resolution requires.

Without the appropriate help to process the experience, insecurely attached children will find themselves with overwhelmingly distressing feelings, which they deal with by either engaging in the insecure template and seeking external methods of self-soothing or by a common trauma response: dissociating. This state of complete detachment includes the inability to think or feel about what has and is happening and the inability to take action to achieve safety.

Martin Dorahy, director of the clinical psychology programme at the University of Canterbury, identifies the role of shame in the victim's sexual behaviour following child sexual abuse.[7] Because they are developmentally not powerful enough to get appropriately angry at the offender (and in the case of a known perpetrator may well love them, too), the child transforms the humiliation of having their body exposed and violated into shame, to cover up hostile feelings. Dissociation is used to maintain this state and, because it is likely to result in impaired risk self-assessment, this puts the abused child at further risk. In the small percentage who go on to offend against others, shame and the resulting dissociation also play a role in disconnecting from any victim empathy and feelings of reparatory guilt.

In a teaching presentation, international child trauma expert Charlotte Dalenberg suggested that child sex offenders may be motivated by catastrophic loneliness. They want their victims to experience a trauma just like theirs so that someone else knows what they feel/felt like, and for that brief time they are no longer alone.

Child sexual abuse creates other particular characteristics, too, that can, for a small percentage of those abused, shape the resulting coping be-haviours towards the sexual abuse of children. US family violence researchers David Finkelhor and Angela Browne have found that where childhood trauma is sexual abuse there are four trauma-causing factors, some of which are common to other kinds of trauma (for example witnessing or being a victim of physical violence), but which in totality co-occur only with sexual abuse.[8] These four dynamics alter children's cognitive and emotional orientation to the world and distort their self-concept, world view and emotional capacities.

Traumatic sexualisation refers to a process in which a child's sexual feelings and attitudes develop dysfunctionally as a result of sexual abuse. It occurs when a child is repeatedly used by an offender for sexual behaviour for which the child is not developmentally ready. Through the exchange of affection, attention and/or gifts for sexual behaviour, the child learns to use sexual behaviour as a strategy for manipulating others to satisfy a variety of developmentally appropriate needs. Traumatic sexualisation also occurs when certain parts of a child's anatomy are fetishised and given distorted importance, and through the misconceptions about sexual behaviour and sexual morality that are transmitted to the child from the offender. It further occurs when very frightening memories and events become associated in the child's mind with sexual activity.

Sexual abuse experiences vary a lot in regard to the degree and kind of traumatic sexualisation they cause. Experiences in which the offender evokes a sexual response in a child are likely to be more sexualising than those in which an offender uses a passive child to masturbate with. Enticing a child to participate is also likely to be more sexualising than when using force, although with force a form of traumatic sexualisation can occur as a result of the fear that becomes associated with sex after such an experience. How much the child understands can also affect the degree of sexualisation. At an early developmental level, not understanding the sexual implications of the activities may be less sexualising (though no less traumatic) than sexual abuse of a child with greater awareness. Children who have been traumatically sexualised learn inappropriate sexual behaviours, develop skewed sexual self-concepts and have unusual emotional associations to sexual activities.

Betrayal occurs when children have been harmed by someone they are reliant on for their survival. The impact of this betrayal is profound and long-lasting.

Powerlessness is experienced in sexual abuse when a child's body is violated with the consequence of all the inherent harm described earlier. This is exacerbated by whatever coercion and manipulation the offender uses as part of the abuse process. The failure of any attempts to be believed and to halt the abuse reinforces this sense.

Stigmatisation occurs through badness or shame being communicated to the child around the experiences. These negative feelings then become incorporated into the child's self-image and impair their self-worth. In the wake of a sexual abuse experience some children are heavily shamed, whereas others are told clearly that they are not at fault. However, even those not overtly shamed can carry a sense of shame due to the complexities previously described.

Children's attempts to cope with the world through these distortions may result in some of the behavioural problems that are commonly noted in victims of child sexual abuse. It's easy to see how each of these dynamics can potentially impact negatively on the developing sexual template, creating self-destructive or other-destructive behaviour.

POTENTIAL SEXUAL IMPACTS OF OTHER FORMS OF CHILD TRAUMA

It's not only child sexual abuse trauma that can impact on the healthy development of the sexual internal working model. Any emotional trauma also has a detrimental effect on attachment, child or adolescent health and well-being,[9] thereby, as we have seen, increasing the risks of later destructive sexual behaviour.

American psychiatrist and trauma expert Bessel van der Kolk has suggested that as the imprint of trauma is found in the limbic system and the brainstem (non-thinking parts of the brain), and as the amygdala (responsible for flight and fight) can remain hypersensitive long after trauma, sexual behaviour can be a way for a trauma survivor to relieve numbness or hyperarousal — that is, to regulate the nervous system.[10]

Forensic psychotherapist Estela Welldon adds to this regulation of the nervous system understanding from a lifetime of working with serious offenders. She identifies sexual offending as a 'manic defence against the dreaded black hole of depression',[11] a survival instinct in those whose developmental years did not provide the basics for well-being. She also notes the extreme lengths to which many trauma-surviving offenders go in order to avoid traumatic memories, thus maintaining an offending cycle if they do not receive effective treatment to resolve trauma.

Another factor can be the intergenerational transfer of trauma. This is where children's psychological well-being is impacted on by such unresolved consequences of the parents' trauma as anxiety, emotional dysregulation or denial, even though the children were not personally exposed to the original trauma.[12]

American professor of psychiatry Robert Stoller outlined an early psychoanalytic perspective in which sexual offending arises from poor parental handling of the childhood experiences of struggling to master the tensions of each libidinal stage: the struggle for control versus humiliation.[13] Humiliation shapes the erotic life only when a parental act of aggression such as sexual or physical abuse is aimed at those parts of the body concerned with erotic or gender behaviour. Then, as an adult, identifying with the aggressor becomes the driver: by acting out the destructive urge the sex offender converts his trauma to triumph. He can make his victim feel powerless, humiliated, terrified, and he can feel in control. The desire to hurt, harm or humiliate is essential to getting turned on. Sexual behaviour is the focus, rather than the partner being the focus — the dangers of intimacy are too great. Rather than lead to intimacy, as it can do in constructive sexuality, eroticism is used as a defence against intimacy.

Parental humiliation is generally seen now to potentially impact more widely on self-concept and emotional regulation, creating a sense of shame, anxiety and low self-esteem. As shown above, these consequences can then play a role in shaping destructive sexual behaviours.

Similarly to Stoller, American psychology professor Raymond Bergner argues that sexual compulsion is a momentarily gratifying but ultimately unsuccessful attempt to recover from degradation, leaving the individual feeling more degraded than before and thus setting them up in a compulsive cycle.[14] For therapy to be successful, it has to address both the drive (the engine of the behaviour, which is the felt sense of degradation) *and* the urge to recover from it.

John Money, a New Zealand-born psychologist and sexologist who worked in the United States from the 1950s onwards, is credited with creating the term 'love map'.[15] This was an early step towards current understanding of a sexual template. He argued that when the right hemisphere of the brain is developing — before age three, and again between five and nine — and the amygdala pathway triggering extreme and unregulated emotion is open, any markedly negative situation corrupts the construction of an appropriate sexual template.

He proposed that paraphilias ('atypical' sexual desires: a term still being used as a diagnostic category when sexual preferences and/or behaviours cause clinically significant distress or impairment) are not generated at random. Rather, he suggested, they are due to a vandalised love map caused by the neglect, traumatisation or suppression of the natural love map development. This creates distortions, omissions or inclusions in the individual's sexual repertoire. This love map pathology manifests in full after puberty and is not subject to voluntary control. Money believed that paraphilias are essentially a developmental disability. While he may well have made some useful contributions towards our understanding of sexual development, he has also been shown to have reflected the prejudices of his era, not least in his very narrow definitions of 'normal'.

In contrast, Jesse Bering, an American research psychologist and author who is currently working at New Zealand's University of Otago, suggests that some children are born with paraphilias.[16] He also acknowledges, however, that the mix of factors that determines an individual's sexuality includes genes, prenatal experiences, brain chemistry, early childhood events, family dynamics, cultural milieu and untold others.

Significant research since Money's era, such as that of Feliti et al. (cited above), has certainly established the ways in which vulnerable populations are formed by adverse childhood experiences. Glyn Hudson-Allez has shown that, through its impact on the formation of the HPA axis (hypothalamic–pituitary–adrenal axis — the central nervous system and endocrine system that together form our central stress-response system), childhood trauma predisposes a child to compulsivity or addiction disorders. The unregulated emotions of an insecurely attached child impact on their behaviour and others' responses to them. The adverse experience is then incorporated into the sexual template. Faced with events that cause extreme emotions of fear, rage and anxiety, an insecure child does not know how or where to turn to for soothing. Oral and genital soothing turns into sexual soothing while they suppress and repress their negativity and turn it firstly onto themselves.

All adolescents experience brain changes that involve pruning out any seldom-used connections formed in childhood between brain cells. Hudson-Allez identifies that in the insecurely attached adolescent these usual brain changes can have dangerous consequences, as options for constructive self-soothing are removed due to disuse. Brains with insufficiently developed adaptive coping strategies may develop amygdala-driven fear states without the ability to stop, think through a situation and choose appropriate action. This could be emotionally overwhelming and can lead to aggression. These adolescents become passive responders to their internal fear states, and their behaviour of course promotes what at a deep level they most unconsciously fear: parental rejection and abandonment. Sex becomes a means of comfort and a search for attachment and can lead to inappropriate sexual behaviour, including child sexual abuse.

Hudson-Allez reports a consistent finding in the literature that a large majority of paedophiles were victims of abuse or trauma in their own childhoods. As we have seen, this inevitably affects their attachment styles and for a minority can lead to inappropriate sexual behaviour, more commonly after the age of eight or nine when the sexual template 'comes online'. She reports that by the time they reach the age of 15, 40 per cent of those traumatised young people whose problematic template involves sexual attraction to children will have already molested a child.

It is clear from this summary of some pertinent literature that if childhood trauma of any form occurs, then children are more at risk of forming destructive behaviours as part of their adaptive coping mechanisms. This risk is greater if they reach adolescence without help to resolve traumatic experiences and achieve secure attachment. Some of the destructive coping behaviour can be sexual, and can involve child sexual abuse. While it is by no means the case that all children who are sexually abused become sexual offenders, it does seem that most child sexual offenders have experienced childhood trauma in some form.

ADULT EROTICISM AND CHILD SEXUAL ABUSE BEHAVIOUR

As outlined in the previous chapter, Jack Morin describes from his work with adults how an individual's core erotic themes, the greatest turn-ons, reflect childhood struggles.[17] He further demonstrates the complexity of sexual behaviour: for example, if the pain of an inability to get the love you needed from a parent is a key problem, then it doesn't lead to you seeking out someone consistently loving, as that would feel alien. Rather, the template leads to attraction to someone who shows ambivalence towards loving. Then if you can get him/her to change their mind, this leads to moments of wonderful, powerful passion when you feel successful. The goal, he suggests, is not to perpetuate the pain by re-enacting but, in the process of re-enacting, to reverse the pain and achieve passion. This finding is consistent with child attachment and trauma research.

While all this may sound like yet more highly complex psychological theorising for what is sometimes described as a basic physiological drive, it is very consistent with the observations of many sex therapists. It also adds to the understanding of the drive to sexually offend using children and the precursors of this drive. Morin enlarges: 'Despite the pain problematic attractions ultimately cause, at critical moments they are gloriously successful at generating ecstatic passion.' Hence the intensity and power of the most exciting turn-ons.

Further, if an individual's eroticism began evolving at a time when experiencing persistent feelings of inferiority (an effect of neglect and abuse), then 'low self-esteem fuses with high arousal', and the results are the most destructive of all turn-ons. Sex can be intensely exciting but neither pleasurable nor satisfying, and the only way to escape the resulting self-hatred is to repeat the pattern; thus the behaviour becomes compulsive and the risk escalates. The psychological process of conditioning (as first demonstrated in Pavlov's famous experiments with dogs) also impacts significantly with sexual arousal. Morin found passionate experiences to be potent reinforcers, no matter what other pain is associated with those passionate moments.

THE IMPACT OF PORNOGRAPHY AND DIGITAL PERVASIVENESS

What is regarded as pornography changes with time, along with other societal trends. A child's exposure to any form of sexually explicit material (SEM) can potentially be harmful in prematurely sexualising them. If not given appropriate support to process what they have seen, the images may be distressing or even overwhelming. As mentioned in the previous chapter, research into the impact of SEM is inconclusive. However, correlations have been shown between more frequent consumption of pornography and youth having unrealistic sexual values and beliefs, higher levels of permissive sexual attitudes, lower self-concept, sexual preoccupation and earlier sexual experimentation.

Pornography that depicts violence has been linked by some with increased sexually aggressive behaviour. Additionally, some research suggests that adolescents who use pornography have lower degrees of social integration, more behavioural problems, a higher incidence of depressive symptoms and decreased emotional bonding with caregivers. Causal connection or direction has not yet been established.

Any pornography involving children is by legal definition a crime scene; the capturing and exchange of such images are child sexual abuse and are thus harmful to children. Illegal internet activities include downloading illegal child images, trading these images with others, producing illegal images of children and contacting minors via the internet for sexual reasons.

The internet operates on market forces of supply and demand; if no one wanted to visit child sexual abuse sites, then few would be available.

Whether viewing SEM is harmful for adults (those featured or those viewing), and an example of destructive sexual behaviour or not, depends on many things. These include your political and moral values, shared agreements reached or not reached within relationships, the duration and intensity with which the material is used and what drives that use. If SEM is a 'drug of choice' from the insecure template, then using it is likely to feel or come to feel compulsive. This puts the viewer at much more at risk: increased tolerance, desensitisation and arousal escalation may result in seeking out more and more edgy materials. As a result, an adult who begins looking online at adult–adult pornography can move into viewing child sexual abuse material.

It also appears that those selling pornography can push the viewers' boundaries by gradually exposing them to materials that stretch their original viewing boundaries. This 'marketing strategy' can catch out formerly law-abiding citizens intent on constructive sexuality, with no minor-attraction previously in their sexual template. Neil Holden has described in his chapter that the police are increasingly seeing this phenomenon.

Anecdotal evidence from sex therapists suggest that those with attention deficit problems resulting in a struggle to stay focused are especially susceptible to becoming reliant on pornography. They and others may become so accustomed to the high levels of visual novelty and stimulation which come with internet porn that the combination of attending to another's arousal, holding their own arousal and reaching orgasm in interaction with a live partner may feel impossible. It's also the case that some things blamed on pornography can be simply bad behaviour, for example pressuring a partner to do things one wants.

Do images create reality? There is disagreement on whether the stimulation of viewing child porn leads to acting out the fantasies. Tolerance or desensitisation is hypothesised to be associated with the urge to escalate in order to keep building arousal. The trancelike 'seeking circuit state' is proposed to flood the mind, interfering with rational thought. There is evidence that those who sexually abuse children have often viewed such materials online. But there is no evidence that such viewing, while illegal in itself, necessarily leads to contact offending. Some viewers appear to have sufficient impulse control, and/or respect for or fear of the law, to avoid contact offending. Or the viewing itself fulfils the need. Or they are not caught in the act of contact offending. Hudson-Allez suggests that for the insecurely attached, the internet comes to feel like a supportive resource that will never abandon: it always provides more, and it's under the user's control.

While not necessarily involving SEM, the extent to which some young people now carry out their social life online, believing that to be meaningful friendship, can leave them vulnerable to not getting their esteem and other needs met effectively and not developing all the skills of effective intimate relationships. Often referred to as 'digital natives', these young people were born into a world where devices providing instant gratification have always been available. In this way the challenges of establishing real-life relationships may never be engaged with and achieved, thus maintaining vulnerability to being victimised and also to developing harmful sexual behaviour as described in the insecure attachment cycle.

Forensic psychologist and sexologist Michael Seto (like Bering, as noted earlier) identifies the possibility that paedophilia is an inborn sexual orientation.[18] He further argues that paedophilic arousal or fantasy, including consumption of sexually harmful online images of children, does not in itself predict contact sexual abuse of children. Rather, major predictors of acting on that fantasy are antisocial traits, the disinhibiting effects of substance abuse, high sex drive, the presence of mental illness and low empathy for the victim. Isolation has also been shown to increase the risk of offending.

He also found that conditioning from early sexual experiences with other children, and the resulting pairing of the physical cues of a young partner with sexual pleasure and arousal, can create enduring sexual interest in children. However, as not all those who have early sexual experiences become paedophiles, he suggests that conditioning is an explanatory factor only for those predisposed by insecure attachment, trauma and inadequate social skills.

In summary, it does seem that the persistent and intense use of SEM arises from a combination of neurological, dopamine-based brain changes and, as described by Morin and others, efforts towards the mastery of past trauma. Anecdotal evidence from sex therapists confirms Morin's finding that individuals seek out porn which reflects their core erotic themes, and that one reason for persisting with its use is because each time they achieve orgasm they have a brief sense of triumphing over a past or present humiliation.

Jay Feierman, an American biologist studying animal models, created a male brain chemistry model of embryonic brain masculinisation and brain feminisation. He suggested that paedophiles had slightly more masculinisation than 'normal males', thus exacerbating the 'usual' masculine attraction to those smaller and weaker than themselves, and slightly less defeminisation, making them less likely to be attracted to 'typical [adult] feminine behaviours'.[19] However, there is as yet no evidence in the field of neuroendocrine research on humans to back this theory.

THE MODELS AND THEORIES DESCRIBED above identify potential precursors of CSA. Of course none of them justifies or excuses destructive sexual behaviour on children. As has already been stated, ultimately the only cause of CSA is that someone has made a choice to gratify their own sexual needs by using a child. And yet to understand the shaping of destructive sexual behaviours is to understand some, if not all, of the drivers of child sexual abuse. From a comprehensive understanding, prevention and treatment efforts can be made more effective.

Can destructive sexual behaviours be changed? There's a big difference between changing one's behaviour and changing who you are. The former is certainly possible, the latter less so. When sexual preferences are conditioned into behaviour following insecure attachment or other child trauma they become open to the possibility of deconditioning and becoming extinguished. Achieving an earned secure attachment in adulthood plays a crucial role in that process. As noted above, those who violate the rights of others may be diagnosed with an antisocial or narcissistic personality disorder. While neither of these disorders necessarily involves child sexual abuse, some who sexually offend may well fit the diagnostic criteria for these disorders. However, these disorders are not generally accepted as causal factors.

Where sexual attraction to children is experienced as an exclusive sexual orientation or has been powerfully, repeatedly reinforced by highly arousing experiences, it is imprinted into the person, tends to be stable over time, and is much more difficult to change. Therapeutic help for such circumstances is generally focused on management, self-acceptance, the development of ethical behaviour and the formation of alternative sexual interests. This task is complex on several fronts. In situations where orientation is exclusively focused on underage children, the task involves an individual having to come to terms with there being no prospect of sexual satisfaction until they can generate an alternative focus. Several international organisations support non-offending individuals with minor attraction: VirPed, Stop It Now and B4U-ACT.

A further constraint is to do with the erotic material that may help minor-attracted adults meet their sexual needs, rather than act them out in contact offending. Some have suggested digitally created images of children for this purpose would be in the interests of protecting real children; however, such material could be risky if accessed by those who would not otherwise have ventured into the domain of sexual attraction to minors. Further, some insecurely attached individuals seeking external means to meet their emotional needs may spend increasing time on the internet, with the result that they and their loved ones miss out on real-world connection. As made clear above, such isolation is a major risk factor for child sexual offending.

18. The pathway forward

ROBYN SALISBURY

WE NOW KNOW MORE THAN ever about the lasting psychological and physiological harm, and growing identification of the epigenetic (intergenerational physiological) harm, that can result from children being sexually abused. For children to be free to be themselves, they need adults to do all they can to provide the conditions that will allow children to develop optimally, and it will surely not come as a surprise to any reader that the way forward must be a very thorough preventative one. This final chapter outlines the requirements for a far safer pathway forward for our children. It is a blueprint for making Aotearoa New Zealand a sexually safe country to grow up in, and it will benefit all of us to make it so.

This chapter can in no way be read as a summary of all the previous chapters, each of which contains significant wisdom. The essential components described below arise from this generous sharing of knowledge. In the interests of brevity, no attributions have been made and no further rationale is offered for each step. For all these reasons, you are advised not to read this chapter until you have read the rest of the book.

My invitation to you, the reader, is to broaden the base of knowledge from which you form or reform your beliefs about addressing child sexual abuse. I have the same reaction of disgust and anger that I believe many others experience in response to each and every child sexual abuse revelation, but it is crucial that we move beyond initial reactivity in order to thoughtfully and intelligently consider all the factors involved in shaping and maintaining harmful sexual behaviours in any individual. Calm consideration is required. Each of us must acknowledge that we do not have expertise in all spheres, but there will be ways in which each of us can effectively contribute. May this book fire your passion to join with others in taking the lead within your domain of wisdom, your sphere of influence.

No single change will fix the problem of child sexual abuse; we need a multi-factorial approach. There are many not-so-complex steps that together can make a huge difference. A combination of all of the steps, with all of us working together, is what is needed. These steps become clear by identifying the essential needs and responsibilities of each of the stakeholders, namely:

- children and young people;
- adults;
- state services;
- communities — local and national, individuals and groups; and
- those sexually attracted to children.

The first group of stakeholders do not hold any responsibilities to fix this problem; they have only needs.

NEEDS OF TAMARIKI/CHILDREN AND RANGATAHI/ YOUNG PEOPLE

In order to be protected from CSA, children have many needs. First, they need skilful parents and age-appropriate ongoing sex education. Later, as they grow, they need protection from being used as sex workers. Those who have been sexually abused or have experienced other forms of trauma need the adults involved to have an excellent understanding of the impact of trauma, and they need to encounter less stigma in reporting it. They also require multi-agency services to streamline and optimise the assessment, investigation and treatment of children who are sexually abused. And they need justice, including the option of restorative justice when appropriate.

Children need understanding and well-informed parents

Parenting is the toughest job I've ever done and I sure was not skilled to tackle the job at the outset. We could probably all use a little help here. There are now some culturally sensitive programmes, services and resources offered in our country, both to prepare for childbirth and to parent through the developmental stages of childhood and adolescence. I later describe research under way for the ongoing development of an excellent such programme that will be the recipient of all royalties from the sale of this book.

Fundamental learning for parents includes grasping the requirements of secure attachment. This will enable infants and, later, children to acquire well-being, along with the life skills, including emotional agility, required to maintain this for themselves as they become independent. Understanding child sexuality, and providing the essential support, knowledge and boundaries to allow this to develop optimally, is another important parental skill set.

Living in a digital world

Given the extensive use of digital devices, coupled with the societal desensitisation to sex over recent years, children and young people urgently need the tools to deal with what they are seeing. They need freedom of access to information and learning in order to be able to feel confident and learn about their own bodies, and to form their own values and learn to act in accord with them. Those children whose body, gender identification or orientation are different from the majority of their peers need to be understood and accepted. Further, children need help to develop a social conscience, to have the skills to engage in respectful relationships and to be able to critique images and values they encounter. All of this learning is an essential component of education, some of which skilful parents can deliver and some of which is the responsibility of the state.

Porn literacy and digital literacy are other essential components of sex education. Given young people's concerns about the widespread availability of pornography and the impossibility of ensuring they are never exposed to it, porn literacy education would enable viewers to form their own opinions about what they are seeing and equip them to discuss their reactions with supportive others.

Rangatahi/young people also need to learn the skills of sexual relationships, including consent. When they reach their teens, young people need and seek opportunities to discuss, question and debate issues of sexuality in open, safe, non-judgemental spaces. Relationships and sexuality are complex for adults, yet we currently don't give young people enough help to learn the necessary skills. Some parents fear that learning about sexuality lowers the age at which their children will become sexually active, but in fact there is significant research to show that the exact opposite happens. When young people are given the tools to make choices about their sexuality, they delay becoming sexually active.

Support for the victims of abuse

A public health campaign to reduce the stigma and shame for children and young people who report sexual abuse, and to allow others to feel able to report it, would be valuable. The sociocultural changes that can be effected through campaigns such as those against smoking around children show the way here. The more children are believed and not shamed when they report CSA, the less those with sexually harmful behaviours can remain hidden.

Additionally, those who experience CSA, along with their whānau/family, need excellent services for assessment, treatment and support from multi-service agencies. For Justice, Corrections and the community to do their part, the court system needs to do more to support victims, rather than merely punish offenders. The ongoing availability of an excellent restorative justice process will, where appropriate conditions are met, help victims and their families find their best way forward.

NEEDS AND RESPONSIBILITIES OF ADULTS

Stopping CSA requires universal, ongoing upskilling for the role of parenting, and help to develop the resources to create a healthy, pro-social life.

Understanding and discussing child sexuality and abuse

Parents need to understand child sexuality development. If our rangatahi/young people are carrying out harmful sexual behaviours, usually on children younger than themselves, then we need to know about it. Reading this book is a start. Boundaries are also required between child sexuality and adults' sexuality — these include managing (and limiting) internet access.

Becoming comfortable about discussing sexuality with one's own children is important. When children risk telling someone about CSA they need to receive optimal, warm, reassuring, well-informed responses. When comprehensive, skilful, age-appropriate sex education is consistently taking place nationally, future generations of parents will have the skills to do this. Given that high states of arousal often flow from the tension between persistent problems and triumphant solutions, the onus is on adults to resolve their persistent problems constructively. The sexual drive can be very powerful — our responsibility is to make ourselves safe drivers.

A lot of parental awareness comes down to our having effective 'radar', to spot when something may be wrong. Children who do not have at least one primary caregiver with a parental protective radar in place are at serious risk in many ways, including of CSA. Mental illness and other life stressors, such as physical illness, trauma and poverty, can interfere with and even remove this radar; hence the importance of adequate funding for mental health services and other social-equity endeavours.

Help for parents

If your own childhood lacked the environment to achieve secure attachment, then developing into a mature, respectful adult requires extra work. It may require professional help. Facing your own shortcomings can also help to avoid stigmatising others for theirs. Each of us has also to become comfortable with ourselves, our interpersonal relating, our body image and our sexuality in order to model that to children, to keep them safe and to deal well with their learning needs. Developing the life skills essential to be able to live life on life's terms and, for those who choose, to achieve mutually satisfying intimate relationships is a further ongoing lifelong need. We have a lifelong responsibility to maintain well-being, itself a vital component of parenting. Compulsory ongoing parent education for all is something I expect many will react strongly against. But why? Public health advocate and former New Zealander of the Year Dr Lance O'Sullivan firmly challenges anyone crying out 'nanny state' in response to initiatives that signal a caring country determined to create safety for children and young people. All children need parents who are attuned and wise about keeping them safe. Supporting parents to achieve this is essential. We need to dare to do something different.

Thus equipped, we can break destructive cycles, including substance abuse as a form of self-soothing or distraction. To do the psychological maturing work outlined above, basic needs such as sufficient food, warmth, security and income are essential prerequisites. There are government-funded endeavours to meet these fundamental external resources. It is important to understand that basic life conditions play an important role in stopping CSA, and to never stop working on social action, including campaigning for fairly paid work.

NEEDS AND RESPONSIBILITIES OF THE STATE SECTOR

No state service or Crown entity can be effective on its own. To address CSA, inter-sector collaboration is essential, as are individuals and community groups engaging with the resulting interventions. Experts in each pertinent service are urgently required to take the lead to produce evidence-based, or at least well-founded, initiatives to meet the needs outlined below. These services include, but are not limited to: Corrections; the ministries of education, health, justice and social development; Oranga Tamariki; New Zealand Police; ACC; district health boards (DHBs); school boards of trustees; and the Office of Film and Literature Classification. All need to be adequately funded and resourced in order to be able to address the following responsibilities.

Prevention of CSA requires research and data collection, effective victim support, primary and secondary prevention initiatives and justice improvements. The development of nationally accepted standard protocols in all these areas is essential. Some initiatives fit into more than one of these categories. For example, excellent early intervention services for victims of CSA will not only help resolve the trauma and thus prevent the developmental, lifelong impact, but could also play a primary prevention role in breaking an offending cycle. Further, such services could provide the evidence police need for an effective investigation and prosecution when appropriate, and treatment for the offender (in prison or in a community treatment programme) would reduce the risk of reoffending, thus playing a secondary prevention role.

Research and data collection

Ongoing research is needed to support and extend the sophisticated understanding of several key concepts in this field. These include: the concept of offender risk in guiding treatment and release decisions; the differences between the seriousness of harm done versus overall risk level; and the ongoing refining of the evidence base about risk assessment, treatment and rehabilitation, reintegration and reoffending. Research to evaluate the outcomes of all initiatives in this field is important for establishing an evidence base for ongoing funding. Research currently under way to explore and develop preventative treatment measures is also crucial.

Support services for victims of trauma

Victims and their whānau/families need nationwide access to optimal, across-service responses. These need to be free of charge, appropriate to the needs of the child, and offered in a cohesive manner so that skilful diagnosis, support, investigation and treatment all run smoothly together. It is hard to imagine improving on the model of a multidisciplinary agency using culturally appropriate approaches with good links to follow-up services in the community.

Various agencies are modelling this approach regionally; the task now is to make it nationally available on a multidisciplinary footing, with clearly established national standard protocols throughout. This requires commitment from the police, Ministry of Health and Oranga Tamariki to provide dedicated staff. At the time of going to print, Oranga Tamariki staff report being stretched too thinly to be able to comply with this requirement.

All those working in child health need to become skilful and confident about understanding CSA: to define what it is (and is not), to know how to identify it and to understand why children will not necessarily disclose. The development of educational resources and tools to this end is crucial. Given the proven significant effects on physical and mental health, and the proven high success rate of early intervention, CSA needs to be given the same serious attention as childhood cancer.

When children do risk telling someone about CSA, they need to receive optimal, well-informed responses. All those working with children, including pre-school education and daycare workers, teachers and youth workers, need to be trained in how to respond appropriately to a child's disclosure. Again, the creation of tools and resources for this purpose is important. Expecting a child to make a detailed disclosure of CSA to a stranger is challenging, if not unrealistic, so familiar adults need to be upskilled.

To be effective, all those working therapeutically with traumatised children require specialist training. I've trained and worked as a counsellor, psychotherapist and psychologist. I've been a parent, and I am a grandmother. Yet at no time did I learn the skills that Sue Glanville has to work with traumatised children. The impacts of trauma on a person differ according to age and developmental stage. Effective therapy for children requires a quite different skill set than when working with adults; therapy for traumatised children requires another skill set again. The complexity should not be underestimated.

Police national management need to ensure the continuing recognition of the importance of fielding specialist child protection teams. When conducted appropriately, the process of reporting CSA, having it investigated and, when evidential thresholds are able to be met, prosecuted, can play a valuable role in the healing process.

The ongoing refining, resourcing and improved running of ACC's Sensitive Claims Service is essential. This agency provides a national team of skilled counsellors and therapists to address, at no cost to the individual, unresolved sexual trauma afflicting many child, youth and adult survivors. All services offered by ACC and their contracted service providers need to be culturally appropriate. A trauma-informed Te Whare Tapa Whā model has been found by contributors to this book to be a very appropriate approach to healing. At the time of going to print, reports of long waiting lists, and of service providers in some locations withdrawing from working for ACC, are a cause for serious concern.

Police, Oranga Tamariki, the ministries of health and education and all allied agencies need to be well informed about underage sex work and the sex-trafficking of our rangatahi/young people. When the factors that make children and young people vulnerable to being exploited in these ways are understood, there should be no judgement or assumptions about choice, thus removing the stigma and so allowing disclosure and asking for help. Upskilling those working with young people would allow adults to open the door to such disclosures. Understanding the chaotic lives that inevitably result is also essential for the efficient support, treatment and police investigation of such crimes. A national plan of action on youth exploitation and a screening measure so victims are picked up by health professionals are important additional initiatives. Further, it is important that police target buyers of underage sex as a preventative intervention. International initiatives to identify those New Zealanders who travel in order to buy sex with children also need support and resources.

Primary prevention initiatives

State agencies have a key role to play in equipping parents, educators, health professionals and communities to create a child-safe environment.

Sexuality education is a fundamental requirement. The Ministry of Education guide recommends that 12–15 hours of sexuality education be provided each year throughout the schooling system as one part of the health and physical education curriculum, but this is often not happening. At the time of writing, teachers report being severely overworked and under-supported. Our current cohort of teachers may well have been educated in a system that also did not adequately address sex education. There is an essential need for ongoing funding and resources in order to upskill and support teachers in the field of sexuality education. The Education Review Office needs to monitor this and hold those responsible accountable. Meanwhile, boards of trustees can play a role in supporting schools to provide sex education and helping parents to understand the need.

Updating legislation and ongoing resourcing is clearly required to allow the Film and Literature Classification Office to further its excellent work, which involves valuable youth-centred research. All caring people need to acknowledge how the market for abusive sexually explicit material is rapidly expanding and that there is no way to completely control this. The promising collaboration of key internet service providers with the Department of Internal Affairs must continue. The insertion of automated warning signs whenever accessing illegal child SEM will deter some users. There may be valuable lessons, too, from some proactive European initiatives currently addressing online hate crime by preventative therapeutic engagement online with individuals identified to have concerning attitudes and preferences.

The Auckland and Waitematā DHBs have developed a child health information link (CHIL) hub aimed at improving the provision of, and collaboration between, all health services available to children for their first six years. This cost-neutral model appears to be an excellent way of supporting and monitoring developmental well-being. It involves the creation of a national register to allow prompt access to all pertinent information on every child, regardless of where they move to in the country.

Outcome evaluations were ongoing at the time of writing. It is to be hoped all other DHBs will follow these initiatives closely. Over time this initiative needs to be extended beyond the age of six.

Good results are emerging from current community-based treatment programmes to help those with sexual behaviours potentially harmful to children; now, there is a need to further fund and publicise them. While waiting to see my GP recently, I noticed that on the slip I was handed for him to mark the services received was the question, 'Would you like help to give up smoking?' I propose the next campaign be, 'Would you like help to stop harmful sexual behaviour?'

Understanding, support and funding are also needed for the development of a residential treatment programme such as that currently being worked on. As with the community-based treatment services, these programmes promote the message that an individual is not guilty or shameful because of their sexual desires, but they are responsible for their sexual behaviour, and getting professional help would be a vital step.

Mental health services funding could be so very valuable if, rather than being exclusively symptom-focused, it was targeted towards supporting the development of an earned secure attachment and then individuation. This preventative measure would produce resilient, mature, pro-social individuals with the life skills to avoid destructive behaviours and to give to their families and communities. In parents, it would ensure an effectively functioning protective parental radar. All those working in the mental health field need to be skilful and alert to recognise the signs of any trauma and to address those.

Police and community-based initiatives to address family harm need to be adequately resourced, not least because of the beneficial impact on reducing CSA, which is more likely to occur in the absence of a protective parental radar. Violence not only impairs such radars, but is also one of the known risk factors in creating child sex offenders.

As signalled earlier, all agencies and community initiatives striving to address such societal stressors as alcohol and other drug abuse, poverty and overcrowding are important. Community and national support following the lead of government and their agencies to help address these issues will help stop CSA. For example, from time to time the New Zealand Drug Foundation highlights the failure to implement key recommendations arising from studies into the harm caused by the abuse of alcohol and other drugs. This is a reminder that positive change requires political will, as well as leadership within the industry and consumer groups.

Secondary prevention initiatives

Given the crucial secondary prevention function of the sex offender register programme, it is essential to adequately resource all the agencies, including the police, Corrections and the Ministry of Social Development, that jointly run it. The development and refinement of a community-appropriate, effective risk-measurement tool is one important part of this resourcing. Community understanding and involvement in integrating released, treated, low-risk individuals back into their communities is another essential part of keeping the children and young people of that community safe.

Such involvement requires a public education initiative, and would be further helped if the media avoided sensationalised reporting. (When media reports provide balanced coverage, the public are less likely to be irrationally reactive.) At the time of publication, the Ministry of Social Development is nearing the end of a major trial to help successfully integrate released offenders. Early indicators from this trial are encouraging, signalling the importance of building relationships of trust as a central factor in preventing reoffending. It is important for this work to continue to be resourced. Much work remains to clarify guidelines, to roll them out nationally, and to staff the work appropriately.

As in other state sectors, all Corrections services, including prisons and probation services, need to follow a respectful, research-based, empathic approach — one that holds hope for positive change, and which is culturally and individually appropriate in recognising that there is not just one model of healing, harm prevention or rehabilitation. (A model that excludes spiritual and other cultural elements risks further colonising harm to Māori and to all those others whose world view encompasses the spiritual and cultural.) Surely many would benefit from a healing approach that incorporates heart, soul and spirit and recognises where we come from, ancestral wisdom and informed intuition. Such an approach has at its centre a meaningful therapeutic relationship. For many of those who have harmful sexual behaviours, such a relationship is their best chance of achieving the maturity that comes with an earned secure attachment.

Justice initiatives

As there are often very complex dynamics occurring during CSA, increasingly so when the abuse is inside the family, judges and juries need a sound knowledge of such issues as the balance of power, the needs of children to please, and the implications of their immaturity. With a full understanding of the impact of trauma and about child sexuality, they would be able to make properly informed decisions.

Further, in our justice system the state carries the burden of proof of guilt. Although child victims' evidence is often prerecorded, currently defence lawyers are still allowed to cross-examine victims intensively, which can be disturbing and confusing for even the most resilient adult, let alone a young victim of sexual abuse. Some defence lawyers can be seen on televised news reports invoking CSA myths, apparently intending to undermine the credibility of the testimony. Juries in such trials sometimes appear not to understand the difference between 'beyond reasonable doubt' and 'absolute certainty'. The former is what they are responsible for establishing. Jury members have at times reported feeling manipulated by power struggles within their membership.

Because of such issues, some concerned parties are calling for specialist CSA courts, along with improvements to current judicial processes. Such proposals demand to be seriously considered and trialled, not least because they would obviate the need for much jury education and training. Maximising the benefits and minimising the jeopardies of telling the truth have also been suggested as ways to increase the frequency of guilty pleas, thus sparing child victims from distressing trials.

Our justice system and the public as a whole need to recognise that a penalty-based approach has a preventative effect only for those who have an understanding of right and wrong and who have grasped that actions have consequences. Sadly, this is beyond the capabilities of many prisoners.

Similarly, calling for greater punishment will do little for many of those with harmful sexual behaviours. Treatment that expertly addresses the developmental and skills learning needs of each individual has been shown to have a greater effect in preventing reoffending. Those who recommend therapeutic jurisprudence — where judges have an extended ability to recommend an appropriate way forward for each individual — appear to understand such factors. As a society we need to support such initiatives.

The Ministry of Justice used to fund couples counselling via the Family Court. The withdrawal of this valuable preventative input currently makes it difficult, and often prohibitively expensive, to receive professional help to resolve a relationship crisis. Given the importance of parental modelling in guiding children through the maze of sexuality and relationships, and the fact that relationship counselling helps parents maintain their protective radar, this is of great concern. Renewed government funding for such services, under the auspices of whichever ministry is deemed appropriate, would help to prevent CSA.

NEEDS AND RESPONSIBILITIES OF THE COMMUNITY

All communities need to know that they, especially their young, are safe to go about their daily lives. Communities thrive when as many of their members as possible are resourced to be all they can and give all they can. Many responsibilities for the public as a whole arise from all the issues I have identified. These will need to be addressed by each of us as individuals as we gather within our communities and take well-informed action in support of the blueprint I have outlined. This action includes facing the facts about child sexual abuse, addressing related societal problems, supporting specialist restorative justice for CSA, and getting one's own house in order. A special request to the media is also included.

A number of key societal principles also require promotion. These include the rights of children to be protected, absolute intolerance of child sexual abuse, and countering the current sexualisation of society. Some of this will be achieved by modelling respect, including the respect for difference, and by teaching all children about their bodies and about consent. We need to put sexuality education higher on the agenda, despite opposition from activist groups. I urge all caring people to lobby their MPs and local schools to provide children of all ages with the tools they need to help keep themselves sexually safe. Society also carries the responsibility to examine and improve influences on sexuality and to stop shaming those who don't fit currently accepted norms, as this puts them at greater risk. Achieving a respectful society also involves recognising and resolving the harm done to tangata whenua by colonisation, and the task of recognising, understanding, valuing and responding appropriately to all differences in our multicultural country.

Communities must face facts

The goal of preventing child sexual abuse demands that members of the community get beyond stereotypes and simplistic punitive measures to face the facts. Enhancing released offenders' well-being and integration back into the community reduces community risk. Given that 84 per cent of those convicted of CSA each year are first-time offenders, we need preventative interventions to help those who sexually desire children and young people. Given that an increasing number of those with sexually harmful behaviour towards children are our young people, we also need to support any national actions to restrict non-compliant ISPs' access to users.

Over 60 per cent of the New Zealand participants in the WHO study reporting CSA had perpetrators from within their family; so it's time to stop projecting the blame onto 'grubby little paedophiles lurking out there'. And given that one in four girls and one in eight to ten boys are suffering from CSA, this is not happening to 'them', it's happening to 'us'. We are the victims; we are the perpetrators.

Churches, too, along with other community institutions, can help by modelling respectful, inclusive, appropriate, well-informed behaviours. In this way they can safely hold victims, families, released offenders and those at risk of first-time offending. All community groups, religious and secular, of course need to ensure their own houses are in order, so as to be widely trusted and effective in this role. At the time of writing, the Catholic Church was still working towards addressing its past failure to respond appropriately to CSA by its own priests. A Royal Commission into Historic Abuse in State Care is seeking to gain an understanding of the extent of sexual harm done to children in the care of the state. The #MeToo movement has raised awareness of how frequently issues of power and consent are ignored. Community groups can provide a sense of belonging, meaning and security essential for well-being, but we still have some way to go.

Addressing serious societal problems

The relevance to CSA of addressing societal issues such as our serious alcohol and other drug problems, poverty, overcrowding and family violence has been described. Sexual violence education, awareness-raising activities, and healthy social norms campaigns all contribute to stopping CSA. Communities also need a trauma-informed approach to dealing with social problems. This helps people understand the impact on children of all forms of deep trauma and how critical an appropriate response is. It also clarifies the need for informed action and for understanding how and why young people get into underage sex work. We must act to improve our systems and culture now. Washington State's Lincoln Alternative High School in the United States illustrated how effective a trauma-informed care framework could be. Staff were trained to respond appropriately to the signs of trauma (for example parental separations or drug or alcohol abuse) in the students' lives and, instead of reacting punitively to undesirable behaviours, counselling and healthcare were provided. Positive outcomes for students included reduced truancy and gang problems, increased graduation numbers and reduced suspensions.

A restorative justice programme is also essential — one that is survivor-informed and nationally available. Project Restore NZ leads by example, and, by mandating its services, so too does the Ministry of Justice, providing an effective healing process to restore victims' sense of self and help whānau/family find their way forward. By involving perpetrators, this service also reduces the risk of reoffending and breaks intergenerational patterns. The trust that runs Project Restore will require ongoing support and funding. We must ensure there is always enough and that there is widespread awareness of its work.

NEEDS AND RESPONSIBILITIES OF THOSE SEXUALLY INTERESTED IN CHILDREN

> Dear all who are sexually attracted to minors
> Taking your needs and desires to a child is not acceptable and never will be. Children are not objects to be used; they are vulnerable and need protection. Be very clear that no intensity of desire justifies this predatory behaviour. I know that for some of you, your desire is for a whole-hearted, loving relationship with a child, and that you strongly believe that this would be wonderful and life-enhancing for both. I'm sorry. The prospect of never being able to fulfil your deepest longing must be horrible. But this 'love' cannot be realised, ever. For all the reasons outlined, bringing an adult's sexual desire

anywhere near a minor is inherently disturbing and destructive behaviour.

There is effective, community-based help for anyone with a sexual interest in children or young people. Your responsibility is to ensure you do not carry out sexually harmful behaviours; please make contact with your local agency, today. Along with other contributors to this book, I am working towards making it even easier and safer for you to ask for the help and support you need to ensure you avoid any, or any further, destructive sexual behaviours. If you have already acted on your urges and have not faced the consequences of that, please do the honourable thing: take ownership of your wrongdoing and contact the police.

With my best wishes

Robyn

Afterword

THE CLOSING WORDS TO THIS last section of the book come from the abuse survivor whose story opened the book: 'I am in no way regretful about telling my story. It's real and it probably demonstrates how many eyes and ears must have been turned off rather than interfere on a child's behalf.'

The goal of this book is to get as many people as possible to turn on their eyes and ears and to dare to take informed action so that our country does a better job of keeping young people safe from sexual abuse.

Imagine if this man's mother (and his father, while he was on the scene) had been supported to understand the needs of their child and helped to meet those needs so that they didn't abandon him. Failing that, imagine if the home into which he was placed had been a well-supported, safe, skilful and loving one. Imagine if he had grown up receiving the message, 'If anyone hurts you, I will love you, believe you and protect you.'

If not, then imagine if at daycare, pre-school and school he had been skilfully taught to understand about his body, his sexuality, privacy and consent, so that, armed with this knowledge, he felt he had permission and the vocabulary to tell his teacher about what was being done to him. Imagine if that teacher had not only been trained in sexuality education but was also well informed about how to respond appropriately to his courage. This would have allowed them to know how to make a notification to the Ministry for Children, which was adequately resourced to help him tell enough of his story to know they had to notify police and to take steps to make him safe.

Imagine if his community had a multi-agency service for abused children, staffed with well-trained experts, which streamlined the involvement of all the necessary agencies. Imagine that a member of the local police child protection team then gathered sufficient evidence to be able to take the matter to court, where skilled professionals safely and successfully detain an offender to ensure they received intensive treatment. Down the track, effective risk-assessment guided decisions about the possibility of release.

Imagine, meanwhile, this boy gently and effectively being enabled to build trust with an expert child trauma therapist. Picture him learning to reclaim a sense of agency, inhabit his body, de-escalate the alarm hormones racing around in his bloodstream and know for sure that he was not to blame for what happened. Imagine him building a sense of self that supported him to resume his education and take his place in the world. Imagine a future for him where he could take part in loving, fulfilling, intimate relationships and where he could feel good about his sexuality and claim its pleasures.

Imagine if he had been born in a country courageous and knowledgeable enough to have widely established all the strengthening layers of prevention against child sexual abuse, along with the currently available community-based treatment agencies. A country also wise enough to have adequately resourced health and treatment services to address the impact of trauma so that any risk of a repeating cycle is removed.

One of the many things that make me proud to be a Kiwi is our 'can do' attitude. We are often down-to-earth, pragmatic and infinitely skilful at creating solutions to problems. The biggest personal wake-up call for me in writing this book has been the reminder that worker ants are far more effective as a team. All those working with children, or contributing help in any way to the domain of child sexual abuse, need to ensure they are aware of all the information in this book. They need to network effectively to share expertise and support, creating a knowledge base that will ultimately enable all of us to help bring about change.

Within this blueprint there are many opportunities for everyone to support initiatives towards making Aotearoa New Zealand a great and safe place for children. My invitation to all readers is to identify where you can best add your energy and take informed action in your community to stop child sexual abuse. Dare to have this grand vision. We can make a difference. We are Kiwis.

Acknowledgements

I STAND ON THE SHOULDERS of many who have come before me. Having read widely, taken part in many training experiences and received the wisdom of many valued local and international colleagues, I make no claims to the originality of my work, but rather express my sincere wishes that what I have gathered together here is encouraging and informative. I have endeavoured to cite sources of information wherever possible.

I have been so very moved by many people's willingness to support this book and its goals in a variety of ways. A huge thank you, firstly, to all the contributors: your wisdom and enormous hard work in the field are greatly valued, as is your making time to write for this project. To those of you who shared some of your personal story in the book: your courage and determination are appreciated and inspirational.

I am deeply grateful to my wonderful husband, Kevin, for his love and support, and for uncomplainingly doing more than his fair share of the division of household labour for the duration of this book's production.

My sincere thanks to Nicola Legat and the staff at Massey University Press. Nicola, your willingness, generosity and skills to advise, support and guide me throughout this process make MUP a great publisher. Thanks, too, to Matt Turner for his editing input. Matt, I am in awe of your extensive knowledge and written language skills.

Six friends and colleagues agreed to provide peer review: Jacky Burgon, Jan Dickson, Donna, Dr Karen Faisandier, Dr Jurriaan de Groot and Professor Louise Signal. Three of my much valued Sex Therapy New Zealand colleagues, Rick Williment, Paula Dennan and Clare Greensmith, gave me feedback on my 'development of sexuality' chapters. Your responses, ideas and eagle eyes helped in many ways, and I knew I was in good hands. Thank you for all you gave me, and please know that your wisdom is embedded in the refined manuscript I was then able to deliver to the publisher.

When I first started researching this book I met Sigrid Lindbolm, a sexual health promotion advisor at my local DHB, and Siobhan Healy-Cullen, a tutor and doctoral student at Massey University who is researching the question of whether pornography is our current form of sex education. Both women are tremendously knowledgeable in their fields and I thank them for their interest, enthusiasm and contributions to this book. I also thank Mark Rainier for his kindness in accessing invaluable resources for me in the early phase of my researching.

Finally, but not least, I acknowledge Tina Malone and Sue Glanville, the warriors fighting for children's well-being who inspired this book, and all other warriors, paid and unpaid, who work to protect children from abuse.

ALL ROYALTY INCOME FROM THE sale of this book will go directly to a fund managed by Te Awa Community Foundation. This fund will provide grants to support Parenting From the Start, a positive, preventative, accessible project that I see as having the potential to support the raising of secure, resilient children who are able to discover all they can be. Parenting From the Start was developed by registered clinical psychologist and mother of four Leith Pugmire and is being evaluated as part of her PhD research. At the core of the project are workshops that summarise the latest multi-disciplinary research about what babies need to grow up happy and healthy and explore childcare in different cultures and across evolutionary history. The workshops integrate findings from psychology, biology, medicine, midwifery, neuroscience and anthropology in a relaxed, non-judgemental, culturally sensitive context where existing parents and those expecting their first baby can explore the evidence underlying various parenting ideas without being 'told' what to do.

Why did I choose this project? From more than three decades of helping individuals to heal from deep pain and helping couples to learn to connect intimately with each other, I am aware of the centrality and necessity of meaningful, responsive human interaction. From the beginning of life until the end, human beings are reliant on healthy connection in order to thrive.

The unaddressed absence of such connection, or factors that significantly interfere with it, have multiple layers of negative consequences. One potential consequence is the terribly destructive behaviour of child sexual abuse. Parents and other caregivers deserve the information and support necessary to assist them in raising their precious tamariki/children and mokopuna/grandchildren from the start.

The goal of the workshops — which have been well received by parents, support people and professionals — is to facilitate participants' informed choice about what's right for their unique whānau/family situation. Topics include early brain development, attachment, and a range of cross-cultural parenting approaches, empowering caregivers to build strong, healthy relationships that children can trust. Traditional Māori parenting is used as an exemplar of the sensitive, responsive care that is consistently associated with optimal child outcomes, and the workshops acknowledge the well-established benefits of 'alloparenting' — the shared childcare traditionally valued and practised by tangata whenua in Aotearoa New Zealand. Utilising a mixture of short movies, kōrero/discussions, presentations and hands-on activities, each workshop can be completed in a single day or split over several sessions.

Leith Pugmire is currently conducting a longitudinal study following Manawatū women from pregnancy until their babies are 18 months old to quantify the impact of the workshops, find out what local parents are doing and investigate how common parenting strategies are working out for them. Her dream is to support parents and communities throughout the country in their vital caregiving work, to develop the strong healthy relationships that form the basis for lifelong mental health, well-being and resilience. I consider this programme of central importance to this book's goal of protecting children and preventing child sexual abuse.

If you wish to further support the charitable trust Parenting From the Start, you can make a donation by visiting https://teawafoundation.org.nz.

Appendix: Children's sexual behaviours

THE FOLLOWING TABLES OUTLINE DEVELOPMENTALLY normal behaviours arising from children's sexual curiosity and learning, according to their age group. These are *not* intended for diagnosing child sexual abuse. If parents or other adults are concerned about a child's sexual behaviour and the child is under three, it is recommended to gently distract them or remove them from the situation, with a brief, calm comment.

For children four and above, adults are encouraged to stay calm, simply state what they see and give the rules about this behaviour, so the child can learn from the situation. They can offer to answer the child's questions at any time or to provide other information. Having quietly addressed the situation, observe. If the behaviour continues to be repeated, guidelines are also given for when to seek professional help. Remember that a child who has been sexually abused will not necessarily go on to abuse others; most do not.

Toni Cavanagh Johnson is a clinical psychologist who has lectured internationally on child sexual abuse and children's sexuality and sexual behaviours. My sincere thanks to Toni for giving me permission to reproduce the following tables.

BEHAVIOURS RELATED TO SEX AND SEXUALITY IN PRE-SCHOOL CHILDREN

Natural and healthy	Of concern	Seek professional help
Touches/rubs own genitals when nappies are being changed, when going to sleep, when tense, excited, afraid or because it feels good	Continues to touch/rub genitals in public after being told 'no' consistently	Touches/rubs self to the exclusion of normal childhood activities. Hurts own genitals by touching/rubbing
Explores differences between males and females, boys and girls	Asks continuous questions about genital differences after all questions have been answered	Plays male or female roles in angry, sad or aggressive manner. Hates own/other sex
Touches the 'private parts' of familiar adults and children with hand or body	Touches/rubs the 'private parts' of familiar children or adults after they have been told consistently not to do so	Sneakily touches/rubs the 'private parts' of adults or children and, if questioned, denies it
Takes advantage of opportunity to look at nude people	Stares at nude people even after having seen many people nude	Asks people to take off their clothes. Tries to forcibly undress people
Asks about the genitals, breasts, intercourse, babies	Keeps asking people even after parent has answered all questions at an age appropriate level	Asks unfamiliar people after parent has answered all questions. Sexual knowledge too great for age
Erections	Very frequent erections	Fearful of erections
Likes to be nude. May show others his/her genitals	Wants to be nude in public after the parent repeatedly and consistently says 'no'	Refuses to put on clothes. Secretly shows 'private parts' in public after many scoldings
Interested in watching people doing bathroom functions	Interest in watching bathroom functions does not wane after days/weeks	Refuses to leave people alone in bathroom. Forces way into bathroom
Interested in having/birthing a baby	Boys' interest does not wane after several days/weeks of play about babies	Displays fear or anger about babies, birthing or intercourse

Natural and healthy	Of concern	Seek professional help
Child stands/sits too close to familiar adults and children	Child stands/sits too close to unfamiliar adults and children	After consistent reminders by the adults, the child stands/sits with his/her body touching familiar/unfamiliar adults, which makes the adults uncomfortable
Uses 'dirty' words for bathroom and sexual functions	Continues to use 'dirty' words at home after parent consistently says 'no' and parents do not swear	Uses 'dirty' words in public and at home after many strong scoldings and parents do not swear
Interested in own faeces	Smears faeces on walls or floor more than once	Repeatedly plays/smears faeces after scolding. Angry when doing it
Plays 'doctor', inspecting others' bodies, including 'private parts'	Frequently plays 'doctor' and gets caught, after consistently being told 'no'	Forces child to take off clothes and play 'doctor'
Puts something in own genitals or rectum one time for curiosity or exploration	Puts/tries to put something in genitals or rectum of self or other after being told 'no'	Any coercion, force, pain in putting or trying to put something in genitals or rectum of self or other person
Plays house, acts out roles of mummy and daddy	Humping other children with clothes on after being told not to	Simulated or real intercourse without clothes; oral genital contact

BEHAVIOURS RELATED TO SEX AND SEXUALITY IN CHILDREN AGED 5–10

Natural and healthy	Of concern	Seek professional help
Asks about genitals, breasts, intercourse	Shows fear or anxiety about sexual topics	Asks endless questions about sex after curiosity satisfied. Sexual knowledge/vocabulary/thoughts too advanced for age
Interested in watching/peeking at people doing bathroom functions	Keeps getting caught watching/peeking at others doing bathroom functions	Refuses to leave people alone in the bathroom
Uses 'dirty' words for bathroom functions, genitals and sexual behaviour	Uses 'dirty' words with adults after the parent consistently says 'no' and punishes child	Continuously uses 'dirty' language even after exclusion from school and favourite activities and parents/relatives do not use these words
Plays 'doctor'. The child inspects another child's body, including 'private parts'	Frequently plays 'doctor' and gets caught after being told consistently not to do so	Forces child to take clothes off and touches/inserts something in child's 'privates'
Boys and girls are interested in having/birthing a baby	Boy keeps making believe he is having a baby after month/s	Child displays fear or anger about babies or intercourse
Touches/rubs own genitals when going to sleep, when tense, excited, afraid or because it feels good. Shows others his/her genitals in a private location	Shows genitals in public. Continues to touch/rub genitals in public after consistently being told 'no'. Rubs genitals on furniture or other objects after the parent says 'no' and punishes child	Shows genitals at school and/or other places to express anger or disdain for authority
Plays house, may simulate all roles of mummy and daddy	Repeatedly humping other children with clothes on. Repeatedly imitates sexual behaviour with dolls/stuffed toys	Humping others while naked. Intercourse with another child. Forcing sexual contact on a child or adult

Natural and healthy	Of concern	Seek professional help
Thinks other gender children are 'gross' or have 'germs'. Chases them	Continues to use 'dirty' language after other children complain	Uses bad language against other child's family. Makes sexual threats
Talks about sex with friends. Talks about having a girlfriend or boyfriend	Sex talk gets child in trouble. Romanticises all relationships. Sexualises all relationships	Talks about sex and sexual acts habitually. Repeatedly in trouble with regard to sexual talk
Wants privacy when in bathroom or changing clothes	Becomes very upset when observed changing clothes, using the toilet or bathing	Aggressive or fearful in demand for privacy
Likes to hear and tell 'dirty' jokes, makes a few sexual sounds	Keeps getting caught telling 'dirty' jokes or making sexual sounds, e.g. moaning	Still gets caught telling 'dirty' jokes or making sexual sounds, even after exclusion from school and fun activities
Plays games with same-aged children related to sex and sexuality	Wants to play games related to sex and sexuality with much younger, older or unknown children	Child/children force others to play sexual games that make them feel uncomfortable
Draws genitals on human figures for artistic expression or because figure is being portrayed in the nude	Draws genitals on some nude figures but not others or on drawings of clothed people. Genitals disproportionate to size of body	Genitals stand out as most prominent feature of drawing. Drawings of intercourse, group sex, sex with animals, sadism, masochism, etc.
Explores differences between adult males and females, boys and girls	Confused about male/female differences after all questions have been answered	Plays male or female roles in a sad, angry or aggressive manner exclusively
Takes advantage of opportunity to look at nude people	Stares/sneaks to stare at nude people after punishment and having seen many people nude	Asks others to take off their clothes. Tries to forcibly undress children or adults

BEHAVIOURS RELATED TO SEX AND SEXUALITY IN CHILDREN AGED 5-10 CONT.

Natural and healthy	Of concern	Seek professional help
Pretends to be opposite gender	Talks very negatively about own gender	Hates/fears being own gender. Hates own genitals
Wants to compare genitals with peer-aged friends	Wants to compare genitals with much older or much younger people	Demands to see genitals, breasts or buttocks of others
Looks at the genitals, breasts or buttocks of others	Stares at the genitals, breasts or buttocks of others, making them uncomfortable	Continuously sneaks and peeks at genitals, breasts and buttocks of others after being caught many times
Interest in touching genitals, breasts or buttocks of other same-age child or have child touch his/hers	Makes others uncomfortable by requests to touch their genitals, breasts or buttocks or have them touch his/her genitals, breasts or buttocks	Coerces unwilling child to touch his/her genitals, breasts or buttocks or allow touching of theirs. Forced or mutual oral, anal or vaginal sex
Kisses/hugs familiar adults and children. Allows kisses/hugs by familiar adults and children	French kissing. Talks/acts in a sexualised manner with unknown children. Fearful of hugs and kisses by adults. Gets very anxious when sees displays of affections. Kisses/hugs unfamiliar adult or child	Talks/acts in a highly sexualised manner with known or unknown adults/children, which makes them feel uncomfortable. Physical contact with any adult causes agitation, anger, fear or anxiety to the child or adult
Looks at nude pictures on the internet, in videos, magazines, etc.	Continuous fascination with nude pictures that gets child in trouble	Wants to masturbate to nude pictures or display them
Erections	Continuous erections or fear of erections	Painful erections or hurting self to stop erection

Natural and healthy	Of concern	Seek professional help
Puts something in own genitals/rectum for the physical sensation or curiosity	Puts something in own genitals/rectum frequently or when it feels uncomfortable. Puts something in the genitals/rectum of other child	Any coercion or force in putting/trying to put something in genitals/rectum of other child. Causes harm to own/others genitals/rectum
Interest in breeding behaviour of animals	Touching genitals of animals	Sexual behaviours with animals

BEHAVIOURS RELATED TO SEX AND SEXUALITY IN PRE-TEENS

Natural and healthy	Of concern	Seek professional help
Uses slang such as: dick, boobs, willy, beaver, pussy, 'do the nasty', home run, etc.	Uses slang with adults/young children after adults consistently say 'no' (when pre-teen knows proper terminology and it is used at his/her home)	Continues to use slang in front of people who find it offensive and/or after exclusion from school and social activities
Uses 'dirty' language with friends when they are alone and know there are no adults around, e.g. 'You're a bitch/dick'	Continues to use 'dirty' language with friends and/or at school after having been caught several times and asked to stop	Directs 'dirty' language at known or unknown people in an aggressive manner or shows disdain and disgust for them
Very interested in sex and sexuality. To explore sex and sexuality goes to video sites, internet, social media, movies, music, television, magazines	Spends considerable amount of time seeking sexual images online, including pornography, to the detriment of school work, family activities and friendships	After being caught and internet access taken away continues endlessly to look for ways to go online. Makes pictures and/or videos of own genitals and/or sexual behaviour. Watches violent porn/child porn
Asks (or does not ask) about sexual topics such as: hair growth, body changes, kissing, intercourse, menstruation, etc.	Very anxious when hears others talk about sexual topics or when talking about sexual behaviour	Endless questions about sex after curiosity satisfied. Talks about specific adult sexual acts with details
Feels OK or very embarrassed when parent/s want to talk to him/her about puberty and/or sexual topics	Denies the parents' right to talk to him/her about sexual topics. Angry with parents for wanting to talk about puberty and/or sexual topics	Cries and runs away as if scared and/or ashamed and/or disgusted regarding puberty and/or sexual topics

Natural and healthy	Of concern	Seek professional help
The changes of puberty may be acknowledged or hidden. Looks at own genital area with hand-held mirror	Wears clothes in such a way that body changes cannot be detected. Refuses to change at PE. Tries to bind breasts so they cannot grow	Obsessed about the changes to his/her body. Finds new hair growth and/or onset of menses disgusting. Cuts body. Genital self-mutilation
Walks around nude or partially clothed in the same gender locker room, at school or with same gender friends at home	Seeks attention while nude in the same gender locker room or with same gender friends at home. Thinks it is 'fun' to flash private parts	After other pre-teens have complained, gets caught again by school authorities for showing private parts
Wants privacy when dressing/bathing and/or attempt to watch people engaged in private behaviours when they don't know it	Gets caught watching/peeking at others when they want privacy and then does it again	After appropriately severe consequences/restrictions continues watching/peeking at people at school/home and/or in public places
Talks about sex with friends. Talks about having a girlfriend/boyfriend. Exaggerates sexual experiences to peers	Talks about sex to known adults/children who do not like it and want it to stop. Oblivious to others' rejection	Saying he/she is older, continuously seeks sexual conversations with adolescents/adults online
Flirts with other pre-teens and young adolescents	Spends excessive amounts of time with people of all ages of their sexual choice. Romanticises many of these relationships, of which none are reciprocated	Seeks sexual attention/behaviour/relationship from parent/s and/or known or unknown people of any age who are firmly put off by the (obsessive) focus on them
Plays games with same-aged children related to sex and sexuality, such as kissing, touching, taking off some, but not all, clothes	Expresses/shows an interest in playing games with children several years younger and/or older related to sex and sexuality	Coerces/tricks (emotionally or physically) others to play sexual games. A group of children forces one or more children to play sexual games

BEHAVIOURS RELATED TO SEX AND SEXUALITY IN PRE-TEENS CONT.

Natural and healthy	Of concern	Seek professional help
Sometimes innocently touches the private parts of peer when roughhousing/wrestling/chasing and/or tickling him/her	Continues to 'innocently' touch private parts of young children/peers/adults when roughhousing/wrestling/chasing him/her after being asked many times to stop	Fondles/grabs private parts of others after being asked many times not to do so and having received appropriately severe consequences
Finds willing friends with whom to dance in an erotic manner which can look like simulating intercourse	Simulates intercourse with same-aged peers who the pre-teen does not really know and/or who do not want to do it	Penetration of vagina or rectum of a little known person with finger, penis or object with or without physical force or emotional coercion
Touches/rubs own genitals when alone	Continues to touch/rub genitals in public places after being told 'no' consistently by parents	Touches/rubs genitals in public after being ridiculed by classmates and censured by school authorities. Inserts unsafe/unhygienic objects in own genitals
Rhythmically rubs own genitals/masturbates in private	Goes to bathroom at school to rhythmically rub genitals/masturbate in private	Rhythmically rubs own genitals/masturbates to the exclusion of other normal pre-teen behaviours. Excessive rubbing hurts genitals
Looks/masturbates to nude pictures/videos	Masturbates to nude pictures/videos and leaves them around where others can see them after being told not to do so	Talks about his/her masturbatory behaviour to people who do not want to hear about it. Masturbates in front of siblings/peers/others
Alone or with friends sneaks to look at sexual activity of animals/people online and/or in printed material	Wants younger siblings to watch sexual activity online or in printed material	Bribes/coerces siblings/peers to watch/act out sexual behaviour seen online or in printed material

Natural and healthy	Of concern	Seek professional help
Posts* online about girlfriend/boyfriend	Sexually suggestive online* language about self, peers, movie stars, etc.	Posts* materials online that are sexually explicit and/or violent in nature about self/others. Lies online about age to attract older persons
Texts* sexual jokes	Texts* 'dirty' jokes about sex to peers who don't want to see or hear them	Texts* (coerces others to text*) nude/semi-nude selfies and/or pictures of self/peers engaged in masturbation, oral/anal sex, intercourse
Draws/doodles/texts* basic sexually explicit images	Draws/doodles/texts* drawings of advanced sexual behaviours	Draws/doodles/texts* sexually explicit images with violent themes
Looks at and/or touches the genitalia of animals once or twice	Likes animals to touch/lick his/her genitals/rectum	Rhythmically stimulates and/or tries to penetrate and/or hurt the genitalia of animals
Talks about wanting to have a baby when she grows up	Visually and emotionally focuses on males of all ages in pursuits of goal of having a baby	Concerned that she might be pregnant. Disgusted by the idea of having something grow inside her
Beginning sexual interest in same/other gender peer	Feels ashamed about sexual interest in same gender peer	Feels suicidal regarding same gender sexual interest
Explores other gender preferences	Unsettled and ashamed about own gender, would rather be other gender, but refuses to talk about it with anyone	Hates own gender. Very upset with current gender, sexual characteristics. Suicidal

* Texts, posts online, emails, chats and other forms of electronic messaging are all included

Notes

Foreword

1. Jonathan Mitchell, 'Brutalised inside and then I had to live with that shame', Male Survivors Aotearoa, 24 April 2019, https://malesurvivor.nz/brutalised-inside-and-then-i-had-to-live-with-that-shame/
2. Statistics from New Zealand Family Violence Clearing House, Data Summary 4, June 2017.
3. Safety of Children in Care, Oranga Tamariki — Ministry for Children, https://www.orangatamariki.govt.nz/statistics/safety-of-children-in-care/

Preface

1. D. T. Kenny, *Children, Sexuality, and Child Sexual Abuse* (New York: Routledge, 2018).

Introduction

1. Anne French, 'Autumn', in *New Zealand Love Poems,* ed. Lauris Edmond (Auckland: Oxford University Press, 2001); David Lyndon Brown, 'The Right Side', in *When Two Men Embrace: The New Zealand anthology of gay and lesbian poetry*, ed. Jonathan Fisher (Christchurch: Giant Press, 1999); Robin Healey, 'Pullover', in Edmond, *New Zealand Love Poems*.
2. Vincent O'Sullivan, *Believers to the Bright Coast* (Auckland: Penguin, 1988).
3. Joyce McDougall, *The Many Faces of Eros* (London: W. W. Norton & Co., 1995).
4. Jack Morin, *The Erotic Mind* (New York: Harper Collins, 1996).
5. R. F. Anda et al., 'The Enduring Effects of Abuse and Related Adverse Experiences in Childhood', *European Archives Psychiatry Clinical Neuroscience* 256, no. 3 (2006): 174–86.
6. V. J. Felitti et al., 'Relationship of Childhood Abuse and Household Dysfunction to Many of the Leading Causes of Death in Adults', The Adverse Childhood Experiences (ACE) Study, *American Journal of Preventative Medicine* 14, no. 4 (May 1998): 245–58.
7. Delphine Collin-Vézina, Isabelle Daigneault and Martine Hébert, 'Lessons Learned from Child Sexual Abuse Research: Prevalence, outcomes, and preventive strategies', *Child and Adolescent Psychiatry and Mental Health* 7 (2013): 22.

8   Sarah D. Goode, *Understanding and Addressing Adult Sexual Attraction to Children* (London: Routledge, 2010).
9   Ibid.
10 Ministry of Social Development, https://www.msd.govt.nz/about-msd-and-our-work/publications-resources/statistics/cyf/findings.html
11 Ministry of Justice, Sexual Offences, June 2018, https://www.justice.govt.nz/assets/Documents/Publications/Sexual-offences-June2018-v2.0.xlsx
12 Diana T. Kenny, *Children, Sexuality and Child Sexual Abuse* (New York: Routledge, 2018).
13 Ministry of Women's Affairs, 'Lightning Does Strike Twice: Preventing sexual revictimisation' (September 2012).
14 David Finkelhor, 'The International Epidemiology of Child Sexual Abuse', *Child Abuse and Neglect* 18, no. 5 (May 1994): 409–17.
15 David Finkelhor et al., 'The Lifetime Prevalence of Child Sexual Abuse and Sexual Assault Assessed in Late Adolescence', *Journal of Adolescent Health* 55, no. 3 (September 2014): 329–33.
16 J. E. Fanslow, E. M. Robinson, S. Crengle and L. Perese, 'Prevalence of Child Sexual Abuse Reported By a Cross-sectional Sample of New Zealand Women', *Child Abuse and Neglect* 31, no. 9 (October 2007): 935–45.
17 S. E. James, J. L. Herman, S. Rankin, M. Keisling, L. Mottet and M. Anafi, *The Report of the 2015 U.S. Transgender Survey* (Washington, DC: National Center for Transgender Equality, 2016).
18 Finkelhor, 'International Epidemiology of Child Sexual Abuse'.
19 Ibid.
20 Joe Kort, 'Homosexuality and Pedophilia: The false link', *In the Family*, Autumn 2003, http://www.joekort.com/articles.htm/Homosexuality_and_Pedophilia

2. Child sexual abuse: A paediatrician's viewpoint

1   J. Anderson et al., 'Prevalence of Childhood Sexual Abuse Experiences in a Community Sample of Women', *Journal of the American Academy of Child and Adolescent Psychiatry* 32, no. 5 (September 1993): 911–19.
2   D. M. Fergusson, M. T. Lynsky and L. J. Horwood, 'Childhood Sexual Abuse and Psychiatric Disorder in Young Adulthood: I. Prevalence of sexual abuse and factors associated with sexual abuse', *Journal of the American Academy of Child and Adolescent Psychiatry* 35, no. 10 (October 1996): 1355–64.
3   T. Van Roode, N. Dickson, P. Herbison and C. Paul, 'Child Sexual Abuse and Persistence of Risky Sexual Behaviors and Negative Sexual Outcomes over Adulthood: Findings from a birth cohort', *Child Abuse and Neglect* 33 (2009): 161–72.

3. Working therapeutically with children who have experienced sexual abuse

1   S. E. Stevens, 'The Relationship Between Counsellors' Orientation, Experiences and Training and their Conceptualisation of their Tasks in the Healing Process in Sexual Abuse Counselling: A qualitative analysis', unpublished master's thesis, Massey University, Palmerston North, 1992.
2   J. Briere, Presentation to NZCCP Conference, Nelson, March 2018.
3   James S. Fleming, 'Erikson's Psychosocial Development Stages', 2004, https://pdfs.semanticscholar.org/ab44/d6a2d3178e4e159108ab5333504d23cc9508.pdf

4   B. E. Saunders, L. Berliner and R. F. Hanson (eds), *Child Physical and Sexual Abuse: Guidelines for treatment* (Charleston, SC: National Crime Victims Research and Treatment Center, 2003).

5   J. S. Feather and K. R. R. Ronan, *Cognitive Behaviour Therapy for Child Trauma and Abuse* (London & Philadelphia: Jessica Kingsley, 2010).

6   O. Taylor, 'Treating Child Trauma with CBT and Sensory Therapy', Te Pou Mental Health Symposium, December 2017.

7   Thank you, Dave Wood.

8   N. Davis, *Once Upon a Time: Therapeutic stories that teach and heal* (Self-published, 1996). For information, visit https://drnancydavis.com

9   P. Stallard, 'Adapting Cognitive Behaviour Therapy for the Treatment and Prevention of Emotional Disorders in Children', training workshop, Auckland, 2018.

10 M. Libeau, 'Self-defence and Personal Safety Classes and Workshops', brochure.

4. Child sexual abuse: A police viewpoint

1   Section 128, Crimes Act 1961 — Sexual violation defined.

2   Section 131A, Crimes Act 1961 — Meeting young person following sexual grooming.

3   Online Child Exploitation Across New Zealand (OCEANZ). For more information, visit https://www.police.govt.nz/advice/cybercrime-and-internet/online-child-safety

4   If pornography has a place, it is *never* with children. The phrase 'child pornography' softens the degrading nature of child sexual abuse imagery and should not be used by police.

5   For Wellington District, apart from Oranga Tamariki, wonderful support agencies such as Wellington HELP (www.wellingtonhelp.org.nz) and Hutt Valley Sexual Abuse Support and Healing (HV SASH, www.hvsash.org.nz) are key in supporting children and families.

6. Te Wairua O Tika

1   E. Bass and L. Davis, *The Courage to Heal* (New York: Collins Living, 1988).

7. Sexuality education in New Zealand: What is (not) happening in schools and why you should care

1   Office of Film and Literature Classification, *NZ Youth and Porn: Research findings of a survey on how and why young New Zealanders view online pornography* (Wellington: Office of Film and Literature Classification, 2018), https://www.classificationoffice.govt.nz/news/latest-news/nzyouthandporn/

2   L. Allen, 'Say Everything: Exploring young people's suggestions for improving sexuality education', *Sex Education* 5, no. 4 (2005): 389–404.

3   K. Fitzpatrick and R. Tinning, 'Health Education's Fascist Tendencies: A cautionary exposition', *Critical Public Health* 24, no. 2 (2014): 132–42.

4   Education Review Office, 'The Teaching of Sexuality Education in Years 7–13' (Wellington: Education Review Office, 2007).

5   Education Review Office, 'Promoting Wellbeing Through Sexuality Education' (Wellington: Education Review Office, 2018).

6   Ministry of Education, *The New Zealand Curriculum* (Wellington: Ministry of Education, 2007), 23.

7   I. O'Neill, 'In Our Own Words: Student experiences of sexual violence prior to and during tertiary education' (Wellington: New Zealand Union of Students' Associations, 2017).

8   R. Tinning, 'Seeking a Realistic Contribution: Considering physical education within HPE in New Zealand and Australia', *Journal of Physical Education New Zealand* 33, no. 3 (2000): 8–21; D. Penney and J. Harris, 'The Body and Health in Policy: Representations and recontextualisation', in *Body Knowledge and Control: Studies in the Sociology of Physical Education and Health*, ed. J. Evans, B. Davies and J. Wright (London: Routledge, 2004), 96–111.

9   Ministry of Education, *Sexuality Education: A guide for principals, boards of trustees and teachers* (Wellington: Ministry of Education, 2015), 11.

10 K. Quinlivan, 'Affirming Sexual Diversity in Two New Zealand Secondary Schools: Challenges, constraints and shifting ground in the research process', *Journal of Gay and Lesbian Issues in Education* 3, nos. 2/3 (2006): 5–33; L. Allen, 'Denying the Sexual Subject: Schools' regulation of student sexuality', *British Educational Research Journal* 33, no. 2 (2007): 221–34; K. Kumashiro, *Troubling Education: Queer activism and anti-oppressive pedagogy* (New York: RoutledgeFalmer, 2002); H. Sykes, *Queer Bodies: Sexualities, genders and fatness in physical education* (New York: Peter Lang, 2011).

11 T. M. Jones and L. Hillier, 'Sexuality Education School Policy for Australian LGBTQI Students', *Sex Education* 12, no. 4 (2012): 437–54.

12 T. M. Jones, E. Gray and A. Harris, 'LGBTQI Teachers in Australian Education Policy: Protections, suspicions, and restrictions', *Sex Education* 14, no. 3 (2014): 338–53.

13 T. C. Clark et al., *Youth'12 Overview: The health and wellbeing of New Zealand secondary school students in 2012* (Auckland: University of Auckland, 2013).

14 K. Fitzpatrick and R. Tinning (eds), *Health Education: Critical perspectives* (London: Routledge, 2014).

15 R. Crawford, 'Healthism and the Medicalisation of Everyday Life', *International Journal of Health Services* 10, no. 3 (1980): 365–88. See also Fitzpatrick and Tinning, *Health Education*.

16 Ministry of Education, *Sexuality Education*, 12.

17 Ministry of Education, *Health and Physical Education in the New Zealand Curriculum* (Wellington: Ministry of Education, 1999); Ministry of Education, *The New Zealand Curriculum*.

18 S. Heaton, 'The Co-Opting of *Hauora* into Curricula', *Curriculum Matters* 7, no. 1 (2011): 99–107.

19 Ministry of Education, *Health and Physical Education*.

20 M. Durie, *Whaiora: Māori health development* (Auckland: Oxford University Press, 1994).

21 B. Hokowhitu, 'If You Are Not Healthy, Then What Are You? Healthism, colonial disease and body logic', in Fitzpatrick and Tinning, *Health Education*, 31–47. For a model of Te Whare Tapa Whā, visit www.health.govt.nz/our-work/populations/maori-health/maori-health-models/maori-health-models-te-whare-tapa-wha

22 F. K. Pulotu-Endemann, 'Fonofale Model of Health', paper presented at the Pacific Models for Health Promotion, Massey University, Palmerston North, 2001. For an explanation of the Fonofale model, visit www.health.govt.nz/.../pacific-peoples-and-mental-health-2008.doc

23 L. Smith, *Decolonising Methodologies: Research and indigenous peoples* (New York: Zed Books, 2013).
24 Ministry of Education, *Sexuality Education*, 8.
25 D. Powell, *Schools, Corporations and 'the War on Childhood Obesity'* (New York: Routledge, 2019).
26 S. Garland-Levett, 'Exploring Discursive Barriers to Sexual Health and Social Justice in the New Zealand Sexuality Education Curriculum', *Sex Education* 17, no. 2 (2017): 121–34.
27 K. Fitzpatrick and R. Tinning, 'Considering the Politics and Practice of Health Education', in Fitzpatrick and Tinning, *Health Education*, 1–14; M. Gard and D. Leahy, 'Dicing with Death: Tensions, contradictions and awkward positions in school health education', in *Health and Physical Education: Issues for curriculum in Australia and New Zealand*, ed. M. Dinan-Thompson (Melbourne: Oxford University Press, 2009), 183–97.
28 Fitzpatrick and Tinning, 'Considering the Politics'.
29 Allen, 'Say Everything'.

8. Technology, new media and child sexual abuse: Time for a change

1 ECPAT International, 'Trends in Online Child Sexual Abuse Material', 2018, https://www.ecpat.org/wp-content/uploads/2018/07/ECPAT-International-Report-Trends-in-Online-Child-Sexual-Abuse-Material-2018.pdf
2 UK Internet Watch Foundation, 'IWF Operational Trends 2014: Overview' (London: Internet Watch Foundation, 2014).
3 Terre des Hommes, 'Webcam Child Sex Tourism' (The Hague: Terre des Hommes, 2013), https://www.terredeshommes.org/resources-press/researches/
4 Josh Constine, 'Microsoft Bing Not Only Shows Child Pornography, It Suggests It', TechCrunch, https://techcrunch.com/2019/01/10/unsafe-search/
5 Office of Film and Literature Classification, 'NZ Youth and Porn: Research findings of a survey on how and why young New Zealanders view online pornography' (Wellington: Office of Film and Literature Classification, 2018), https://www.classificationoffice.govt.nz/news/latest-news/nzyouthandporn/
6 Barnardo's, 'Police figures reveal rise of almost 80% in reports of child-on-child sex offences', press release, 3 February 2018, https://www.barnardos.org.uk/news/Police_figures_reveal_rise_of_almost_80_in_reports_of_child-on-child_sex_offences/latest-news.htm?ref=121581
7 Netsafe, 'Teens and 'Sexting' in New Zealand: Prevalence and attitudes' (Wellington: Netsafe, 2017), https://www.netsafe.org.nz/teens-sexting-report/
8 Sonia Lewycka et al., 'Downwards Trends in Adolescent Risk-taking Behaviours in New Zealand: Exploring driving forces for change', *Journal of Paediatrics and Child Health* 54, no. 6 (June 2018): 602–8, https://onlinelibrary.wiley.com/doi/full/10.1111/jpc.13930
9 Aja Romano, 'A New Law Intended to Curb Sex Trafficking Threatens the Future of the Internet As We Know It', *Vox*, 2 February 2018, https://www.vox.com/culture/2018/4/13/17172762/fosta-sesta-backpage-230-internet-freedom

10. Kia Marama: Providing child sex offender treatment in prison

1 Ministerial Committee of Inquiry into the Prisons System, *Prison Review — Te Ara Hou: The new way* (Wellington: Government Printer, 1989).

2   D. A. Andrews and James Bonta, *The Psychology of Criminal Conduct* (Cincinnati: Anderson, 1998).

3   B. Rutherford, 'The Therapeutic Community Project at Kia Marama', unpublished report (Wellington: Department of Corrections, 2001).

4   A. Frost, 'New Connections: The engagement in group therapy of incarcerated men who have sexually offended against children' (Christchurch: University of Canterbury, 2000).

5   L. Moore, 'A Comparison of Offence History and Post-release Outcomes for Sexual Offenders Against Children in New Zealand Who Attended or Did Not Attend the Kia Marama Special Treatment Unit', master's thesis, University of Canterbury, 2012.

11. Singing my soul back into being

1   The transgender performer Carmen (née Trevor) Rupe (1936–2011) was the first Māori drag performer. The Balcony was her Wellington strip club.

12. Hurt people hurt people

1   G. F. McKibbin, C. Humphreys and B. Hamilton, '"Talking About Child Sexual Abuse Would Have Helped Me": Young people who were sexually abused reflect on preventing harmful sexual behaviours', *Child Abuse and Neglect* 70 (2017): 210–21.

2   T. C. Johnson, *Helping Children with Sexual Behavior Problems: A guidebook for professions and caregivers* (South Pasadena, CA: Institute on Violence, Abuse and Trauma, 2014); T. C. Johnson, *Understanding Children's Sexual Behaviours: What's natural and healthy* (self-published, 2013).

3   K. Epps and D. Fisher, 'A Review of the Research Literature on Young People Who Sexually Abuse', in *The Handbook of Clinical Intervention with Young People Who Sexually Abuse*, eds G. O'Reilly, W. L. Marshall, A. Carr and R. Beckett (Hove: Brunner-Routledge, 2004), 62–102.

4   K. Flanagan and K. Hayman-White, 'Sexual Abuse Counselling and Prevention Program: Five-year review of work with victims and adolescent perpetrators of sexual abuse' (Melbourne: Children's Protection Society, 1999).

5   Office of Film and Literature Classification, *NZ Youth and Porn: Research findings of a survey on how and why young New Zealanders view online pornography* (Wellington: Office of Film and Literature Classification, 2018), https://www.classificationoffice.govt.nz/news/latest-news/nzyouthandporn/

6   J. Worling and N. Långström, 'Assessment of Criminal Recidivism Risk with Adolescents Who Have Offended Sexually', *Trauma, Violence and Abuse* 4 (2003): 341–62.

7   I. Lambie and M. Stewart, 'Community Solutions for the Community's Problem: An outcome evaluation of three New Zealand community child sex offender treatment programmes', *International Journal of Offender Therapy and Comparative Criminology* (August 2011); Ian Lambie, *Getting It Right: An evaluation of New Zealand community treatment programmes for adolescents who sexually offend. Ka pu e ruha, ka hao te rangatahi* (Wellington: Ministry of Social Development, 2007).

8   L. Ayland and B. West, 'The Good Way Model: A strengths-based approach for working with young people, especially those with intellectual difficulties, who have sexually abusive behaviour', *Journal of Sexual Aggression* 12, no. 2 (2006): 189–201.

9   T. Ward and T. Gannon, 'Rehabilitation, Etiology, and Self-regulation: The Good Lives Model of sexual offender treatment', *Aggression and Violent Behavior* 11 (2006): 77–94.

13. The Good Lives Model of rehabilitation

1. Mayumi Purvis, Tony Ward and Simone Shaw, *Applying the Good Lives Model to the Case Management of Sexual Offenders: A practical guide for probation officers, parole officers, and case workers* (Brandon, VT: Safer Society Press, 2013).
2. T. Ward and C. Fortune, 'The Role of Dynamic Risk Factors in the Explanation of Offending', *Aggression and Violent Behavior* 29 (2016): 79–88; T. Ward and T. Gannon, 'Rehabilitation, Etiology, and Self-regulation: The Good Lives Model of sexual offender treatment', *Aggression and Violent Behavior* 11 (2006): 77–94.
3. M. Purvis, T. Ward and G. Willis, 'The Good Lives Model of Offender Rehabilitation', in *The Safer Society Handbook of Adult Sexual Offense Assessment and Treatment*, eds M. Carich and S. Mussack (Brandon, VT: Safer Society Press, 2014), 193–220.
4. Purvis, Ward and Shaw, *Applying the Good Lives Model*.
5. C. M. Chu and T. Ward, 'The Good Lives Model of Offender Rehabilitation: Working positively with sex offenders', in *Positive Criminology*, eds N. Ronel and D. Segev (Abingdon, UK: Routledge, 2015); C. A. Fortune, T. Ward and R. Mann, 'Good Lives & the Rehabilitation of Sex Offenders: A positive treatment approach', in *Positive Psychology in Practice*, 2nd edn, eds A. Linley and S. Joseph (West Sussex, UK: John Wiley & Sons, 2015); N. Leaming and G. M. Willis, 'The Good Lives Model: New avenues for Māori rehabilitation?', *Sexual Abuse in Australia and New Zealand* 7 (2016): 59–69; C. Lorito, B. Vollm and T. Dening, 'The Individual Experience of Ageing Prisoners: Systematic review and meta-synthesis through a Good Lives Model framework', *International Journal of Geriatric Psychiatry* (in press); D. M. Loney and L. Harkins, 'Examining the Good Lives Model and Antisocial Behavior', *Psychology, Crime and Law* (in press); R. E. Mann, S. D. Webster, D. Schofield and L. W. Marshall, 'Approach Versus Avoidance Goals in Relapse Prevention with Sexual Offenders', *Sexual Abuse: A Journal of Research and Treatment* 16 (2004): 65–76; A. M. Martin, B. Hernandez, E. Hernandez-Fernaud, J. L. Arregui and J. A. Hernandez, 'The Enhancement Effect of Social and Employment Integration on the Delay of Recidivism of Released Offenders Trained with the R & R Programme', *Psychology, Crime and Law* 16 (2010): 401–13; E. Taylor, '"I Should Have Been a Security Consultant": The Good Lives Model and residential burglars', *European Journal of Criminology* (in press); L. Van Damme, C. Fortune, S. Vandevelde and W. Vanderplasschen, 'The Good Lives Model Among Detained Female Adolescents', *Aggression and Violent Behavior* 37 (2017): 179–89; L. Van Damme, M. Hoeve, R. Vermeiren, W. Vanderplasschen and O. F. Colins, 'Quality of Life in Relation to Future Mental Health Problems and Offending: Testing the Good Lives Model among detained girls', *Law and Human Behavior* 40 (2016): 285–94; J. Ware and D. A. Bright, 'Evolution of a Treatment Programme for Sex Offenders: Changes to the NSW custody-based intensive treatment (CUBIT)', *Psychiatry, Psychology and Law* 15 (2008): 340–49; G. Willis and T. Ward, 'The Good Lives Model: Evidence that it works', in *What Works in Offender Rehabilitation: An evidence-based approach to assessment and treatment*, eds L. Craig, L. Dixon and T. A. Gannon (West Sussex, UK: John Wiley & Sons, 2013), 305–18.
6. D. A. Simons, B. McCullar and C. Tyler, 'Evaluation of the Good Lives Model Approach to Treatment Planning', paper presented at the 25th Annual Association for the Treatment of Sexual Abusers Research and Treatment Conference, Chicago, Illinois, September 2006.
7. L. Harkins, V. E. Flak, A. Beech and J. Woodhams, 'Evaluation of a Community-based Sex Offender Treatment Program Using a Good Lives Model Approach', *Sexual Abuse: A Journal of Research and Treatment* 24 (2012): 519–43.

8   T. A. Gannon, T. King, H. Miles, L. Lockerbie and G. M. Willis, 'Good Lives Sexual Offender Treatment for Mentally Disordered Offenders', *British Journal of Forensic Practice* 13 (2011): 153–68.

14. Assessing risk and treatment change, and the shift towards prevention

1   M. C. Seto, *Pedophilia and Sexual Offending Against Children: Theory, assessment, and intervention* (Washington, DC: American Psychological Association, 2008).

2   J. Bonta and D. A. Andrews, *The Psychology of Criminal Conduct*, 6th edn (New York: Routledge, 2016).

3   J. Vess and A. Skelton, 'Sexual and Violent Recidivism by Offender Type and Actuarial Risk: Reoffending rates for rapists, child molesters and mixed-victim offenders', *Psychology, Crime and Law* 16 (2010): 541–54.

4   Bonta and Andrews, *The Psychology of Criminal Conduct*.

5   https://www.psynergy.ca

6   S. Beggs, 'Within-treatment Outcome Among Sexual Offenders: A review', *Aggression and Violent Behavior* 15 (2010): 369–79.

7   M. E. Olver, S. C. Wong, T. Nicholaichuk and A. Gordon, 'The Validity and Reliability of the Violence Risk Scale — Sexual Offender Version: Assessing sex offender risk and evaluating therapeutic change', *Psychological Assessment* 19, no. 3 (2007): 318.

8   S. M. Beggs and R. C. Grace, 'Assessment of Dynamic Risk Factors: An independent validation study of the Violence Risk Scale — Sexual Offender version', *Sexual Abuse* 22 (2010): 234–51; S. M. Beggs and R. C. Grace, 'Treatment Gain for Sexual Offenders Against Children Predicts Reduced Recidivism: A comparative validity study', *Journal of Consulting and Clinical Psychology* 79 (2011): 182–92.

9   M. J. Howell, S. M. Beggs Christofferson and M. E. Olver, 'Evaluating the Inter-rater Reliability of the Violence Risk Scale-Sexual Offense Version (VRS-SO) In a Community-based Treatment Setting', *Sexual Offender Treatment* 12 (2017), http://www.sexual-offender-treatment.org/160.html

10 New Zealand Ministry of Justice, 'Number of people convicted of sexual offences against a child or young person (aged 16 years or younger) in 2015, by offending history, 2016', unpublished dataset prepared for S. M. Christofferson.

11 S. M. Hudson, D. S. Wales, L. Bakker and T. Ward, 'Dynamic Risk Factors: The Kia Marama evaluation', *Sexual Abuse* 14 (2002): 103–19; L. Moore, 'A Comparison of Offence History and Post-release Outcomes for Sexual Offenders Against Children in New Zealand Who Attended or Did Not Attend the Kia Marama Special Treatment Unit', unpublished doctoral dissertation, University of Canterbury, Christchurch, 2012.

12 S. Dickson and G. M. Willis, 'Primary Prevention of Sexual Violence in Aotearoa New Zealand: A survey of prevention activities', *Sexual Abuse* 29 (2017): 128–47.

13 K. M. Beier et al., 'Encouraging Self-identified Pedophiles and Hebephiles to Seek Professional Help: First results of the Prevention Project Dunkelfeld (PPD)', *Child Abuse and Neglect* 33 (2009): 545–49.

14 M. C. Seto, 'Is Pedophilia a Sexual Orientation?', *Archives of Sexual Behavior* 41 (2012): 231–36.

15 S. Jahnke, R. Imhoff and J. Hoyer, 'Stigmatization of People with Pedophilia: Two comparative surveys', *Archives of Sexual Behavior* 44 (2015): 21–34.

16 Child Welfare Information Gateway, 'Mandatory Reporters of Child Abuse and Neglect' (Washington, DC: U.S. Department of Health and Human Services,

Children's Bureau, 2016), https://www.childwelfare.gov/topics/systemwide/laws-policies/statutes/manda/
17. Australian Institute of Family Studies, 'Child Family Community Australia (CFCA) Resource Sheet: Mandatory reporting of child abuse and neglect', 2017, https://aifs.gov.au/cfca/publications/mandatory-reporting-child-abuse-and-neglect
18. Health Information Privacy Code (1994); Oranga Tamariki Act (1989).
19. www.dont-offend.org
20. K. M. Beier, D. Grundmann, L. F. Kuhle, G. Scherner, A. Konrad and T. Amelung, 'The German Dunkelfeld Project: A pilot study to prevent child sexual abuse and the use of child abusive images', *Journal of Sexual Medicine* 12 (2014): 529–42.
21. S. M. Christofferson, 'Is Preventative Treatment for Individuals with Sexual Interest in Children Viable in a Discretionary Reporting Context?', *Journal of Interpersonal Violence* 34, no. 20 (October 2019): 4254–80.
22. F. J. Thain, 'Preventing Child Sexual Abuse: Exploring public support for establishing pre-habilitation services in New Zealand', unpublished honours research project, University of Canterbury, Christchurch, 2017.

15. Restorative justice: Enabling a new 'normal' after sexual violence

1. 'Project Restore NZ — A Summary' is an evolving document you can request.
2. Ministry of Justice, *Restorative Justice Standards for Sexual Offending Cases*, 2013.
3. S. Julich, K. McGregor, J. Annan, F. Landon, D. McCarrison and K. McPhillips, 'Yes, There Is Another Way!', *Canterbury Law Review* 17 (2011): 222–28.

16. The development of constructive sexual behaviours

1. A. Morgentaler, *The Viagra Myth: The surprising impact on love and relationships* (New York: Jossey-Bass, 2003).
2. D. Siegel, *The Developing Mind: How relationships and the brain interact to shape who we are*, 2nd edn (New York: Guilford Press, 2015).
3. K. M. Faisandier, 'Effective Intimacy? Evaluating intimacy-focused therapy for out-of-control sexual behaviour', doctorate thesis, Massey University, 2015.
4. A. D. Ménard et al., 'Individual and Relational Contributors to Optimal Sexual Experiences in Older Men and Women', *Sexual and Relationship Therapy* 30 (2015): 78–93.
5. A. P. Zoldbrod, *Sex Smart: How your childhood shaped your sexual life and what to do about it* (Oakland, CA: New Harbinger Publications, 1998).
6. B. Zilbergeld, *The New Male Sexuality* (New York: Bantam, 1999).
7. J. Morin, *The Erotic Mind* (New York: HarperCollins, 1996).
8. D. Schnarch, *Passionate Marriage* (New York: W. W. Norton & Co., 2009).
9. M. S. Seto, *Pedophilia and Sexual Offending Against Children: Theory, assessment and intervention* (Washington, DC: American Psychological Association, 2008).
10. Carl Jung, 'The Philosophical Tree', in *The Collected Works of C. G. Jung 13: Alchemical studies* (Princeton, NJ: Princeton University Press, 1945).
11. M. Klein, *Sexual Intelligence* (New York: HarperCollins, 2012).

17. The development of destructive sexual behaviours

1. G. Hudson-Allez, *Infant Losses; Adult Searches: A neural and developmental perspective on psychopathy and sexual offending* (London: Karnac Books, 2011).
2. A. N. Schore, *Affect Regulation and the Repair of the Self* (New York: W. W. Norton & Co, 2003).
3. B. Perry, DSAC (now MEDSAC) training workshop.
4. J. Briere, 'Risky Behaviour: Treating self-endangering behaviours from an attachment/trauma perspective', workshop, Wellington, 2018.
5. P. Rich (ed.), *Attachment and Sexual Offending* (New York: John Wiley & Sons, 2006).
6. T. Ward, S. M. Hudson and W. M. Marshall, 'Attachment Style in Sex Offenders: A preliminary study', *Journal of Sex Research* 33, no. 1 (1996): 17–26.
7. M. J. Dorahy et al., 'Shame, Dissociation, and Complex PTSD Symptoms in Traumatized Psychiatric and Control Groups: Direct and indirect associations with relationship distress', *Journal of Clinical Psychology* 73, no. 4 (April 2017): 439–48.
8. D. Finkelhor and A. Browne, 'The Traumatic Impact of Child Sexual Abuse: A conceptualization', *American Journal of Orthopsychiatry* 55, no. 4 (October 1985): 530–41.
9. V. J. Feliti et al., 'Relationship of Childhood Abuse and Household Dysfunction to Many of the Leading Causes of Death in Adults', *American Journal of Preventive Medicine* 14, no. 4 (May 1998): 245–58.
10. B. A. van der Kolk, *The Body Keeps the Score: Brain, mind, and body in the healing of trauma* (New York: Penguin, 2015).
11. E. V. Welldon, 'Dancing with Death', *British Journal of Psychotherapy* 25, no. 2 (2009): 149–81.
12. Van der Kolk, *The Body Keeps the Score*.
13. R. Stoller, *Perversion: The erotic form of hatred* (London: Karnac Books, 1986).
14. R. M. Bergner, 'Sexual Compulsion as Attempted Recovery from Degradation: Theory and therapy', *Journal of Sex and Marital Therapy* 28, no. 5 (2002): 373–87.
15. J. Money and M. Lamacz, *Vandalized Lovemaps: Paraphilic outcome in seven cases of pediatric sexology* (Buffalo, NY: Prometheus Books, 1989).
16. J. Bering, *Perv: The sexual deviant in all of us* (New York: Scientific American/Farrar, Straus & Giroux, 2013).
17. J. Morin, *The Erotic Mind: Unlocking the inner sources of passion and fulfillment* (New York: Harper Perennial, 1995).
18. M. C. Seto, *Pedophilia and Sexual Offending Against Children: Theory, assessment and intervention* (Washington, DC: American Psychological Association, 2013).
19. J. Feierman (ed.), *Pedophilia: Biosocial dimensions* (New York: Springer-Verlag, 1990).

About the contributors

Jennifer Annan, Masters Ed. (Counselling), is a senior survivor specialist and founding member of Project Restore NZ. She has worked with survivors in all aspects of disclosure since 2001 and brings a valuable insight into how restorative justice may meet the needs of survivors and how to best support them in this. She continues to look for innovative ways of supporting survivors in their healing journey through restorative processes.

Sarah Beggs Christofferson, PhD, PGDipClinPsyc, is a senior lecturer in clinical psychology at the University of Canterbury and a registered clinical psychologist. Her research interests include assessment and treatment of sexual offending behaviour, assessing therapeutic change, and sexual abuse prevention. Sarah has a special interest in ethical and legal matters as they pertain to clinical practice and research, and serves on the Human Ethics Committee of the University of Canterbury. She is chair of the Institute of Criminal Justice and Forensic Psychology, and maintains a clinical practice consulting to various agencies.

Professor Dawn Elder is a paediatrician and HOD of the Department of Paediatrics and Child Health at the University of Otago, Wellington. She has performed many new patient assessments in the context of allegations of child sexual abuse and also medically assesses children with histories of child abuse and neglect. Dawn regularly teaches at the New Zealand Police College. She has acted as an expert witness before both the Criminal and Family courts. She was a member of the Family Violence Death Review Committee from 2011 to 2016, and is currently clinical lead of the New Zealand Paediatric Society Child Protection Clinical Network.

Dr Katie Fitzpatrick is an associate professor at the University of Auckland. Her teaching and research focus is on sexuality, health and physical education. Katie has published over 50 journal articles and book chapters, and six books. She also led the writing of the policy *Sexuality Education: A guide for principals, boards of trustees and teachers* (Ministry of Education, 2015) and co-authored a resource text for mental health education: *Mental Health Education and Hauora: Teaching about resilience, interpersonal skills and wellbeing* (NZCER, 2018).

Sue Glanville (formerly Hutchinson) has worked with children, young people and families for more than 30 years, initially as a residential social worker with adolescents in the care of Child Youth and Family (now Oranga Tamariki) and as a clinical psychologist with Oranga Tamariki Specialist Services. From 2003 Sue worked at Puawaitahi, a co-location of Auckland District Health, New Zealand Police and Oranga Tamariki child abuse specialists in a child-centred, collaborative multi-agency approach to providing services for children, young people and families affected by child abuse. Sue has a longstanding interest in psychological trauma and the development of effective interventions for children with abuse-related trauma.

Alexandra Green is Manager Psychological Services at Kia Marama Special Treatment Unit. She has worked at Kia Marama STU, which specialises in the assessment and treatment of men who have committed sexual offences against children, since 2002. Alex attained registration as a psychologist through the New Zealand Psychological Society, and holds a postgraduate diploma in mental health from the University of Otago and a Master of Science from Massey University. Her previous roles have included working with clients of the Child, Adolescent and Family Mental Health Service at the Southland DHB, subsequent to spending two years at a Child, Youth and Family residence in Christchurch, before joining Ara Poutama, the Department of Corrections.

Neil Holden is a police manager who has spent the majority of his career as a detective in the Criminal Investigation Branch (CIB). Most of his operational time was at Porirua, where he ran a busy Child Abuse Team and CIB office. After a period working in detective training, Neil undertook a role at national headquarters with oversight and coordination of child protection and adult sexual assault across New Zealand. More recently he has returned to management of frontline services, focusing on sexual crime in the Wellington region.

Deanna Hollis is a registered social worker and has been the manager of WellStop Central Region for over six years. Prior to this role, her background was in mental health and forensics. Deanna has worked in the social work profession for almost 20 years, and regardless of the focus of work has always been struck by the impact that harmful sexual behaviour has on individuals, and the ripple effects of this type of behaviour and its strong links to trauma, not only for those harmed, but also those doing the harming. While she acknowledges the importance of work with victims, without focusing on work with those at risk of offending, the cycles are unlikely to change.

Shirley Jülich, PhD, is a senior lecturer in the School of Social Work, Massey University. She has researched and published in the fields of restorative justice and sexual violence since the mid-1990s. She was a member of the first restorative justice provider group, Te Oritenga, and a founding member of Project Restore NZ.

Lisa Markwick, MSc, PGDipClinPsyc, is Executive Director of Project Restore NZ. Her experience and interest is in deep, long-term systemic impact and the leadership of such transformative organisations or communities. Her experience of over 30 years as a clinical psychologist is the backdrop for her understanding of the effects and impact of sexual harm on individuals, whānau and communities. Lisa has been a mindful leadership coach and mentor for over 15 years. At Project Restore NZ, as well as navigating the organisation towards the strategic intention of ending cycles of sexual violence in New Zealand, she sees her role as growing and supporting her team to thrive and offer their very best to the world. Project Restore NZ has come a long way over the past 15 years — from a paradigm-breaking and creating founder-lead practice to a sustainable ever-evolving charitable trust serving the community nationwide with its innovative model of restorative justice.

Hinewirangi Kohu Morgan is a poet, activist, artist and psychotherapist who has provided healing for rape victims. For the past decade she has also been working with Māori sexual offenders. She has presented internationally at a United Nations forum on healing indigenous youth in detention and custody. Two Māori Television documentaries in 2014 and 2017 explored her work and her personal healing journey after childhood rape experiences by an uncle. Hinewirangi was a major contributor to the Mauri Ora distance learning programme aimed at reducing disparities in Māori health by training health providers in cultural competency. She is Kahungunu, Ngāti Ranginui and Ngāti Porou.

Mayumi Purvis, PhD, is a clinical criminologist, counsellor, researcher and university lecturer. She is academic course coordinator for a post-graduate certificate in sexual offender management at the University of Melbourne, as well as a Monash University lecturer in ethics for counsellors. Mayumi has previously worked in a range of different roles including senior positions within Corrections, offender case management, and has also worked as a consultant trainer for correctional agencies around Australia. During her time in Corrections, Mayumi's most notable achievement was the development and implementation of a sex offender Specialist Case Management Model into Community Correctional Services, which was the first of its kind to operationalise the Good Lives Model into case management practices.

Robyn Salisbury is a clinical psychologist based in Palmerston North who has been specialising in relationship and sex therapy for over 30 years. She began by training as a marriage guidance counsellor in the early 1980s in Lower Hutt, then as a psychotherapist and psychologist. She has been writing newspaper and online columns on issues of sexuality since 2006, and in 2009 published *Staying in Love*, a guide for couples. She was the founding director of Sex Therapy New Zealand, where she developed and presented training courses in many aspects of sexuality for a range of professionals, and she established a national referral network for those seeking sex therapy. Since 2010 Sex Therapy New Zealand has been directed by four original members of the team.

David Shanks is New Zealand's chief censor and leads the Office of Film and Literature Classification. David has led large legal divisions, and held senior roles in both private and public sector organisations, but he has always been most fascinated by the interface between technology, public policy and social change. Now as chief censor he works to protect New Zealanders from harmful content — while upholding our rights to freedom of expression in an ever-changing digital environment.

Dr Natalie Thorburn is a registered social worker and researcher working primarily in the fields of sexual violence, family violence and sexual exploitation. Her PhD thesis explored the experiences of underage New Zealanders who were forcibly prostituted by partners, gangs or family members. Natalie is also the policy advisor for the National Collective of Independent Women's Refuges and is on the board of ECPAT Child Alert.

Ciaran Torrington is an ACC-registered sexual abuse therapist and assessor who also works to tackle community violence. She lives in the Far North, where she has worked in the healthcare sector of the Kaitāia community for over 19 years. Since 2014 Ciaran has campaigned for more support for survivors in Kaitāia. She developed the concept Te Wairua O Tika ('the spirit of belonging to right'). In 2018, along with other survivors, Ciaran founded HEALnz, a trauma charity. She has received Best Contribution to Social Good by an Individual — Social Innovation Awards and a Local Hero medal for her work.

Tony Ward is Professor of Clinical Forensic Psychology at Victoria University of Wellington and a fellow of the Royal Society of New Zealand Te Apārangi. He has taught clinical and forensic psychology at Deakin, Melbourne and Canterbury universities and has been director of Kia Marama, a specialist treatment unit for men who have committed sexual offences against children. His current research projects include: explanation and inquiry in research and practice — this includes the nature of psychopathology and crime related problems such as protective and dynamic risk factors; normative issues in clinical practice; and change processes in the psychopathology and forensic/correctional domains.

Index

A

ACC 114, 116, 118, 263, 265
adolescents *see* young people
adophile 22, 88
Adverse Childhood Experiences (ACEs) Study 61
age of legal sex 22
agency 69, 96, 101, 195, 198, 275
aggressive behaviour 67, 74, 251
alcohol *see* substance use and addiction
anger 67, 74, 112, 185, 235, 247
antisocial behaviour 64, 66, 185, 195, 196, 255, 256
anus 56; complaints of anal pain 55
anxiety 66, 68, 76, 104, 184, 235, 250
apology 221, 225
arousal 21–22, 58, 187, 227, 233, 235, 253, 254
assessment and diagnosis 60–61, 68–69; differential diagnosis 68–69
attachment relationships 69, 74, 98–99, 228–31, 232, 235, 236, 240, 255, 260, 267; disorders 68; impacts of trauma and sexual abuse 66, 67, 249, 251, 255, 256; insecure attachment and sexuality 242–46, 253, 255, 256; offenders 185, 187, 188, 231, 246, 255, 256, 257; and recovery from trauma and child sexual abuse 67, 71, 246; and vulnerability to abuse 104, 105, 106
attention-deficit hyperactivity disorder (ADHD) 68–69
Automated Sexual Recidivism Scale — Revised (ASRS-R) 161

B

beatings *see* physical abuse
boys, sexual abuse of 37–39, 44, 53, 110–11
brain, impact of trauma on development 20, 22, 68–69, 96–97, 109, 110, 249, 250, 251
bullying 118, 190

C

capacity building 131, 193, 196, 202
caregivers *see* parents and caregivers
censorship 134, 135–36, 140; pre-internet regulation 137–38
child health information link (CHIL) 266–67
Child Protection Protocol (CPP) 81–82, 83
child sex dolls 144
child sexual abuse 60–61; definition 20–21, 59, 61; impacts (*see* harm caused by child sexual abuse); increasingly younger children 138–39; myths and misunderstandings 48–59; personal accounts 37–39, 44, 109–10, 111, 113–14, 168–69, 274–75; prevalence 23–25, 47, 59–60, 65, 80, 97, 271; public awareness 47–48; secrecy 52–53, 65, 88; *see also* harm caused by child sexual abuse; offenders; prevention; risk factors for child sexual abuse; victims
Child Sexual Abuse Data Summary 23–24
children: access to pornography 137, 140–42, 144, 183; needs 259–61; objectification 188, 239; perpetrators of child sexual abuse 21, 24, 92, 111–12, 141, 180, 181–86; sexual attraction to children 237–38, 246, 252, 255, 256–57, 271, 272–73; sexual behaviours

between children 20–21, 49–50, 180; sexualisation 137, 253; sexuality and sexual behaviours 48–50, 120, 147, 181, 228–29, 232–33, 238, 260–62, 279–85; shifts in risk behaviour 144–45; treatment for children with harmful sexual behaviour 186; young children's sex play and exploration 21, 49, 50, 142–44, 181–82, 280–85; *see also* trauma; young people

coercion 50, 92, 94, 100, 105, 181, 182, 228, 237, 248, 284, 285, 287, 288, 289

cognitive behavioural therapy (CBT) 155, 186

collaboration 85, 115–16, 146, 147, 189–90, 210, 226, 263, 266; *see also* multi-agency centre model

community needs and responsibilities 270–72

Community of Change 158–59

community-based treatment agencies 179, 180, 186, 210–11, 267; *see also* WellStop Central

consent to sex 20, 22, 100, 102, 106, 124, 141, 147, 182, 184, 260, 261; minors deemed incapable 20; *see also* informed consent

coping responses 67–68, 97–98, 102, 190, 252; ways of enhancing coping 74–76

counselling 114, 198, 223, 225, 265, 269, 270, 272

court system and cases 84, 85–86, 89–91, 118, 261, 269; *see also* juries

crime by abused children 33, 34, 35, 64

cultural issues 128–29, 225, 226, 268; *see also under* Māori

D

Dark Net 139
Davis, Nancy 75–76
deepfake technology 144
defiance 74
delinquency 64
Department of Corrections 155, 156, 161, 164, 179, 186, 261, 263, 267, 268
depression 66, 104, 110, 184, 249, 253
diagnosis *see* assessment and diagnosis
differentiation (individuation) 235–36, 240, 267
digital technology 136–37, 138–39, 140, 142–45, 186, 255, 260; *see also* images and videos; internet; online offending
disclosure 25–26, 45, 52–53, 54, 66, 72, 75, 83, 106, 113, 114, 117, 264, 265; about sexual abuse by women 181; accusations of lying 54, 57; delays 58; false allegations 55; misinterpretation of things said by very young children 54–55, 73; young girls' understanding of their genital anatomy 56–58; *see also* reporting
dissociation 23, 37, 97, 101, 110, 118, 188, 246, 247
distress tolerance 96, 98
district health boards (DHBs) 62, 70, 116, 263, 266–67
DNA 59, 84
drugs *see* substance use and addiction
Dunedin Multidisciplinary Health and Development Research Study 24, 60
dysthymia 110

E

ECPAT (End Child Prostitution and Trafficking) International 138–39
emotional abuse 60, 66, 70, 72
emotional effects of child sexual abuse 39–40, 42, 64–65, 66, 68, 96, 101
emotional regulation 74, 102, 158, 187, 198, 202, 230, 246, 250
empathy 147, 198, 230; impact of pornography 141; offenders 154, 158, 164, 185, 222, 231, 247, 255; parents and caregivers 98; in relationships 42, 125; therapists and other professionals 75, 102, 225, 268; victims 40, 72, 112, 167
eroticism 19–20, 233–36, 237, 240, 250, 252–53, 257
evidence 26, 84, 90, 114, 263, 269; interviews 54, 57, 84–85, 113–14, 117–18
evidence-based practice 65–66

F

family members: intergenerational harm and hurt 80, 218, 225, 249, 258, 272; lack of family membership 30–33, 42–43, 44; strengthening of relationships by restorative justice 220, 226; support of abused children 66, 68, 73, 85; *see also* father–daughter normal interactions; parents and caregivers; siblings
family members as offenders 52–55, 97, 99, 136, 139, 157, 168, 223, 248, 269; child not supported by alienating parent 224–25; lack of support for offenders by other family members 163; meeting and questioning

by victims 171, 220, 223; misinterpretation of statements by very young children 54–55; objectification of victims 188; statistics 24, 184, 271; step-relatives 142; support for mothers when partners are offenders 85–86

family support by agencies and therapists 66, 68, 85–86; *see also* support agencies and services

family therapy 186

family violence 60, 92–93, 99, 102–03, 104, 182–83, 184, 188, 189, 224, 267, 271

father–daughter normal interactions 48, 49, 50–51

fear 15, 23, 26, 66, 74, 76, 104, 105, 106, 124, 164, 188, 213, 219, 235, 243, 248, 251

Films, Videos and Publications Classification Act 1993 137–38, 187

financial reparation 222, 225–26

Fonofale model 128

forensic tests and evidence 58, 84; and identity of offender 59

Fortnite porn 141

friendships 40, 41, 42, 52, 54, 86, 89, 124, 151, 199, 255; *see also* interpersonal skills; relationships

G

gender: beliefs and inequality 99–100, 101, 103, 106, 127, 238–39; offenders 22, 24, 25, 38, 39, 48–49, 52–53, 110–11, 158, 181, 183; victims 25, 53, 110–11

genitals: children's awareness of gender differences 48, 49, 280, 282; complaints by children of pain 55; concerning behaviours of children and young people 280, 281, 282, 283, 284, 285, 286, 287, 288, 289; exposure 20, 280, 282; genital-to-genital connection 57; pre-pubertal children 56, 286, 287, 288, 289; touching 24, 51, 57, 280, 282, 288; use of correct terms 55–56

gonorrhoea 59

Good Lives Model 186, 188, 191, 193–94, 204; causes of crime 195; conceptualisation of offending behaviour 194–95; core concepts 196–200, 201; empirical research 203–04; four key problems that diminish human well-being 200, 202–03; offender collaboration with workers 195–96

Good Way Model 186

Google 140, 141, 145

government agencies and services 30, 45, 50, 52, 55, 85, 263–70; *see also* New Zealand Police; Oranga Tamariki; Puawaitahi; support agencies and services

grooming 20, 84, 86, 88, 105, 136, 138, 187

guilt 44, 66, 114, 147, 218, 220, 235, 247

H

harm caused by child sexual abuse 20, 21, 22–23, 25, 44–45, 60, 61, 64, 66–68, 86–87, 97, 101, 110, 168–71, 208, 218, 258; intergenerational harm and hurt 80, 218, 225, 249, 258, 272; offenders' belief that abuse not harmful to the child 21, 185, 188, 208; *see also* specific types of harm, e.g. emotional effects of child sexual abuse

Harmful Digital Communications Act 2015 143

hauora concept 128

HEALnz 108, 118–19

health education 123, 125–26, 127–28, 131–32, 133

hebephile 22

heteronormativity 126–27

homelessness 96, 100, 101, 104

hue 172, 174–75

hymen 56, 58

I

images and videos: censorship 135–36; of child sexual abuse 136, 139, 141, 144, 146, 187–88, 253, 254–55; of children 20, 21, 136–37, 139, 140, 253, 255, 257; critiquing images and values 123, 260; deepfake technology 144; of young people 22, 137, 142–44; *see also* pornography; sexually explicit material (SEM)

individuation (differentiation) 235–36, 240, 267

informed consent: to restorative justice conference 223; to therapeutic work 71–72

intergenerational harm and hurt 80, 218, 225, 249, 258, 272

internet 83, 122–23, 136, 137, 187, 239–40, 253–54; digital filter to block access to CSA material sites 146; role of major corporations 140, 141, 145, 146, 266; sexually explicit material (SEM) 138, 140, 144, 239–40, 253–57, 266; *see also* Dark Net; digital technology; images and videos; online offending

Internet Watch Foundation (UK) 139

interpersonal skills 66, 124,

126, 158, 195, 229, 243, 245, 262; see also friendships; relationships

J

Johnson, Toni Cavanagh, *Children's Sexual Behaviours* 181
juries 57, 84, 112, 118, 269; see also court cases

K

kaupapa Māori approach 159
Kia Marama special treatment unit, Rolleston Prison 154–61, 164–65, 212; effectiveness 161–63

L

labia 56–57
LGBTQI issues and inclusion 126–27, 129, 145
Libeau, Morgan 76
love-illusion 105, 106

M

Māori: conceptions of body and well-being 115, 128; decolonisation and healing 176–77, 178; impact of colonisation 175–76, 177, 268, 270; kaupapa Māori approach 159; parenting 278; restorative justice processes 221
Māori Women's Centre for sexually abused women, children and men 177
mass allegation investigation (MAI) 82
masturbation 51–52, 181, 187, 227–28, 235, 284, 288, 289
'Mates and Dates' programme 131
media reporting 50, 53, 111, 123, 124, 136, 151, 156, 157, 183, 268, 270; see also social media
Medical Sexual Assault Clinicians Aotearoa (MEDSAC) 116
medication 68–69
memories 50–51, 59, 70–71, 109
men: child sexual abuse by men 22, 24, 25, 38, 52–53, 97, 110–11, 158; normalisation of male violence 96
mental health issues 20, 55, 60, 66, 68–69, 73, 101, 160, 184, 255, 262, 267; caregivers 60
#MeToo movement 99, 147, 238–39, 271
Microsoft Bing search engine 140
Ministry of Education 124–25, 128, 130, 132, 263, 265, 266
Ministry of Justice 24, 264, 270, 272
Ministry of Social Development 186, 263, 268
multi-agency centre model 77, 107, 259, 261, 264; see also collaboration; Puawaitahi

N

neglect 30–33, 34–36, 40, 41–42, 45, 60, 70, 188, 189
Netsafe 143
New Zealand Curriculum (Ministry of Education) 125, 128, 132
New Zealand Family Planning 130
New Zealand Family Violence Clearing House 23–24, 25
New Zealand Police 23, 24, 60, 61, 62, 70, 113, 114, 116, 219, 263, 264, 265, 267; Child Protection Team 79–82, 83–91, 265; community relationships 116–18; OCEANZ unit 83; prevention of child abuse 91–93; training and working in child abuse field 80–81, 83–84
'nudes' 143
nudity 48–50

O

objectification 188, 238, 239
'objectionable' material 138, 187
offenders 82–83, 84, 180–81; belief that abuse not harmful to the child 21, 185, 188, 208; childhood experiences of abuse 165, 182–83, 184, 185, 188, 189, 218, 224, 246–48, 251–52; children 21, 24, 92, 111–12, 141, 180, 181–86, 226; gender 22, 24, 25, 38, 39, 48–49, 52–53, 110–11, 181, 183; in institutions, religious orders or organisations 225–26, 271; known to the child 54, 97, 136, 157, 164, 247; a neighbour's experience 150–52; offending-related thoughts and fantasies 186, 213; online offending 83, 137, 138–39, 143–46; opportunistic offenders 21, 87, 88–89; police investigations 89–91; preferential offenders 21, 83, 87–88; proof of identity 59; registers 92, 268; reintegration following imprisonment 160, 163–64, 165, 268, 271; secrecy 52–53; strangers 53–54; young people 13, 112, 181, 183–86; see also family members as offenders; men — child sexual abuse by; paedophiles; penalties; reoffending; restorative justice; risk factors for child sexual abuse; suspects; therapy and support for offenders; women — child sexual abuse by
Office of Film and Literature

Classification 134, 135–36, 263, 266
online offending 83, 137, 138–39, 143–46, 187–88; role of major internet corporations 140, 141, 145, 146
online safety resources 148
Oranga Tamariki 23, 60, 61, 62, 70, 81–82, 85, 186, 189, 226, 263, 264, 265
overcrowded homes 92

P

paedophiles 21, 53, 88, 111, 139, 140, 151, 186–87, 207, 251, 255–56
paraphilia 250–51
parent–child interaction therapy 71
Parenting From the Start 277–78
parents and caregivers 51–52, 60, 67, 87; couples counselling 270; emotional responsiveness 96, 98–99; mother's support of offender 224–25; needs and responsibilities 67, 259–60, 261–63, 267; in restorative justice conferences 218, 220, 223–24; role in child safety 92; support by agencies and therapists 66, 67, 68, 85–86; support of abused children 66, 68, 73, 85, 113; views on sexuality education 123–24, 126; *see also* attachment relationships
Parker, James 116–17
parole 159–60, 162–63, 164
peer interactions 69, 98–99, 101, 102, 185, 229, 240
penalties 56–57, 90, 91, 210, 269, 271; imprisonment 114, 151, 153, 156–57, 159–60, 162–63, 208, 210, 220, 221–22
perpetrators *see* offenders
personality disorders 66
physical abuse 35, 36–37, 38, 39, 60, 66, 70, 96, 99, 100, 102, 103, 105, 106, 184, 189, 225, 247, 249
police *see* New Zealand Police
pornography 84, 88, 92, 123, 137, 138, 140, 145, 184, 187, 188, 190, 239, 253–54, 255–56, 260; access by children and young people 137, 140–42, 144, 183; virtual reality and augmented reality 144; *see also* images and videos; sexually explicit material (SEM)
post-traumatic stress disorder (PTSD) 110, 115, 118
poverty 92, 96, 100, 103, 104, 118, 262, 267, 271
power and powerlessness 21, 23, 53, 99–100, 101, 181, 182, 221, 224, 234, 248, 249, 269, 271
prevention 91–93, 146–47, 189–90, 207, 211–15, 219, 258, 263, 269, 271; primary prevention 212, 263, 266–68; secondary prevention 212, 263, 268
primary human goods (PHGs) 194–200, 202–03; compared to goals 200, 201
prisons 155, 156–57, 159–60, 177–78, 210, 221–22, 268
probation 160
Project Restore NZ 216, 217–26, 272
prostitution *see* sex work; sex-trafficking of adolescents; underage sex work (USW)
psychological effects of child sexual abuse 64, 65, 66, 67, 168–71
The Psychology of Criminal Conduct 156
psychosocial development: Erikson's stages 29, 69; impact of trauma and abuse 41–42, 66, 96
Puawaitahi 60, 62, 70, 72, 77, 80
puberty 56, 58, 250, 286, 287

R

registers of offenders 92
regressive behaviour 66–67, 109
rehabilitation *see* therapy and support for offenders
reintegration of offenders 160, 163–64, 165, 268, 271
relationships 123, 125–26, 129–30, 147, 187, 199, 230, 260; impact of child sexual abuse 42, 43–44, 66, 101; peer relationships 69, 98–99, 101, 102, 185, 229, 240; and risk of offending 163, 207; therapeutic work 158, 159; *see also* attachment relationships; friendships; interpersonal skills
reoffending 156, 157, 158, 160–61, 162, 164, 177, 184–86, 193, 208–11, 221, 268, 269, 272
reporting 25–26, 37, 45, 52, 84–85, 89, 114, 213–14; *see also* disclosure
resilience 12, 62, 68, 108, 125, 231, 246, 267, 269, 277, 278
respect 80, 89, 90, 92, 106, 116, 120, 123, 154, 159, 195, 202, 204, 239, 260, 268, 270, 271
restorative justice 216, 217–24, 259, 261, 272; goals 219–21; Māori processes 221; process 221–23; specific processes for children 218, 221, 223–24
re-victimisation 25
risk factors for child sexual abuse 92–93, 186, 188–89, 190, 193, 195, 205, 207–11, 222, 246–57, 263–64, 267
risk–need–responsivity

Index 309

treatment model 156
Roper Commission (Ministerial Committee of Inquiry into the Prisons System 1989) 155
Royal Commission into Historic Abuse in State Care 271

S

SAFE community-based treatment agency 180, 186
Saunders, Benjamin 70
secrecy 52–53, 65, 88
self-blame 66
self-empowerment courses 76–77
self-harming 67, 73, 98, 101, 102, 118, 198, 200
self-soothing 51–52, 70–71, 74, 189, 230, 231, 246, 251, 262
semen 58, 59
Sentencing Amendment Act 2014 219
sex-trafficking of adolescents 95, 103–04, 106–07, 265–66; distinguishing features 104; recruitment and entrapment 103, 104–06
sex work 169; *see also* underage sex work (USW)
sexting 143
sexual and gender diversity 25, 126–27, 129, 132, 187, 234, 236–37, 260, 270
sexual behaviours 20; acquisition 228–29; between children 20–21, 49–50, 180; by children and young people 21, 49–50, 51–52, 142–44, 181–82, 228–29, 260–61, 272–73, 279–89; children exposed to adult sexual behaviour 182, 188; constructive behaviours 227–28, 240; destructive behaviours 237, 241, 246–57
sexualisation of society 92, 136–37, 183, 190, 260, 270; children and young people 137, 143–44, 253; traumatic sexualisation 247–48
sexuality 19–20; attraction to minors 237–38, 246, 252, 255, 256–57, 271, 272–73; children and young people 48–49, 120, 147, 181, 228, 232–33, 238, 260–62; milestones in development 232–33; optimal 232, 240; social influences 236–39
sexuality education 120–21, 122–26, 132–33, 147, 184, 189, 259, 261–62, 266, 270; cultural concepts and content 128–29; learning and meaningful assessment 131–32; need for change 129–31; what is taught 126–28
Sexuality Education (Ministry of Education) 124–25, 132–33
sexually explicit material (SEM) 138, 140, 144, 239–40, 253–57, 266
shame 14, 29, 31, 69, 235, 237–38; about pornographic images 142, 143, 187; and disclosure 26; family 225; male victims 25; offenders 91, 188, 250; underage sex workers 97, 98, 107; victims 44, 45, 70, 87, 97, 142, 147, 247, 248, 261
Short Intervention Programme (SIP) 160
siblings: aggression toward younger siblings by abused children 67; attachment relationships 66; protection of younger sisters by older sisters 52–53; sexual abuse by 21, 24, 226; sexual behaviours between 21
social justice 126, 127–28, 262
social learning-based group treatment 155, 158–59
social media 92, 122, 138, 141, 143–44, 145, 255, 286
social well-being 101, 126, 163, 199, 202, 203, 255, 267
societal norms and behaviours 146–47, 212, 236, 270
spirituality 199, 268
Starship National Children's Hospital 62
step-porn 142
stigma 82, 84, 89–90, 91, 97, 102, 107, 190, 213, 248, 259, 261, 265
STOP community-based treatment agency 180, 186
stories, use in therapy 75–76
Stout, Teri 118–19
strangers, child sexual abuse by 53–54
substance use and addiction 60, 66, 98, 101, 102, 104, 118, 145, 169, 170–71, 184, 187, 198, 200, 202, 255, 262, 267–68, 271, 272
suicidal children and young people 73, 87, 98, 113, 118, 167, 168, 289
support agencies and services 17–18, 60–61, 73, 85, 101–03, 107, 115–16, 118–19, 261, 264–66; *see also* government agencies and services; Puawaitahi
survivors *see* victims
suspects 87–91

T

Te Piriti special treatment unit, Auckland Prison 157–58, 160
Te Wairua O Tika 108, 119
Te Whakaruruhau 177
Te Whare Tapa Whā model 115, 128, 177, 265
teachers: child sexual abuse by 53; role in reporting child abuse and neglect 37, 45
Terre des Hommes 139
therapy and support for

offenders 185, 189–90, 207, 222–23, 256–57, 263, 268; children and young people with harmful sexual behaviour 186; confidentiality 213; expectations 72–73; Māori processes 115, 128, 159, 176–77, 178; matched to risk level 208–09; Waikeria Prison 176, 177–78; *see also* community-based treatment agencies; Good Lives Model; Kia Marama special treatment unit, Rolleston Prison; Te Piriti special treatment unit, Auckland Prison; WellStop Central

therapy and support for victims 61, 65–66, 71–77, 116, 222–23, 261, 263, 264–66; caring purpose 72, 75; Trauma Informed Te Whare Tapa Whā (TITWTW) 115, 118–19, 265; trauma-focused cognitive behaviour therapy (TF-CBT) 70–71, 73; *see also* restorative justice; support agencies and services

TOAH-NNEST (Te Ohaakii a Hine — National Network Ending Sexual Violence Together) 116

touching 20, 24, 25, 39, 43, 51; genital area 57

toys, use in therapy 71, 74, 75

trauma: impact on brain development 20, 22, 68–69, 96–97, 109, 110, 249, 250, 251; mental health implications 101; offenders 183, 187, 188–89, 190, 248, 249–52, 255; sexualisation 248; therapies and support services 70–71, 102, 114–15, 186, 190, 218, 226, 259, 263, 264–66, 271–72;

and vulnerability to exploitation 96–98, 103, 218, 251

trauma-focused cognitive behaviour therapy (TF-CBT) 70–71, 73

Trauma Informed Te Whare Tapa Whā (TITWTW) 115, 118–19, 265

trust 66, 68, 69, 101, 221, 246, 268; trusted and supportive adults 73

U

underage sex work (USW) 95, 265–66, 272; consequences 101–03; preceding circumstances 96–100

University of Canterbury 155, 161–62, 210, 212

V

vagina 56–57; use of term 55–56

victim impact statement 220

victims 80, 81–83, 98, 110, 113–14; encounters with court system 84; gender 25, 53, 110–11; ignored and unheeded 87, 113, 114, 115–16; initial victimisation and secondary abuse 103; non-judgemental understanding by police 86–87; personal accounts 37–39, 44, 109–10, 111, 113–14, 168–69, 274–75; physical examinations 56–57; relationships with abusers in sex-trafficking 104–06; re-victimisation 25; shame 44, 45, 70, 87, 97, 142, 147, 247, 248, 261; use of term 'survivor' 110; *see also* coping responses; disclosure; harm caused by child sexual abuse; restorative justice; sex-trafficking of adolescents; therapy and support for

victims; underage sex work (USW)

Violence Risk Scale — Sexual Offender version (VRS-SO) 161, 209–11

virginity 57–58

W

Waikeria Prison 176, 177–78

WellStop Central 179, 186–90

whakapapa 173–74, 175, 176

withdrawal, abused children 67

women: child sexual abuse by women 22, 24, 25, 39, 48–49, 53, 110–11, 158, 181; objectification 238, 239; responsibility 112–13

World Health Organization Multi-Country Study on Violence against Women 24

Y

young people: abuse of 22, 24, 48, 53, 58, 64, 88–89, 96, 97, 155; access to pornography 137, 140–42, 144, 183, 253; attachment status 230, 235, 246, 251, 252; exploration of identity 69, 98–99, 240; false allegations of abuse 55; images and videos 22, 137, 142–44; needs 259–61; perpetrators of child sexual abuse 13, 112, 181, 183–86; sexualisation 137, 253; sexuality and sexual behaviours 260–61, 286–89; shifts in risk behaviour 144–45; *see also* child sexual abuse; children; sex-trafficking of adolescents; trauma; underage sex work (USW)

YouTube 140

Index 311

First published in 2020 by Massey University Press
Private Bag 102904, North Shore Mail Centre
Auckland 0745, New Zealand
www.masseypress.ac.nz

Text copyright © individual contributors, 2020

Design by Kate Barraclough
Cover photograph by iStock

The moral right of the authors has been asserted

All rights reserved. Except as provided by the Copyright Act 1994, no part of this book may be reproduced, stored in or introduced into a retrieval system or transmitted in any form or by any means (electronic, mechanical, photocopying, recording or otherwise) without the prior written permission of both the copyright owner(s) and the publisher.

A catalogue record for this book is available from the National Library of New Zealand

Printed and bound in New Zealand by Printlink

ISBN: 978-0-9951230-0-7
eISBN: 978-0-9951230-9-0